p86 dark pool definition

p130 40 dark pools do 65% all trades

138 footnote 7

142 1999 NYSE had 82 ... its names

155 Flash Crash $700bn each way = $1.4tn

hate 506 NYSE + NASDAQ had already non-profit exchange

1997 ECN's started for profit ~100% computerized + by-passed the market makers

led directly to HFT.

2003 avg share 500 HFT 200
S " " 200   .75%

161. volatility

167 Accenture's stock price

183 Summary on Flash Crash

p130 BATS launch

195 Dave Wield CFO Roundtable } No IPO's

Broken Markets

Broken Markets

How High Frequency Trading and
Predatory Practices on Wall Street
Are Destroying Investor Confidence and
Your Portfolio

Sal Arnuk
Joseph Saluzzi

Vice President, Publisher: Tim Moore

Associate Publisher and Director of Marketing: Amy Neidlinger

Executive Editor: Jim Boyd

Operations Specialist: Jodi Kemper

Assistant Marketing Manager: Megan Graue

Cover Designer: Chuti Prasertsith

Managing Editor: Kristy Hart

Project Editor: Jovana San Nicolas-Shirley

Copy Editor: Apostrophe Editing Services

Proofreader: Gill Editorial Services

Indexer: Lisa Stumpf

Senior Compositor: Gloria Schurick

Manufacturing Buyer: Dan Uhrig

© 2012 by Sal Arnuk and Joseph Saluzzi

Publishing as FT Press

Upper Saddle River, New Jersey 07458

FT Press offers excellent discounts on this book when ordered in quantity for bulk purchases or special sales. For more information, please contact U.S. Corporate and Government Sales, 1-800-382-3419, corpsales@pearsontechgroup.com. For sales outside the U.S., please contact International Sales at international@pearsoned.com.

Printed in the United States of America

First Printing May 2012

ISBN-10: 0-13-287524-1

ISBN-13: 978-0-13-287524-0

Pearson Education LTD.

Pearson Education Australia PTY, Limited.

Pearson Education Singapore, Pte. Ltd.

Pearson Education Asia, Ltd.

Pearson Education Canada, Ltd.

Pearson Educatión de Mexico, S.A. de C.V.

Pearson Education—Japan

Pearson Education Malaysia, Pte. Ltd.

The Library of Congress cataloging-in-publication data is on file.

We dedicate this book to the executives at the major U.S. stock exchanges, to high frequency trading firms, to lobbyists, and to numerous other conflicted parties in Washington, D.C., and Wall Street. Without your actions, we would never have become outraged enough to write this book.

Contents

Foreword

by Former U.S. Senator Ted Kaufman

I didn't know a great deal about high frequency trading and the negative effect it was having on the financial markets and the economy when I became a United States Senator early in 2009, taking the seat vacated by Vice President-elect Joe Biden. But thanks to Sal Arnuk and Joseph Saluzzi of Themis Trading, I learned quickly.

During the Bush II administration, I became concerned about changes in the rules on short selling. Along with Republican Senator Johnny Isaakson, I wrote to SEC Chair Mary Schapiro, asking her to follow up on her confirmation hearing pledge to look into reinstating the "uptick rule," which had been removed in what former SEC Chair Chris Cox admitted had been a mistake. Short sellers play an important role in maintaining an orderly market. But there also are predatory bears. If not policed, they could have a devastating effect by creating a never-ending, negative feedback loop. The uptick rule helped to prevent that by prohibiting the shorting of a security unless the most recent trade was an increase in price.

As it turned out, I lost the battle to reinstate the rule. The main force pushing back was a new group on Wall Street called high frequency traders (HFT). Intrigued, I began to look into what HFT was all about.

One of the great things about being a United States Senator is the access you to have to experts willing to educate you on issues. While my staff and I met with a number of people who claimed to know a lot about HFT, I quickly learned that the ones who made the most sense and had the best take on what was happening were Sal and Joe. They founded Themis Trading and are experts in equity trading on behalf of institutional customers, such as mutual and pension funds. They quickly gave me and my staff an education on HFT that was the best I had heard.

After we talked to Sal and Joe and others and deeply studied the issue, I wrote to SEC Chair Schapiro in August 2009, outlining my concerns about the present market structure and HFT. I spoke many times in the next year on the Senate floor about the dramatic changes taking place in our equity markets, explaining obscure practices like colocation, naked access, flash orders, and the proliferation of dark pools. But mostly I spoke about the explosion in HFT, which had come to dominate the equity markets and account for well more than half of all daily trading volume.

My message was straightforward: The technological advances and mathematical algorithms that have allowed computers to trade stocks in millionths of a second in and of themselves are neither good nor bad. Indeed, as an engineer, I have a deep appreciation for technological progress. But technology cannot operate in a vacuum, and it should not dictate how our markets function. Simply put, technology must operate within a framework that ensures integrity and fairness.

That is why our regulatory agencies are so critically important. While technology often produces benefits, it also can introduce conflicts that pit long-term retail and institutional investors against professional traders who are in and out of the market many times a day. As Chair Schapiro has consistently asserted, including in a letter to me more than two years ago, "If...the interests of long-term investors and professional traders conflict...the Commission's focus must be on the protection of long-term investors."

Many people have asked me why I focused so intently on the arcane details of how stocks are traded. There are several reasons.

- First, we must not just look backward and analyze the factors that brought about the last financial crisis. We must also be proactive and identify brewing problems before they create a new crisis.

- Second, we have to protect the credibility of our markets. The two great pillars upon which America rests are democracy and our capital markets. But there is more at stake than a structural risk that could bring our markets once again to their knees, as occurred on May 6, 2010, during the Flash Crash. There is a real perceptual risk that retail investors will no longer believe that the markets are operating fairly, that there is simply not a level playing field. If investors don't believe the markets are fair, they won't invest in them. And if that happens, we can all agree our economy will be in serious trouble.

- Third, we should have learned the lesson from derivatives trading. When we have opaque markets, disaster is often not far behind. It is hardly surprising that high frequency trading deserves a watchful, and possibly critical, government eye. It is simply a truism that whenever there is a lot of money surging into a risky area, where change in the market is dramatic, where there is no transparency and therefore no effective regulation, we have a prescription for disaster. We had a disaster in the fall of 2008, when the credit markets suddenly dried up and our markets collapsed. The Flash Crash was a near-disaster.

The SEC continues to study the causes for the Flash Crash. I hope the agency has moved much closer to truly understanding the dramatic changes in market structure that have taken place in the past few years, the potential ramifications of HFT, and its impact on retail and institutional investors.

But this is about more than investor confidence. The primary function of our capital markets is to permit companies to raise capital, innovate, grow, and create jobs. Publicly traded companies employ millions of Americans and are at the heart of our economy. Their stock symbols should not be used simply as the raw material for HFTs and exchanges and other market centers more concerned with churning out trade volume than with serving long-term investors and supporting fundamental company value.

Perhaps it is not surprising that our initial public offering markets have deteriorated dramatically and seem to work only for the largest offerings worth several hundred million dollars. Indeed, the IPO situation today is so dire that had it been the case two decades ago, many of our most famous U.S. corporations, including Apple, Intel, and Oracle, might never have been nurtured—or perhaps even born. A leader in documenting this has been David Weild, Capital Markets Advisor at Grant Thornton, founder and chairman of Capital Markets Advisory Partners, and former vice chairman of NASDAQ. He links this phenomenon directly to the rise of high frequency trading under a one-size-fits-all set of market rules that favors efficiency of trading above all else. David has written a guest chapter in the latter part of this book that details his eloquent arguments.

I believe the Securities and Exchange Commission is undergoing an extraordinary turnaround. After years of deregulation fervor, which sapped morale and led to an egregious case of regulatory capture, we now have an emboldened agency, with a beefed up enforcement division, a serious chair, and an invigorated staff.

The Commission must still reform the way it gathers the facts it needs to study market issues and particularly high frequency trading. Evidence-based rule-making should not be a one-way street in which all the "facts" are provided by those whom the SEC is charged with regulating. We need the SEC to quickly implement a consolidated audit trail so that objective and independent analysts—by academia, private analytic firms, the media, and elsewhere—are given the opportunity to study and discern what effects high-frequency trading strategies have on long-term investors. It is important that we find whether there are strategies that are manipulative.

We cannot afford regulatory capture or consensus regulation, in any government agency, but especially at the SEC, which oversees such a systemic and fundamental aspect of our entire economy. Colocation, flash orders, and naked access are just a few practices that were fairly widespread before ever being subjected to regulatory scrutiny. For our markets to remain credible—and it is essential that they do so—it is vital that regulators be proactive, rather than reactive, when future developments arise.

Since leaving the Senate, I have continued to speak out on market structure issues and HFT. Because if we fail, if we do not act boldly, if the status quo prevails, I genuinely fear we will be passing on to my grandchildren a substantially diminished America—one where saving and investing for retirement is no longer widely practiced by a generation of Americans and where companies no longer spring forth from the well of capital flows that our markets used to provide.

Wall Street is a business, like any other business in America. But it is also different in an important way. It is Wall Street that gathers up the hard-earned cash of millions of Americans and allows them to invest in capital markets that have been the envy of the world.

These markets, like all markets, will ebb and flow. But they should never be brought down by inherent structural problems, by trading inequities, or by opaque operations that shun transparency.

Wall Street holds a piece of American capital, our collective capital, and it has a real and profound responsibility to handle it fairly. But that entails another obligation as well: to come to the table and play a constructive role with Congress and the SEC in resolving its current issues—especially the possibility of HFT manipulation and systemic risk. For too long, many on Wall Street have urged Washington to look the other way, to accept the view that all is fine. If Wall Street does not engage honestly and constructively, then these issues must be resolved without their input.

And resolve them we will. The credibility of our capital markets is too precious a resource to squander; it is a fundamental pillar of our nation. And if it is now threatened, Congress and the regulatory agencies surely must act. We can fashion a better solution with industry input. Not a biased solution, but a better solution—one that should benefit Wall Street in the long term, one that must benefit all Americans now.

This book will open your eyes, as Sal and Joe did mine. There have been many dramatic changes in our markets in recent years, and even sophisticated investors may know little or nothing about them. With Sal and Joe as your guides, you will come to understand these changes and what they have meant to individual investors and our capital markets. Sal and Joe believe the system is broken, and they are right. They explain how it happened and what must be done to fix it.

I hope this book reaches a wide audience and that its readers urge their representatives in Congress to do what must be done to restore credibility and fairness to our markets.

Acknowledgments

Never in our imaginations did we ever think we would write a book, let alone one that featured market structure and high frequency trading! Well, we did, but not alone. This book was based on decades of experience trading for our institutional clients. So, ultimately, it was our clients who made this book possible, and we owe them the heartiest of thanks. We also want to thank our families for putting up with our missing weekends as well as our being cranky when we fell behind schedule. Likewise, we need to tip our hats to our Themis team—Paul, Victor, Scott, Caroline, Anna, and Aviva—for picking up the slack when we needed you. Thank you to our publisher, Jim Boyd, and his team for their patient guidance. Finally, we owe a great deal of appreciation to our many friends behind the scenes who unfortunately cannot be named. They have been incredible sources of information, ideas, and inspiration. Thank you all.

About the Authors

Sal Arnuk is partner, cofounder, and co-head of equity trading of Themis Trading, LLC, a leading independent agency brokerage firm that trades equities for institutional money managers and hedge funds. Arnuk has extensive experience in equities trading and is an expert in electronic trading and market structure. Prior to founding Themis in 2002, he was with Instinet Corporation, where he headed the team responsible for equity sales and trading for institutional money managers, for more than 10 years.

His opinions are sought by leaders, regulators, market participants, and the media and are presented via white papers and Themis' widely read blog. He is a frequent speaker at industry conferences, such as Trader Forum, Waters, National Organization of Investment Professionals (NOIP), and Fusion IQ's Big Picture, on issues involving market access, algorithmic trading, and other sell- and buy-side concerns.

He also provides expert commentary for media outlets such as the Associated Press, BBC Radio, Bloomberg TV and Radio, BNN, CNBC, Fox Business, NPR, *Barron's*, *The New York Times*, *The Wall Street Journal*, *USA Today*, *Time*, *Los Angeles Times*, *Bloomberg News*, *Pensions & Investments*, and *Advanced Trading*.

Arnuk earned an MBA in finance from New York University's Stern School of Business and a Bachelor's degree in finance from SUNY Binghamton University.

Joseph Saluzzi is partner, cofounder, and co-head of equity trading of Themis Trading, LLC. Saluzzi has extensive experience in equities trading and is an expert in electronic trading and market structure. Prior to Themis, he headed the team responsible for equity sales and trading for hedge fund accounts at Instinet Corporation for more than 9 years.

Saluzzi has provided analysis to regulators, including the Securities and Exchange Commission and as a member of the Commodity

Futures Trading Commission's new Subcommittee on Automated and High Frequency Trading.

He has appeared or been quoted on market structure issues by media outlets such as CBS's *60 Minutes*, BBC Radio, Bloomberg Television and Radio, CNBC, Fox Business, BNN, *The New York Times*, *The Wall Street Journal*, *USA Today*, *Reuters*, *Associated Press*, *Los Angeles Times*, and *Bloomberg News*. Saluzzi also has authored articles for *Traders Magazine*, *Dow Jones*, *Journal of Investment Compliance*, and *Journal of Indexes*.

He earned an MBA in finance from the University of North Carolina at Chapel Hill and a Bachelor's degree in finance from New York University.

Introduction

The stock market has devolved. Make no mistake, it is broken.

Its primary purpose *had always been to facilitate capital forma-tion*. Companies that needed funds have always looked to the equity markets to issue stock. The funds they raise via an initial public offer-ing, or IPO, are put to work to generate earnings. The increased earn-ings drive the share price of their stocks higher, *and investors and savers accumulate wealth*. That increased wealth, in addition to their wages, *drives consumers to spend and buy*. And that spending and buying in turn drives demand for corporate goods and services, which in turn drives additional corporate profits, and the cycle continues.

The stock market is the mechanism where IPOs trade among sec-ondary investors and traders. If the secondary market is liquid with lots of transactions and trading, then investors feel confident that they can take a risk and buy shares in a company because they could easily exit their investments, should they want.

This linkage has always been crucial to our nation's greatness and is why America has always been held up as the beacon of capitalism worldwide.

Sadly, today, the primary purpose of the stock market is not capital formation. Investors are an afterthought. *The primary purpose of the stock exchanges has devolved to catering to a class of highly profitable market participants called high frequency traders, or HFTs, who are interested only in hyper-short term trading, investors be damned.* The stock exchanges give these HFTs perks and advantages to help them be as profitable as possible, even if doing so adversely affects you, the investors, because HFT firms are the exchanges' biggest customers.

These HFTs use high-powered computers to automatically and algorithmically trade in and out of securities in speeds measured in microseconds (millionths of a second). Although there are few HFTs relative to the number of investors in the marketplace, the following is generally estimated in the industry:

- HFTs account for 50–75% of the volume traded on the exchanges each day and a substantial portion of the stock exchanges' profits.
- While smaller HFTs churn hundreds of millions of shares per day, a few of the larger HFTs each account for more than 10% of any given day's trading volume.
- HFTs earn anywhere from $8 billion to as much as $21 billion a year that comes at the expense of long-term investors—you and the institutional investors that manage money on behalf of you.

These HFTs are always hungry for situations for their algorithms to arbitrage. They are hungry, just like Seymour, the man-eating plant from *Little Shop of Horrors*. And stock exchanges, brokerage firms, technology providers, and consultants spend every waking moment figuring out how they can help their largest customers make more money—new ways to feed Seymour.

When you think about the stocks in your 401k plans, how do you imagine that they trade today? What images come to your mind? Do you think of bustling trading floors in a metropolitan city money center, with humans hustling about screaming, signaling, gesturing, hustling, and interacting? Do you think of Eddie Murphy and Dan Akroid in the climactic final exchange scene in the film, *Trading Places*? Do you think of the movie *Wall Street*? Do you think of Maria Bartiromo reporting from the floor of the NYSE amid a sea of mostly male blue coats, trading on behalf of mutual funds, traders, and investors?

Or, do you realize that today the floor of the NYSE is really a prop for television, and that all the majority of trading is done and housed in a suburban warehouse in New Jersey, housing billions of dollars worth of technology and servers owned or leased to HFT firms?

Our point is obviously that the markets have changed drastically in the past decade, and not all the stakeholders have realized this or the implications of those changes.

Our brokerage firm, Themis Trading, has spent the past decade navigating the equity trading landscaping on behalf of our clients, who are long-term institutional investors. We have accumulated in-the-trenches expertise trading stocks in dozens of exchanges and alternative trading systems. We have experience trading with multitudes of technologies. Prior to our careers at Themis, we spent the better part of a decade as sales-traders at the world's first premier electronic brokerage firm, Instinet, and we spent years before that working at Morgan Stanley in the late 1980s. We have learned to adapt to the ever-changing equity trading landscape. Our front row seats and participation in the markets, throughout the many structural and technological changes that they have undergone, have given us our most important asset: perspective. We have seen the good and bad parts of our market structure in the 1990s and the 2000s, as well as today. We know what works, what doesn't, and what is problematic—and why.

While trading equities for clients, we have uncovered many unfair practices and outright shenanigans. We have spent a significant amount of energy and time raising these issues to our industry. We have participated in conference panels, appeared on CNBC, Bloomberg TV, and even *60 Minutes*. We have given testimony to our regulators—the Securities and Exchange Commission and Commodity Futures Trading Commission. And we have actively blogged our opinions and findings on our firm's website. Initially, our voice was a small and lonely one. Over the past several years, however, we believe we have made great strides in broadening the discussion about our market structure's conflicts of interests, and about high frequency trading.

We question the roles of stock exchanges and HFT firms, the value they are adding, and the damage they are doing. It is common to hear in the media how HFT has reduced costs for investors by lowering commissions and narrowing the spread between the prices investors can buy and sell stocks. We see it differently. Although spreads may be narrower in perhaps 5% of the most actively traded names, they are wider in the other 95% of the market. So while our current markets have solved the "problem" of how investors can trade the top 100 companies for a spread measured in pennies, with little or no commission, they have created many other problems, such as extreme volatility and lack of support for small and midcap emerging companies.

Why did we write this book? The discussion and debate around the workings of our capital raising superhighway needs to be had by the much larger and more mainstream stakeholders: investors. For too long, the HFT and market structure debates have been monopolized by a small group of industry insiders, regulators, and groupthinkers. In the process, our markets have morphed into an insanely complex web of conflicted stock exchanges, dark pools, alternative trading systems (ATSs), and liquidity providers. We want to call attention to these conflicts and issues more broadly. We want you to understand how our markets actually work and why they morphed the way they have. It was no accident.

Perhaps you are reading this book because you have heard about high frequency trading on the evening news or from our appearance on *60 Minutes* and are curious about all the buzz.

Perhaps you are reading it because you have noticed high frequency trading as a term associated with volatility, and the way the stock market has moved the last few years has made you concerned about the safety of your investments.

Perhaps you are reading *Broken Markets* because you wonder why correlation in the stock market, or the degree to which individual stock prices tend to move together, has never been greater. That's because asset pricing in the stock market is largely the result of high frequency algorithmic automated traders, who make up most of the volume. They know nothing about the underlying companies whose shares they churn. They don't even know the names or lines of business of the companies they trade. They don't care, and there is a downside and a danger to that.

Perhaps you are reading this book because you want an answer to why the market can drop a thousand points within minutes, only to rebound just as fast, as the markets did in aggregate during the Flash Crash of May 6, 2010. Did that day frighten you? Make you lose enough confidence that you withdrew your money from the market? If you did, you were not alone. Some $232 billion has been withdrawn from domestic equity mutual funds between May 2010 and January 2012.[1] However, if you did understand what caused the markets to drop that day and stayed in the market, you would have caught a major bullish move up.

Perhaps you are reading this book because you are "in the industry" and agree with our viewpoints—or you flat out disagree with us.

Whatever reason you picked up this book, we are hopeful you will come away from *Broken Markets* with an understanding of how and why our stock markets have changed in the past 15 years. We hope you will see the danger created for retail and institutional investors, as well as the United States and perhaps the world economy. We hope you will be outraged, as we are. We hope that you will be so outraged that you will make it known to your political representatives. Our short-sighted myopic tinkering with our market's foundation has been done for the benefit of few, at the expense of many.

We wrote *Broken Markets* quite simply to try to explain the markets' complexity to an audience that does not only include the most sophisticated industry insiders. Although we wish our markets operated in a manner simple enough that the majority of us could understand it, unfortunately, today's markets do not operate in simple and intuitive ways. Hopefully, we can illuminate the murkiness to help you understand the highway upon which your investments are traveling.

If you are a buy-and-hold investor or a retail trader, we want you to come away understanding new dangers in our market structure that never existed before. We want you to understand that your costs are not just a commission or a bid-ask spread. Your every investment move, order, and trade is recorded and sold/provided to hyper-efficient, short-term HFT firms by the exchanges, similar to how your Internet-browsing is recorded by your search engine provider. However, while your browsing habits are sold to advertisers who make money attempting to sell you goods, your trading data is sold to HFT firms who trade around you and against you, and at your expense.

If you are a chief financial officer or investor relations officer at a publicly traded company, we hope this book helps explains some of the gyrations that your stock may be taking during the day. You probably have lost a lot of "color" on your stock since the specialist model disappeared and may be struggling to understand why your stock is suddenly going up—or down. This book will fill in the blanks for you. We also hope that you will add your voice to the market structure debate.

Ultimately, we hope you enjoy the read!

—Sal and Joe

Endnote

1. Investment Company Institute, "Long-Term Mutual Funds Flows Historical Data," February 29, 2012, Investment Company Institute website, http://www.ici.org/research/stats.

1

Broken Markets

Are you an investor? Are you a stock market aficionado who loves to learn about companies, industries, and the variables that tie them to a stock price? Do you have an online brokerage account at Fidelity or TD Ameritrade, for example?

Do you watch Bloomberg TV or CNBC? Do you read *The Wall Street Journal* or the *USA Today* "Money" section? Did you once fall in love with Maria Bartiromo on TV?

Do you enjoy the feeling that each day in the market is a new puzzle to figure out? Do you like seeing your well-chosen investments appreciate over time so that you can retire and live out your dreams? Have you ever felt excited talking about a stock, good or bad, at a party?

Did the market scare you during the financial crisis in fall 2008? How about spring 2009? Does your brow furrow trying to understand how the market could move so drastically and with such speed?

Do 500-point Dow moves intraday concern you? How about 1,000-point moves? If you trade with *stops*, have you always been mortified and angry about how "they" seem to take your stock to that price level, trigger your stop loss, and then take the stock back from that limit?

Do you understand how—or where—stocks trade today? Do you think that you should?

Because the title of this book is *Broken Markets*, it is fair to assume that we believe that there's something wrong with the stock market. It has changed so drastically, and so quickly, from the model that it was based on for more than a century. The stock market used to be a system—and a place—where investors traded capital. Now it is a loosely connected mess of more than 50 different exchanges, dark pools, and alternative trading venues focused on short-term trading. What was an imperfect, yet elegant, oligopoly of a few stock exchanges has become horribly fragmented, operating at insane speeds, in a crazy dance of arbitrage.

The market is like a shattered vase that is now held together with glue called *high frequency trading (HFT)*, and that glue is weak— very weak. In addition to fragmentation, under the cover of the digital revolution, conflicted stakeholders—stock exchanges, brokers, and owners of ATSs (alternative trading systems)—have

- Enlisted their own regulators to help them create a mechanism that places high-speed trading interests above the interests of all other market participants, particularly investors.

- Converted member-owned nonprofit legal structures into ones that are for-profit, which have enabled them to embark upon new business models centered around the creation and distribution of data feeds.

- Perverted the true purpose and usage of tools like dark pools from mechanisms to effect large block trades for large mutual and pension funds to a means to feed internalization and proprietary HFT.

- Introduced new systemic risks resulting in markets that can violently careen out of control as they did on the May 6, 2010 Flash Crash.

- Extracted the economics away from brokerage activities that nurture young companies and their IPOs.

Why Has Our Stock Market Structure Changed So Drastically?

The market has been hijacked. An evolved class of leveraged short-term, high-speed traders, sometimes called *high frequency traders*, who trade massive amounts of shares based on proprietary algorithms, has eclipsed other types of traders.

In the not-so-distant past, as little as ten years ago, most stocks were listed on the New York Stock Exchange (NYSE) or on the NASDAQ. When you, your mutual fund manager, or other fund managers wanted to buy or sell, a broker who was a member of the exchanges would execute the trade on your behalf in fairly centralized locations. You paid a commission or incurred a spread cost.

If the stock was listed on the NYSE, your order would be executed there, via your broker, with your instructions (that is, limit, market, stop loss, or good-till-cancel). Your order would make it to a specialist on the floor of the exchange who would execute it according to specific rules. The specialist's role was to match buyers and sellers, in a fluid way, whether they were on his limit book or against an order "in the crowd." In exchange for doing this, the specialist was allowed to trade alongside orders, taking advantage of his being privy to all the order flow.

If your stock was listed on NASDAQ, your order was represented and executed against an electronic dealer market. Those dealers would compete for your orders by adjusting their "market." If a NASDAQ market maker was a better buyer of the stock, he would post a competitive bid that was equal to or higher than the other prevailing bids. If he was a better seller, he would post an offer price equal to or lower than the prevailing offers by other dealers. These market makers not only facilitated customer order flow, but similar to the specialists on the NYSE, they also traded for their own accounts.

The history of the NYSE dates back to a 1792 pact, called the Buttonwood Agreement, named for the tree under which the agreement was signed. Twenty-four brokers signed the document, which established rules for the buying and selling of equity ownership in American corporations. These rules of conduct and fair play served as the foundation for all securities trading globally for a century, and volume on the exchange steadily grew.

The significance of integrity and fair play was so important to the Board of the NYSE that when it expanded into a new building on Broad Street, the building featured an incredible sculpture by John Quincy Adams Ward titled "Integrity Protecting the Works of Man." This sculpture features a 22-foot figure of Integrity in its center, with Agriculture and Mining to her left, and Science, Industry, and Invention to her right. How wise that NYSE Board was to recognize that economic growth and the stock market are intertwined. How wise for that NYSE Board to recognize that *integrity forms the basis for trust and confidence. How wise for that NYSE Board to recognize the link between the stock exchange and capital formation!*

Of course, over time, technologies evolved. Computers have made the markets faster and more efficient. Technological advances have empowered retail and institutional investors who can deal more directly in the marketplace, with fewer intermediaries, more control, and lower costs. The benefits have been substantial, to be sure. However, one class of market participants, HFT firms, has leveraged technology as well with automated programs that generate massive volumes for the stock exchanges. As they have grown, HFT firms have used their economic clout to extract an increasing number of perks and advantages from the exchanges, tilting the zero-sum game that is the stock market in the favor of HFTs versus investors.

When Did HFT Start?

We initially spotted HFT at work early in our careers, when we were sales traders at Institutional Network, otherwise known as

Instinet, the world's first electronic brokerage firm. Like the NYSE, Instinet was an order-driven market, but it was anonymous, with no specialists to facilitate order flow. In the 1990s, Instinet captured a huge market share in the block trading of NASDAQ stocks. Institutions and fund managers loved the ability to trade in between NASDAQ market maker spreads, which, at the time, were averaging more than 32 cents. Instinet filled a real need. Institutional fund managers wanted to trade their orders with more control and freedom. They wanted to trade their orders themselves rather than through a broker, and they wanted to do so at reduced costs. Each day, they routinely negotiated and traded blocks ranging from 25,000 to 1,000,000 shares. Each year, their number of trades increased.

Then Instinet began courting a new type of trader. These traders promised large volume, albeit in small size trades of a few hundred shares at a clip. In exchange, these traders wanted insanely low commission rates and access to Instinet's top-of-book and depth-of-book data. These traders wanted to feed their computer models all Instinet's order flow information, including best bids and offers, their sizes, as well as information about the other orders in each stock's limit book. It was a win for Instinet in terms of increased volume. Instinet could pitch that volume as an attribute in attracting new buy-side institutions that would pay higher commission rates.

Some might say it was wise for Instinet to court these automated trading firms. However, the flow these firms pumped into Instinet was predatory. We had never seen anything like it before. The institutional clients complained immediately. If an institutional client placed a bid to buy 5,000 shares at 24 1/8, the automated trading firms instantly placed a bid for a few hundred shares at 1/64 higher (the minimal allowable increment). They did this with every stock. If the institutional clients canceled their bids, the automated traders instantly canceled their higher bids as well.

Allowing these automated traders into the network ran counter to the philosophy Instinet had pioneered since its inception, which was helping institutions trade blocks electronically. It also felt plain wrong. These automated trading firms were nothing more than high-speed scalpers and the first high frequency traders. Instinet enabled them for fear that its order flow would go to the newer upstart electronic crossing networks (ECNs). Eventually, this type of order flow spread to all the other electronic venues in addition to Instinet.

The SEC became concerned, not about the scalping, but that the retail public was seeing one set of prices, while other market players saw better prices on the ECNs. In response, the SEC proposed Regulation ATS (Alternative Trading System), which mandated all orders go to a public quote. Instinet fiercely lobbied against it. Management had employees calling clients and urging them to write comment letters to the SEC. Instinet claimed that such a rule would create a commoditized limit order book, which would "crush innovation." In reality, Instinet was afraid of losing the special selling appeal of its own private stock market, with meaty institutional orders that the SEC, if they had their way, would forcibly make available to all traders through all systems. No doubt, management was also worried that the automated traders might not pay for the privilege of jumping 1/64 ahead of investor orders if the automated traders could do it to the entire market.

The SEC had its way. Reg ATS passed. Spreads between bids and offers tightened due to the competition. Instinet had to compete by having the fastest platform, and it did well. So, too, did the automated traders. They had a much larger body of water to swim in—and hunt. HFT exploded in volume as more firms entered the space. It would eventually peak in late 2009 with an estimated 70% of all volume in the market.

As HFT grew, so did the structure risks. The market is like an ocean. To the extent that there are many different trading styles and participants interacting with each other, the market is healthy, like a body of water teeming with many species. One player may have a subsecond time horizon, another a minute, another ten years. They might be value investors, chart readers, or earnings momentum players. However, when one participant accounts for so much volume and has eclipsed so many other participants, and its trading styles and horizons prevail, the ecosystem is in disequilibrium. One of its more predatory species, such as a shark, has become overwhelmingly dominant. And it is unsustainable.

How Did HFT Become So Big?

After the SEC implemented Reg ATS and decimals, spreads narrowed drastically: from quarters, to eighths, to sixteenths, to 3 cents and lower. The average amount of money a short-term trader could make per trade dwindled sharply, and automated trading firms in Darwinian fashion made up for that with sheer volume of trades. *Their growing volumes were on all of Wall Street's radar.* Brokerage firms, new electronic venues, and the major stock exchanges all took notice.

In the new millennium, when the SEC again set about to modernize its rules about stock trading, the agency sought a massive amount of input from all the players. The result was the Regulation National Market System, otherwise known as Reg NMS, which was authored by many industry participants in collaboration with the SEC. Proposed in late 2004, Reg NMS was supposed to serve as the framework for the evolving stock markets for the coming century. Due to delays, lobbying, industry comment letters, and reworking, it wasn't implemented until late 2007.

Reg NMS created the concept of a National Best Bid and Offer (NBBO). The NBBO was an aggregation of the best priced orders on all exchanges and ECNs, and it was *protected*. This meant that if one market center, say the NYSE, had a participant with an order to buy stock at $10.00 and did not have a matching sell order at $10.00, while another exchange, say NASDAQ, did, then the NYSE would have to route out that buy order to NASDAQ, which would then match the buy and sell order. As a result, Reg NMS *commoditized trading destinations.* Speed of execution became paramount. The slower, specialist-oriented NYSE was forced to become a fast, electronic market.

By the time Reg NMS was implemented, the stock exchanges had beefed up their systems, changed from member-owned, nonprofit corporations, to for-profit exchanges, and many of them became publicly traded companies. Although some say the exchanges did this to respond to Reg NMS while at the same time to protect themselves, they did it with an "eye on the prize," lobbying for the regulations to turn out exactly as they wanted, when they wanted it. You can't help but wonder whether the changed market structure is less the result of "unintended consequences" and more of a well-executed plan.

The changes brought about by Reg NMS have turned the market from an investor-focused mechanism, which welcomes traders and investors of all types and speeds, to a subsecond, trader-focused mechanism, where the concerns and confidence of investors are an afterthought. These changes are hurting you by making the market more dangerous and prone to another severe crash. This crash may start with a news event—a default on debt in Europe, an economic crisis in Asia, or a major bank bankruptcy in the United States. But make no mistake, the real reason will be that the stock market is based on business models that are rife with conflicts of interest that cater to hyper-short-term traders. *The real reason for the crash will be structural.*

Why Have We Allowed This to Happen?

Part of it is that intense lobbying by Wall Street, including the exchange operators, pushing for this to happen with regulators and politicians in DC. A larger part of the answer is we have all been told a nice story about cheap $8 or lower commission trades, ample liquidity, and inexpensive trading costs. We all bought into the notion that our markets are so tight and efficient that there is no downside, only upside due to the new efficient ways the markets work.

There are reasons why brokerage firms offer $8 trades to retail investors, when so often that fee doesn't cover costs. Today, these brokerage firms make money off retail orders in different ways. Money that used to be made mostly through commissions is now made through *trading around that order flow*. For example, your online broker likely sells your order to a "market maker," rather than routing it to an exchange. That market maker is an HFT expert and gets first crack at deciding whether to be on the other side of your order or route it to an exchange. It makes this decision based on its internal short-term price prediction models. Armed with up-to-date information on all the retail order flow that they buy, its algorithm decides whether your retail order is "dumb" or "informed" and acts accordingly.

At times, HFT has a parasite/host relationship with investors. HFT works well only when there are sufficient hosts in the pool upon which to feed. When the hosts dwindle, due to lack of confidence in the system, and funds flow out of equities, HFT firms suffer. They begin to trade with and against themselves. The more the equity markets become unbalanced, the more HFT predatory effects become visible. Picture a watering hole in the wild teeming with crocodiles. Other animals aren't afraid to drink at the hole because they don't see the crocs beneath the surface. If there is a drought, however, the water line drops. The crocs become visible, and the other animals stay away.

There also is a big structural risk in the way retail orders are handled today. Take the May 6, 2010 Flash Crash, for example. Most Americans are aware of the market's jaw-dropping 700 point decline and frenetic rise again that day. Billions of dollars of asset value were erased and almost restored in a period of minutes. Had the decline happened near the closing bell, you could not even begin to guess the damage that might have been inflicted on world markets in a domino effect. A big part of why the market unraveled that day is a direct result of HFT market makers who had purchased retail order flow from investors. At blazing speeds, they picked orders to which they wanted to be the contra-side and routed all others in such a way as to sell major well-known, well-capitalized stocks down to a penny.

Since 2008, we have been warning in our writings and TV appearances that HFT market makers would shut down and run for the hills at the first sign of stress. Under duress, HFTs would not be *liquidity providers*. They would be *demanders and consumers* of liquidity the likes of which the public has never seen. Their speed and information advantage on May 6, 2010 ensured that scared retail investors never had a chance. The story of the Flash Crash is that the market failed that day. It was exposed as a conflicted and rigged game in which only the connected insiders stood a chance. Every investor and market participant in the United States had been sold a lie: HFT liquidity was a blessing that lowered costs and helped investors, and it would be there in stressful markets like the market makers and specialists that it replaced.

Will There Be Another Market Crash?

No doubt. With each passing month, order, transaction, and data speeds increase. Trading is done on increasing numbers of exchanges, linked together by HFT pricing and rebate-induced arbitrage. The markets have become even more fragmented.

The leverage employed by HFT firms remains at extremely high levels, similar to the 40-1 debt to equity ratio used by MF Global, which amplified the disastrous effects of its poorly chosen bets. Because HFT firms' strategy is to start and end each day owning nothing, they have little tolerance for adverse "bets." When they are "wrong," their technology and speed enables them to dump their inventory in such a ferocious manner that limit order books quickly thin out in terms of price and depth. Because their algorithmic models price securities with such an emphasis on *nearby prices* and *robust uninterrupted pricing data flow*, when that data displays discrepancies, they withdraw their "liquidity provision" and shut down.

The Joint CFTC-SEC Advisory Committee, set up to study and report findings on the events of May 6, 2010, summed it nicely: "In the present environment, where high frequency and algorithmic trading predominate and where exchange competition has essentially eliminated rule-based market maker obligations...even in the absence of extraordinary market events, limit order books can quickly empty and prices can crash."[1]

Another concern is the market's *instrument makeup.* In 2010, Exchange Traded Products (ETP), including its biggest category, exchange traded funds, or ETFs, reached an asset under management (AUM) level of $1.3 trillion.[2] Only ten years prior, ETP AUM totaled a mere $66 billion.[3] This represents nearly a 19-fold increase. Each year stock exchanges, which are struggling to list shares of promising companies in the form of IPOs, manage to set new records in the number of ETPs and ETFs they list for trading. NYSE-Arca listed a record 300 new ETPs in 2011 versus 220 in 2010.[4] The result: More and more volume on exchanges is in the form of derivative products, of which an increasing number are leveraged and a large percentage of the trading is done by HFTs.

On calmer, benign days in the market, you can argue that HFT firms may do a good job of arriving at a fair price for large capitalization, highly liquid stocks such as Bank of America. However, in thinner issues that trade less often, HFT may not do such a good job. Although HFT is agnostic to the merits, fundamentals, and prices of the stocks it is flipping, it prefers liquid, lower-priced stocks because it can trade more shares of those for the same amount of capital deployed.

On volatile days, however, HFT exacerbates and amplifies price moves in short amounts of time. It's like lemmings. Lemmings behave normally when their population is in check, but their population is wildly erratic. They migrate in a massive group when population density swells. The group moves together in lockstep and walks off cliffs or jumps into large bodies of water in mass with horrific results. HFT has been around for nearly 15 years, its "population" swelling only fairly recently, corresponding with the implementation of Reg NMS. Their strategies are similar, frequently depending on speed to differentiate their success. HFT decides how, where, and when to buy and sell stock by examining relationships of data points immediately near each other. This modus operandi can cause them to chase stock prices up and down a ladder wildly. On May 6, 2010, HFT algorithms sold Accenture Corp. (ACN) down to pennies and Phillip Morris (MO) from $48 down to $17 and right back up to $46.

Where's the SEC in All This?

In the 1990s, *information superhighway* was the popular term used to describe the Internet. You can think of the stock markets as the *capital superhighway*. Movement of capital on this highway from savers and investors to businesses of all sizes must be safe, orderly, and reliable for all market participants, regardless of their "speed." If not, then the connection between Wall Street and Main Street is broken.

The Securities and Exchange Commission was created by the 1934 Exchange Act to bring confidence back to the markets in the midst of the Great Depression after the 1929 Crash. There was great fear that confidence had evaporated. If that confidence were to be reinstated, folks would buy and sell stocks again and make markets liquid. That would inspire investing, which would fuel the economy and the need for funds to grow businesses.

According to the SEC's website, its mission is to "protect investors, maintain fair, orderly, and efficient markets, and facilitate capital formation." This means that in policing the markets, and in crafting rules to keep up with technological innovation, the SEC should make sure that capital formation, and the catering to investors (as opposed to traders), is always front and center. This means that the SEC must always remember to keep that linkage between Wall Street and Main Street healthy and thriving. If Main Street is left out of the thought process, if it loses faith in the stock market as an investment vehicle, investors will "take their marbles and go home."

News flash: It's already happening. More than a quarter of a trillion dollars have been withdrawn from domestic equity mutual funds since May 2010.[5] This is horrible for two reasons. One, new and existing businesses need funds to grow, innovate, and hire. If American businesses don't get these funds, our economy stagnates, we fall behind other nations, and our standard of living drops. Two, these longer term investors are, and have always been, a source of real stability to the market. Their bids and offers provide liquidity that, unlike that of HFT, is deep and unfleeting.

The mission statement also claims that the SEC is focused on protecting investors and maintaining a fair, orderly, and efficient market. Insider trading cases, including the recent, high-profile prosecution of Raj Rajaratnam from Galleon Group, certainly protect us from those gaining unfair advantages at the expense of long-term investors. However, the Rajaratnam case—the largest insider trading scandal in our nation's history—centers around only $53 *million* in ill-gained profits. Compare that to the SEC's failure to stop the $68 *billion* Bernie Madoff Ponzi scheme, despite being tipped multiple times.

Although we praise the SEC for going after Rajaratnam, we can't help but be disappointed in the agency's seeming lack of action around HFT and the conflicts of interests in our market structure. HFT firms generate between $8 billion and $21 billion a year in profits. Tradebot, an HFT firm based in Kansas City, Missouri, in 2008 said it had not had a losing day in four years.[6] The last few years have shown quarterly earnings from big banks engaged in HFT. Several, including Goldman Sachs, have had quarters without one day of incurring a net trading loss. You might think, especially after the Madoff scandal, that these recurring, out-sized profits at the expense of investors would make the SEC call out the troops.

To appease the public, agency executives certainly appear to say the right things. In a December 3, 2009 letter to U.S. Senator Ted Kaufman, SEC Chair Mary Schapiro wrote the following:[7]

> Next month we hope to seek public comment, through a concept release or similar document, on a range of issues relating to dark liquidity in all of its forms, as well as the impact of high frequency trading in our markets. Among other things, we are likely to seek input on the various strategies used by high frequency traders and any special trading advantages they may enjoy, including through colocation arrangements. I am committed to pursuing the goal of improved intermarket surveillance as a means to strengthen our markets, deter and ferret out wrongdoing, and augment public confidence.

Although the SEC and CFTC have had their hands full with the post-financial crisis Dodd-Frank regulation to control risk at large banks, there is another element at play. You see, the SEC created all the regulations to "modernize" the markets over the past 15 years. It has written and revised the rules with the input of the stock exchanges and large brokerage firms—input that in many cases came from industry personnel who once worked at the SEC.

In other words, the SEC is the creator of our Franken-Market. And, as actor Colin Clive cried in the famous 1931 film about Mary Shelley's monster, *"It's alive!"*

Endnotes

1. Joint CFTC-SEC Advisory Committee on Emerging Regulatory Issues, "Recommendations Regarding Regulatory Responses to the Market Events of May 6, 2010": 2, http://www.sec.gov/spotlight/sec-cftcjointcommittee/021811-report.pdf.

2. Srichander Ramaswamy, "BIS Working Papers No. 343: Market Structures and Systemic Risks of Exchange-Traded Funds," Bank for International Settlements website (April 2011), http://www.bis.org/publ/woks343.pdf.

3. SEI Knowledge Partnership, "Exchange Traded Products: A Look Ahead," (2008), SEI website, http://www.seic.com/docs/IMS/Exchange Traded Products A Look Ahead.pdf.

4. NYSE Euronext, "NYSE Euronext Maintains Leading Position in Global Exchange Traded Products Market," NYSE Euronext website (Jan. 12, 2012), http://www.nyse.com/press/1326363007979.html.

5. Investment Company Institute, "Long-Term Mutual Funds Flows Historical Data," February 29, 2012, Investment Company Institute website, http://www.ici.org/research/stats.

6. Julie Creswell, "Speedy New Traders Make Waves Far from Wall St.," *The New York Times*, May 16, 2010, http://www.nytimes.com/2010/05/17/business/17trade.html?dbk.

7. Mary L. Schapiro (Chairman, Securities and Exchange Commission), letter dated Dec. 3, 2009 to Edward E. Kaufman (U.S. Senator), Zero Hedge website, http://www.zerohedge.com/sites/default/files/12-3-09%20SEC_Schapiro%20response%20to%20Kaufman.pdf.

2

The Curtain Pulled Back on High Frequency Trading

On the morning of June 2, 2010, Sal Arnuk was on the Acela train to Washington, DC. He was thinking about what he wanted to say later at the SEC's Market Structure Round Table. The panel was convened to bring the SEC up to speed on the structure of the markets that the agency played such a large role in creating between 1997 and 2007. In particular, the SEC wanted to understand the growth of the monster called HFT. Sal had been invited to speak. To say he was intimidated was an understatement.

Sal called the Themis Trading desk to speak to his partner Joe Saluzzi for some last-minute feedback. "Stop it," interrupted Joe. "You know this stuff cold. I have just one bit of advice for you. It works for me every time I get nervous before I go on TV. Go around the corner to that coffee shop we stopped in after our last SEC visit, and order a double espresso. Boom. Then, get in there and have fun."

I'm nervous, Sal thought. *The last thing in the world I want is coffee.* To steel himself, he sat back in his seat and reviewed the case against HFT. Although he wasn't sure how he was going to say it, he was very sure of his purpose: To make known the dangerous aspects of HFT and of conflicts of interests in our market structure....

What Is High Frequency Trading, and Who Is Doing It?

High frequency trading (HFT) is a vague term that the industry and regulators struggle to define. The Commodity Futures Trading Commission has even formed a sub-committee to understand it. Generally speaking, however, HFT is automated trading by sophisticated computer programs in stocks, ETFs, bonds, currencies, and options. Computers decide what security to trade, at what price, quantity, and timing, and feed the orders electronically into the market for execution.

This typically involves:

- Large technological expenditures in hardware, software and data
- Latency sensitivity (order generation and execution taking place in sub-second speeds)
- High quantities of orders, each small in size
- Short holding periods, measured in seconds versus hours, days, or longer
- Starts and ends each day with virtually no net positions
- Little human intervention

Will Psomadelis, Head of Trading at Schroeder Investment Management, in a paper titled "High Frequency Trading - Credible Research Tells the Real Story," found that HFT "returns are abnormally high, with Sharpe ratios often in the order of nine or double digits. Well-known names in the HFT space include GETCO, Infinium, and Optiver."[1]

Although initial perceptions focused on how HFT has shrunken spreads and generated liquidity that investors could embrace, in recent years those perceptions have turned quite negative. HFT's reputation has gotten so poor that lobbyists hired by HFT firms have tried to change the name or discourage its use in the media. In a 2010 newsletter, Joe Ratterman, the president of BATS, a stock exchange that caters to HFT firms, urged the industry to resist using the term. "Put HFT on your firm's restricted word list," he said. As an alternative, he suggested "Trading and Market Automation, or TMA," adding that BATS members should "preserve our current equity markets against *baseless sound bites* from those who don't fully understand the markets."[2]

The reality is it doesn't matter what you call it. It is what it is. No amount of lipstick can make a pig pretty, except maybe to another pig.

Recently in 2011, we spoke at Barry Ritholtz's *Big Picture Conference*, a gathering of industry participants in New York City focused on pressing issues in global economics and markets. We gave a presentation titled "High Frequency Trading and Its Threat to the Markets." The gist of that presentation is the guts of this book. Our markets have been purposely morphed into a system designed to cater to an evolved class of hyper-short-term day traders. Those traders enter and cancel thousands of orders per second. The stocks they trade are meaningless to them; they are but currency.

High frequency traders need high-computing power and ultra-low latency (high speed). They get it by renting server space from the stock exchanges. They also need to access big amounts of data, which they analyze and run though algorithmic trading programs to detect patterns in the markets. They get the data from the stock exchanges, too. Then they trade, capitalizing on those patterns. And, in many cases, the exchanges pay them to trade.

In our *Big Picture Conference* presentation, we spoke about a few types of HFT:

- "Market making" rebate arbitrage (we use quotations around "market making" because we really don't see how it even closely resembles real market making)
- Statistical arbitrage

- Latency arbitrage
- Momentum ignition

Market Making Rebate Arbitrage

This is probably the largest bucket of HFT. It is the style and strategy especially catered to by all the for-profit exchanges.

With the exchanges becoming for-profit, and, in many cases, converting to publicly traded companies, such as the NYSE or NASDAQ, they now care very much about how to keep growing revenues. Their largest traders by volume are most willing to pay for the exchange's expensive services, such as enriched data feeds and colocation. Their largest traders are the HFT designated market makers (DMMs) and supplemental liquidity providers (SLPs). DMMs and SLPs are the modern electronic replacements of the human specialists and market makers of yesteryear whose jobs were to match customer orders as well as maintain "a fair and orderly market."

In 1933, the number of specialist firms on the NYSE totaled 230. By 1983, acquisitions and mergers had reduced that number to 59. By 2001, there were only 10.[3] Today only four DMMs control the trading on the NYSE: Goldman Sachs, Knight, Barclays, and newcomer GETCO. They are the HFT powerhouses on Wall Street. Most industry professionals we talk to believe these four horsemen are responsible for 40–50% of all trading on the NYSE. With their electronic savvy and prowess, they optimize their automated trading programs to maximize the money they earn from trading as well as from rebates paid to them by NYSE. DMMs make money not only from buying stocks and selling them higher, but also from the exchanges, which reward them with rebates for "adding liquidity." The exchanges have adopted complex pricing mechanisms that reward the adding of liquidity with a small rebate, while charging a small fee for the taking of liquidity. Due to these exchange rebates, DMMs can make money even when they buy and sell at the same price. A critical factor in doing this is speed. Key for the DMMs' success, therefore, is being as close as possible to the exchange.

DMMs have several things tipping the scales in their favor versus traditional investors and traders. Their colocated speed and technology almost always places them at the top of the queue at any price. They also are allowed *parity* by the NYSE. Parity enables them to buy alongside other customer orders, without having to wait for the orders to be filled. This is a huge benefit that vastly increases the money they can make. It enables them to analyze all orders to decide which ones are the most profitable to trade. Some market structure experts believe DMMs earn only 1/10 of a penny per trade, although we are skeptical of that low figure.[4]

DMMs run on virtual autopilot, flipping stocks with the aim of maximizing their rebates. Whether intraday markets are directionless or trending, their technological prowess and speed gets them to the best prices for their own account faster than any other participant. In one of our earlier white papers, "What Ails Us About High Frequency Trading," we made the following analogy:[5]

> Imagine you are at the grocery store. You take your cart to one of five apparently empty checkout lines. Suddenly, nine carts instantaneously appear ahead of you. You scratch your head and move to lane two. The same thing happens. You soon find that whenever you move into a new lane, a multitude of carts appear ahead of you in line. Why? Because the supermarket has sold the right for those carts to do so. Thus, you can never be at the head of the line, no matter what you do, short of paying the exchanges a large fee to have that same right...

You may frequently hear that DMMs "provide liquidity" to the rest of the market by always trading. In reality, they provide liquidity only when they want and turn it off when it gets too risky. When they do turn it off, the markets become anything but "fair and orderly."

And when do they turn it off? When the market gets stressed. When that happens, there are delays and inconsistencies between the data feeds connecting the plethora of exchanges and trading venues. HFT computer programs can't determine the "correct" prices of securities. With that kind of uncertainty, the programs exit their positions and "liquidity provision." Spreads widen. And sometimes, such as the May 6, 2010 Flash Crash, there is a "liquidity vacuum." Andy Haldane, the Executive Director of Financial Stability at the Bank of England, in a July 8, 2011 speech titled "The Race to Zero," described this as "adding liquidity in a monsoon and absorbing it in a drought."[6]

Statistical Arbitrage

Statistical Arbitrage (AKA, "stat arb") has been in operation for decades. The type of example most often given is when IBM is trading "rich" in London and "cheap" on the NYSE, the stat arb guys will simultaneously short it in London and buy it back on the NYSE. Oh, if it were only that simple today.

Today, the stat arb guys are trading "rich" versus "cheap" in more than 50 fragmented destinations. And they have Wall Street's greatest success/growth story of recent years, the proliferation of thousands of exchange traded funds (ETFs)—think mutual fund-like baskets that trade real-time—to give them even more baskets to statistically compare and trade.

Today, they can arb State Street's SPY versus Vanguard's VOO, as well as against the underlying stock prices those baskets represent. They can track the correlation of different ETFs and trade any number of Delta One relationships. (Delta One refers to the near one-to-one tracking relationships between certain derivatives—like some ETFs and equity swaps—and the underlying basket of securities that they are tracking.) Despite the massive job loss on Wall Street, there is robust demand for math whizzes on nearly every big bank Delta

One desk. These desks have become the most consistently profitable units at nearly all investment banks. They create swaps, track relationships between thousands of instruments, and capitalize on them. These desks are nothing without their HFT capabilities.

Although the name Delta One implies low-risk trades, that is a faulty assumption. In September 2011, UBS announced to a shocked financial community a more than $2 billion loss by one of its "rogue traders." Kweku Adoboli worked in its global synthetic equities division, buying and selling ETFs, bonds, and commodities, such as metals. He worked on UBS' Delta One desk, and his faulty bets in EuroStoxx, DAX, and S&P500 ETFs was the talk of the Street for months. He had disguised the risk of his trades by using "forward settling" ETF cash positions.[7]

Statistical arbitrage trading generates massive volumes in ETFs. Those massive volumes generate massive profits for the exchanges, as well as the ETF industry. The proliferation of ETFs even has the granddaddy of indexing, Jack Bogle, founder of Vanguard, concerned about their outsized effect on risk and volatility. In a September 19, 2011 CNBC interview, he noted that when he advocated and pushed the merits of indexing in the mid-1990s, it was 3% of the marketplace. Today, it is in excess of 25%. In a *Wall Street Journal* interview on September 10, 2011, when asked whether he thought indexing had gotten out of hand, he commented, "Unequivocally, yes. It has been bastardized. ETFs are often great big gambling, speculative instruments that have destabilized the market." According to Bogle, by creating instruments that get flipped all day long, ETFs are extracting wealth from investors, who, he warned, need to put their hand over their wallets quickly.

It is ironic to note that the firm Bogle founded, Vanguard, has become such a large player in the ETF industry now that Bogle has retired. Vanguard's comments in the media and letters to the SEC take a tone that is the polar opposite to his well-known, seasoned and sage reasoning.

Is all HFT statistical arbitrage inherently bad? We would argue that some of this is indeed healthy. However, we can't help but wonder whether many ETFs have been developed for the express purpose of computerized arbitrage trading because that generates volume for the exchanges and big fees for the ETF creator. Unfortunately, the exponential rise of these instruments has increased the correlation between many asset classes. This hurts long-term investors: It makes presumably "safe" portfolios, with a traditional mixture of assets designed to offset each other, increasingly risky.

Another downside is that, because of so much trading in these ETFs, and the speed of that trading, errors that occur in the marketplace become instantly and widely reflected. We have seen where an errant trade in one thin stock, perhaps due to a real-life "fat finger," results in another stock trading down $10, causing sudden drops in "related" ETFs and other securities within those ETFs. You might even have experienced one of your stop loss orders trigged unintentionally as a result.

Market Structure and Latency Arbitrage

This strategy is designed to exploit built-in weaknesses in the market structure. While Reg NMS was being proposed, debated, and enacted between 2004 and 2007, the stock exchanges were busy readying business models in which they amped up the speed of their trade handling ability to cater to HFT. The exchanges built data centers to rent out colocation space to HFT firms to give them an edge in accessing the exchanges' matching engines. The exchanges knew very well that future revenue growth was going to come from technology services as opposed to matching trades.

These exchanges also are responsible for maintaining the publicly available stock quotes, commonly called the Security Information Processor (SIP). This is the quote that most investors see when they look at their data terminals, or if they watch quotes stream on their online broker's website. It is also the speed that the national best bid and offer (NBBO) updates for most dark pools, although not all. (Dark pools contain trading that is not generally available to the public: the orders and quotes in them are not visible like an exchange's quotes are.) The SIP speed is slower than the speed of the exchanges' direct data feeds, which are sold to collocating HFT firms so they can act on the data faster than anybody else.

This speed or latency advantage enables HFT firms to reengineer the NBBO faster than it is disseminated by the SIP. HFT firms can in effect see the future. They know what the quote of any given stock will be microseconds before those looking at the public SIP. If the actual price for a stock is higher than what is available on the slower markets, HFTs swoop in, buy it, and sell it at the higher price. It is like betting on a horse race when you know who the winner will be. It also functions as a kind of tax on investors. The money garnished comes directly from investors, who pay more for stocks they buy and receive less for stocks they sell.

HFT latency arbitrage has as its roots the predatory trading of past market structures. In the late 1980s and 1990s, a group of trading participants, collectively called SOES Bandits, was notorious for picking off market makers that were too slow to update their quotes. SOES stood for Small Order Execution System, which the bandits abused. Ironically, SOES was designed to help retail investors get trades done in a timely fashion. SOES Bandits spooked market makers, with the result being wider spreads to compensate for the risk of getting picked off by the bandits. SOES Bandits were a bane on capital markets in those times. HFT firms, enabled by the stock exchanges, are their direct descendants.

Perhaps similarly, late trading in mutual funds was a strategy whereby traders were taking advantage of slow-to-update (once per day) mutual fund net asset values (NAVs). Here, too, the "late trading" was done at the expense of long-term investors. The mutual fund timing scandal eroded investor confidence. Regulators acted, in the form of a 2003 bill called the Mutual Fund Investor Confidence Restoration Act.[8] We point this out to illustrate that there were times in our past when regulators acknowledged the detriment to investors of practices that took advantage of slower market participants, who traditionally have been investors as opposed to traders.

Momentum Ignition

This type of HFT is perhaps the most secretive. It tries to "trick" larger, institutional orders away from true supply and demand metrics. We first began to notice it when we would bid for a stock in order to accumulate a large position for our clients, and, upon entry of every bid that we made, automated front running was triggered. An offer gets lifted in front of us. Then another. Then the rapid-fire order sequence continued, where bids were entered ahead of us, canceled, and then entered again only higher, and then canceled again. Often this sequence involved hundreds or even thousands of entered orders and cancellations, whereby only a few hundred shares ultimately get executed by the HFT firms. Market participants frequently hear that the reason HFT firms enter and cancel 95% of their orders without a trade is because HFTs are just "managing risk" in their market making activities. In reality, HFT firms are trying to create momentum. They are trying to mislead institutional algorithmic orders into following along these price changes, which are created with the intention to manipulate a stock higher after the HFT firm has already bought the stock at a cheaper price.

These manipulative strategies are what first alerted us to the dark side of HFT. Sometime in 2007, one of our customers criticized our executions in a most passionate way:

"Geez guys. What gives?" he complained over the phone. "Every time I put you in motion, my friggin' stock dances and takes off. What the hell are you guys doing? You are supposed to be electronic trading experts and you are screwing me. Uncle. I give up!"

We were crushed by his criticism. He was right. Our whole careers we had prided ourselves on our ethics, on our no-conflict agency model, and most important, on our ability to navigate "the new markets." And we were letting one of our best customers down. We knew we had to get to the bottom of it. We looked at our own methods to see whether what we were doing had changed. We consulted other brokers to see what they were experiencing. They confirmed the same insanity that we saw. Although we hadn't changed how we traded for our clients, the marketplace certainly had. Our client's words inspired us to understand Wall Street's new, technology-enhanced "plumbing" to correct how we were unwittingly telegraphing our clients' intentions to opportunistic scalpers.

The cost to investors when momentum ignition succeeds is not "a penny or two," as HFT firms claim. We have seen these HFT algorithmics take small- and mid-cap stocks up 50 cents on just a few thousand shares. When we recognize the strategy and cancel our interest from the market, the stock reverts back to our initial price nearly all the time. Then we can go back to accumulating shares for our long-term clients at the lower prices. Until the cycle starts again.

We have heard representatives from smaller, independent HFT firms defend their activities as healthy for the market, as they achieve "price discovery" most efficiently for the markets, which is a goal all investors should want.[9] We say hogwash. Momentum ignition does not bring about price discovery. It distorts it. A telling example of a "price discovery" algorithm is what happened to the book *The Making of a Fly* on Amazon. In an April 25, 2011 article, *Amazon seller lists the book at $23,698,655.93-plus shipping*,[10] CNN reported how predatory algorithms drove up the price of the book from $199 to $24 million in ten days. It was not due to small supply and rabid demand. One algorithm was pricing the book at 1.27 times the price of the other algorithm, which in turn would revise its price to 0.998 times the price of the first algorithm, creating a positive feedback loop.

Momentum ignition is extremely damaging to long-term investors. It does not cost pennies; it costs them quarters, and it ferociously distorts the price discovery process.

How the World Began to Learn About HFT

While HFT has been steadily expanding since the millennium and exponentially since the implementation of the SEC's Reg NMS in 2007, it stayed out of the mainstream media until mid-2009. Over the July 4 weekend, Sergey Aleynikov was arrested by the FBI at Newark Airport for stealing code from his prior employer, Goldman Sachs, and trying to bring it to his new job as an HFT programmer at Teza Technologies, where he was set to triple his $400,000 salary. According to Assistant U.S. Attorney Joseph Facciponti, Goldman raised the alarm that "somebody who knew how to use this program could use it to manipulate markets in unfair ways."[11] Aleynikov was found guilty under the Economic Espionage Act in December 2010 and began serving an eight-year sentence at a federal prison. His conviction was reversed by a higher court in February 2012.

Nonetheless, that July 4 weekend started a scramble for information about HFT and how it could manipulate markets. Our 2008 white paper, "Toxic Equity Trading on Wall Street," shot up in the Google search rankings and went viral. The paper demonstrated in lay terms how HFT was costing investors millions of dollars via automated market making and predatory algos.[12]

The week following Aleynikov's arrest, our phones rang off the hook. Callers ranging from journalists to politicians were starved for information on the financial industry's best kept secret. We took turns answering the calls and giving media interviews. It was exciting for us, to be sure, and we were thankful to have a platform to tell of dangers that we saw in the marketplace. On CNBC, with Steve Liesman and Michelle Caruso Cabrerra, Joe faced off against an HFT practitioner, Irene Aldridge of Able Alpha Trading.

Cabrerra opened by saying, "There's a controversy brewing on Wall Street about a new trend called High Frequency Trading. Critics say it's hosing the little guy, making him pay more for stocks than he would.... Joining us now is one of the guys who started the controversy, Joe Saluzzi, co-head of Equity Trading at Themis Trading. That's because he wrote three white papers that everyone is talking about...."[13]

The segment intended by CNBC to be five minutes was extended to eight. Aldridge tried to say that there was nothing wrong with HFT; all it did was bring in computers and mathematics to the trading process.

Joe brought up flash orders, exchange colocation, rebate trading, as well as the difference between volume and liquidity. "Liquidity can go away tomorrow," he said. "If they (the HFTs) decide to shut the computer, we're down 70% on volume. They can shut their computers off on a bad day."

Sadly, the Flash Crash would prove his point within a year. Steve Liesman interrupted with some great questions. Why wasn't there one speed for all investors? Why wasn't there a speed limit on our financial superhighway?

HFT was dragged out into the sunlight. Our papers and that CNBC interview captured the attention of the SEC's Trading and Markets Division, which invited us to address the entire SEC on-site and bring them up to speed on our views on HFT. We did this in November 2009 and again in June 2010.

The SEC's Round Table on Equity Market Structure—or Sal Goes to Washington

On June 2, 2010, Sal went to Washington to participate in the SEC-sponsored Round Table on Equity Market Structure. Invitees came from all parts of the industry: brokerage firms, exchanges, mutual fund investors, dark pool operators, execution cost specialists, HFT market makers (DMMs), smaller HFT firms, academicians, and latency experts. Since the Aleynikov arrest for stealing code that ostensibly could be used to manipulate markets and the Flash Crash only weeks prior, the pressure was on our regulator to explain to the public how our markets could morph into a structure that would allow market plunges with such jaw-dropping speed and ferocity.

It was the end of May when we received the call from Jamie Brigagliano, a senior SEC staffer, inviting us to testify. We eagerly accepted. How could we be anything other than excited that the SEC was taking seriously the issues we had been speaking about since 2005 and even more aggressively since 2007, when Reg NMS was implemented? Sal asked Brigagliano whether our testimony could take place earlier rather than later, as the round table was on Sal's 20th wedding anniversary. Brigagliano responded dryly, if not incredulously, that the SEC would do its best to get Sal home to see his wife. Brigagliano added that we should expect an email with a list of industry participants who would be on the panel with Sal.

That email came, and our jaws dropped. The list included the CEOs of several prominent HFT firms, senior executives of exchanges selling products to HFT firms, and senior executives and CEOs of brokerage firms selling sponsored access and "latency consulting" to HFT firms. Ours was the sole voice that would take a contra-stance to the entire pro-HFT "more liquidity, tighter spreads, our-markets-are-better-than-ever" crowd.

Our initial pride and excitement was instantaneously replaced with dread and anxiety over what we should say and do. Was it a set-up? How could the American public expect a fair shake and honest fact-finding examination when it was seeking expert commentary from the very folks who had such a strong hand crafting of the SEC regulations that created our Franken-Markets in the first place? Can you imagine the Food and Drug Administration examining the safety of cigarette smoking by soliciting 95% of its input from Big Tobacco?

To prepare our arguments, we called the office of U.S. Senator Ted Kaufman of Delaware. Sen. Kaufman had replaced Joe Biden when the latter became vice president. Sen. Kaufman quickly developed into a knowledgeable Beltway insider and courageous voice always questioning the status quo on Wall Street. If anyone could tell us how to act on Washington panels, we figured it would be Ted and his chief of staff, Jeff Connaughton.

They, too, were shocked at the makeup of the SEC's panel. Senator Kaufman acted the next day. He crafted a speech and read it on the floor of the Senate.[14]

> The SEC has picked one voice for the panel—Sal Arnuk of Themis Trading—who has been a vocal and intelligent critic of high frequency trading.
>
> He has valiantly raised questions about market structure and the trading advantages that high frequency traders enjoy, but he is being asked to go up against six Wall Street insiders who will no doubt be primed to argue against his position.
>
> People wonder why Americans have such little faith in Washington, DC. Talk about a stacked deck.
>
> I fear that an industry-stacked panel in the upcoming round-table on high frequency trading will be more of the same and

will once again dismiss fundamental reforms, ultimately leaving retail and long-term investors with half-measures or none at all.

Why? Because repeatedly we see that regulators are dependent almost exclusively for the information and evidence they receive about market problems on the very market participants they are supposed to be confronting about needed changes.

The panel's makeup changed the next day. Three panelists were added with a historical perspective more aligned with investors than Wall Street trading firms: Kevin Cronin, director of Global Trading at Invesco Management, one of the world's largest long-term investors and money managers; Mark Grier, vice chairman of Prudential Financial; and Dr. Michael Goldstein, Professor of Finance at Babson College.

We sighed in relief. We knew Cronin's mutual fund trading expertise would translate into wise and credible long-term investor perspective. And we knew how powerful a presence he was as a speaker. Likewise, we were confident that Dr. Goldstein's research on spreads and market structure, spanning several decades, would make him a perfect counterbalance to the many pro-HFT panelists.[15]

We began preparing. We grilled each other, with Victor Gonzalez, a long-time Themis team member, playing "devil's advocate." He is a pit bull, always instrumental in toughening our performance in public. Finally, in the waiting room at 100 F Street, while other panelists sat around, Sal played over and over in his mind what he wanted to say, trying to steady his nerves after reluctantly downing the double espresso Joe had recommended.

Unexpectedly, SEC Chair Mary Schapiro entered the room, walked up to Sal, and introduced herself. They shook hands. In front of some of Wall Street's biggest names, Schapiro told Sal, loud enough so everybody could hear, "I want to complement you on your Concept Release Comment Letter; it was one of the very best I have read."

Throughout the room, everybody's eyes burned holes in Sal's chest.

He felt good.

All nine panelists gave opening statements, followed by a question and answer period with the SEC commissioners and staff. The session ran more than 95 minutes. The lines were clearly drawn. Rich Gorelick, CEO of RGM Advisors, an HFT firm; Steve Schuler, CEO of GETCO, an HFT firm; and Jeff Wecker, CEO of Lime Brokerage, an HFT-sponsored access firm, all drove home how valuable their companies were to the markets. Their rallying points were their liquidity provision, contribution to price discovery, narrow spreads, and fairness. (Anyone can choose to buy colocation space and data feeds from the exchanges, they explained.)

Challenging them was Kevin Cronin, head of trading at Invesco, Dr. Goldstein, and Sal. Their counterpunches centered on market fairness; rigged games; the effect on investor confidence; conflicts of interests between the exchanges, brokers, and HFT firms; trading speed limits; and the real definition of quotes and liquidity.

Cronin questioned the value of firms such as RGM front-running his bids, which tend to be sizeable and much more than a 100-share HFT bid, and playing a rebate collection game to the point that it discourages Invesco from even placing its bids in the public markets. Dr. Goldstein brought up trading speed limits, noting that the markets do not seem to be allocating capital any better than they did in 2007, when speeds were substantially slower. He asked, "At what point are we trading too fast?"

Sal attacked the two-speed market: one for investors and the public SIP, and a second for HFT firms purchased from the exchanges through data feed and colocation access. When the discussion honed in on the value of quotes and liquidity, Sal's money line hit home: "What value is there to a quote that you can't access?" He was referring to the capability of HFT firms to unfairly see slower orders in the marketplace and cherry-pick when they wanted to interact with them.

After the panel concluded, venerable *Barron's* Washington editor, Jim McTague, approached Sal and complimented him on his fearlessness. "Sal, you hit them hard," McTague said. "I don't think Steve [Schuler, CEO of the GETCO HFT firm] was pleased though, judging by his face." McTague would subsequently visit our office and pick our brains about HFT in preparation for his book, *Crapshoot Investing.*[16]

Then Schapiro walked up to Sal. She shook his hand and told him to get on the next train home for his anniversary. We like to think the SEC was pleased that they had heard both sides of the HFT argument.

60 Minutes—or Joe Makes It to Primetime

Our white papers, Joe's CNBC and Bloomberg TV interviews, the revelation that our markets could be manipulated by algorithmic code, our discussions with Senator Kaufman and his staff, and our SEC testimonies were thrusting HFT out from the dark. The topic caught the attention of *60 Minutes.* Coleman Cowan, one of the show's producers, contacted us in October 2010.

Cowan was referred to us by Jeff Connaughton, Sen. Kaufman's Chief of Staff. We were more than happy to provide any background that Coleman needed. We wanted to make sure *60 Minutes* understood all sides of the story. After months of extensive research, to our surprise, Coleman asked us to be part of the program.

We filmed the appearance on June 16, 2010. The crew arrived about two hours before the interview began and transformed our trading room into a mini-television studio. Cameras and lights were everywhere. We needed to turn our air conditioner up high to keep the room cool. Unfortunately, the noise interfered with the audio, and we had to turn it off. The place turned into a sauna.

Steve Kroft, *60 Minutes'* long-time correspondent, was extremely well prepared. He arrived with a binder packed with notes and information. His interview with Joe lasted several hours and touched on almost every angle of HFT. Coleman told us the piece would run in the fall, but he couldn't reveal when. On October 10, 2010, the segment, *How Speed Traders Are Changing Wall Street*, aired. Just one week after the SEC report on the Flash Crash, the HFT community was exposed on prime time television.

Kroft introduced the broadcast, explaining:[17]

> It may surprise you to learn that most of the stock trades in the U.S. are no longer being made by human beings, but by robot computers capable of buying and selling thousands of different securities in the time it takes you to blink an eye.
>
> These supercomputers—which actually decide which stocks to buy and sell—are operating on highly secret instructions programmed into them by math wizards who may or may not know anything about the value of the companies that are being traded.
>
> It's known as high frequency trading, a phenomenon that's swept over much of Wall Street in the past few years and played a supporting role in the mini-market crash last spring that saw the Dow Jones Industrial Average plunge 600 points in 15 minutes.

Kroft also interviewed Manoj Narang, CEO of HFT firm Tradeworx, from their offices in Red Bank, New Jersey; Larry Liebowitz, chief operating officer of NYSE; Sen. Kaufman; and SEC Chair Schapiro. Kroft would later comment that the segment was one of the most difficult he had ever done; it was challenging to turn such a technical subject into a mainstream piece, and only one HFT player would talk.

All in all it was a balanced and highly informative piece. While outstanding reporting on HFT had been done for years by bloggers with surprising thought-reach, firstly and most notably Zero Hedge, *60 Minutes* took the subject matter to ordinary investors and citizens. It also lit a match on Wall Street. Here is how *Traders Magazine*, a leading industry publication, described the morning after, in an article titled, "Sellside Moves to Protect Buyside from HFT Onslaught":[18]

> Talk about the power of television. On Monday morning, Oct. 11, 2010, the phones in Credit Suisse's Advanced Execution Services department were ringing more than usual.
>
> On the other end were anxious customers asking the big broker what it was doing to protect their orders from predatory black-box traders. They had all watched *60 Minutes* the night before, when the popular television program explored the world of computerized trading and the role of high-frequency traders.
>
> Reporter Steve Kroft interviewed Joe Saluzzi, co-head of agency brokerage Themis Trading, who told Kroft that high-frequency traders were using their superior firepower-i.e., speed-to push prices up or down, to the disadvantage of the institutional investor.
>
> "They're parasites who exploit technological advantages to suck money out of the market," Saluzzi told Kroft. "They add no value." The trader added that he "spots signs of predatory behavior every day."

After being so quiet for so long, other institutional buy-side firms were starting to speak up.

Endnotes

1. Will Psomadelis and Stuart Baden Powell, "Special Report: High Frequency Trading—Credible Research Tells the Real Story," Schroder Talking Point website, (Nov. 30, 2011), https://c.na3.content.force.com/servlet/servlet. ImageServer?id=01550000000rlr3AAA&oid=00D300000000M2BEAU.

2. Joe Ratterman (chairman, BATS Exchange), letter to BATS Exchange customers and members of the trading community, BATS website (2010), http://www. batstrading.com/resources/newsletters/2010-03-Commentary.pdf.

3. Brian C. Hatch and Shane A. Johnson, "The Impact of Specialist Firm Acquisitions on Market Quality," *Journal of Financial Economics* 00 (2001) 000–000: 2, *Journal of Financial Economics*—Rochester website, http://jfe.rochester.edu/01484.pdf.

4. *The New York Times* "High Frequency Trading (updated Oct. 10, 2011)," Times Topics website, (Feb. 16, 2012), http://topics.nytimes.com/topics/reference/timestopics/subjects/h/high_frequency_algorithmic_trading/index.html.

5. Sal L. Arnuk and Joseph Saluzzi, "What Ails Us About High Frequency Trading?": 3, Themis Trading website, http://www.themistrading.com/article_files/0000/0508/What_Ails_Us_About_High_Frequency_Trading_--_Final__2__10-5-09.pdf.

6. Andrew Haldane, speech titled "The Race to Zero,": 14, given at the International Economic Association 16th World Congress in Beijing, China on July 8, 2011, Bank for International Settlements website, http://www.bis.org/review/r110720a.pdf.

7. Tracy Alloway, Izabella Kaminska, and Megan Murphy, "Opportunities to hide in murky world of ETFs," FT.com (September 19, 2011), http://www.ft.com/cms/s/0/3d8a135c-e2bd-11e0-897a-00144feabdc0.html#axzz1odETBFkl.

8. Nadia Papagiannis, "Market Structure Arbitrage: Fast Trading Techniques That Are Making Some Investors Furious," *Morningstar Alternative Investments Observer* vol. 2, no. 4 (4th q. 2010): 5, Morningstar Advisor website, http://advisor.morningstar.com/Uploaded/PDF/AIO_QuarterlyQ42010_NonACC.pdf.

9. *Futures Industry*, "SEC Roundtable Reveals Sharp Differences of Opinion on High Frequency Trading," Futures Industry website (June 2, 2010), http://www.futuresindustry.org/ptg/sec-roundtable-reveals-sharp-differences-of-opinion-on-highfrequency-trading.asp.

10. John D. Sutter, "Amazon Seller Lists Book at $23,698,655.93—Plus Shipping," CNN Tech, CNN.com (April 25, 2011), http://articles.cnn.com/2011-04-25/tech/amazon.price.algorithm_1_first-book-algorithms-amazon-com?_s=PM:TECH.

11. David Glovin and Christine Harper, "Goldman Trading-Code Investment Put at Risk by Theft (Update 3)," Bloomberg website (July 6, 2009), http://www.bloomberg.com/apps/news?pid=newsarchive&sid=ajIMch.ErnD4.

12. Sal L. Arnuk and Joseph Saluzzi, "Toxic Equity Trading Order Flow on Wall Street: The Real Force Behind the Explosion in Volume and Volatility," Themis Trading website (December 17, 2008), http://www.themistrading.com/article_files/0000/0348/Toxic_Equity_Trading_on_Wall_Street_12-17-08.pdf.

13. Joseph Saluzzi (cofounder, Themis Trading), interview on CNBC, YouTube website (July 24, 2009), http://www.youtube.com/watch?v=_A28Zy9vR_A.

14. Edward E. Kaufman, speech to the U.S. Senate on May 27, 2010, University of Delaware Library website, http://green.lib.udel.edu/webarchives/ kaufman.senate.gov/press/press_releases/release/-id=1144e076-2fea-47fd-ad43-c6893f17bc2c.htm.

15. See all of Michael A. Goldstein's works at the Babson College website, http:// faculty.babson.edu/goldstein/.

16. Jim McTague, *Crapshoot Investing: How Tech-Savvy Traders and Clueless Regulators Turned the Stock Market into a Casino* (New Jersey: Financial Times Press, 2011), http://www.ftpress.com/store/product.aspx?isbn=0132599686.

17. Steve Kroft, "Wall Street: The Speed Traders," 60 Minutes Oct. 10, 2010, CBS News website, http://www.cbsnews.com/video/watch/?id=6945451n.

18. Peter Chapman, "Defending the Turf: Sellside Moves to Protect Buyside from HFT Onslaught," Traders Magazine.com (May 12, 2011), http://www.tradersmagazine.com/news/sellside-defends-buyside-hft-107526-1.html.

3

Web of Chaos

Joe Saluzzi was a guest on CNBC's "Street Signs" segment with Brian Sullivan and Herb Greenberg. It was the afternoon of October 10, 2011. The discussion centered on the volatility caused by high frequency traders and confidence in our stock market structure.

"Ninety billion has come out of domestic equity funds since May," Joe said. "It tells you the confidence is not there.... The markets are broken."

Greenberg agreed. The next day the veteran business journalist penned a scathing article on the cable channel's website, titled, "Yes Virginia, the Markets Are Broken." Joe was right, he wrote. "And I'll take it one step further: Until further notice, investing the old-fashioned way is dead—maybe forever. Yes, maybe this time it really IS different."[1]

We first started noticing in 2007 just how badly our markets are broken. It stung when one of our best customers criticized our trading abilities. Although we had become accustomed to penny-jumping, automated scalpers since the mid-1990s, something had changed. With the mere entry of small, 300-share limit orders, we began to notice increased "wiggle" in the form of the following:

- **More quote-flickering:** When we sent to take stock offered on an exchange, the offer would mysteriously rise or disappear just as we arrived.

- **More penny-jumping:** Each time we would buy or sell stock, it seemed that others were tipped off to our intentions in real time.

45

- **More impact on prices:** Even small purchases would cause stock price movement away from us in ways much more noticeable than we had ever seen before in our careers.

As agency stock brokers with a fiduciary duty to get our clients the best prices, we had to get to the bottom of it. We started digging into the "plumbing"—how our orders are actually sent to exchanges and how the exchanges work. We looked at all the different order types, many of which were far cries from those traditionally used by agency brokers.

We looked at the information being disseminated on the stock exchanges' proprietary data feeds and who was receiving them. We had always assumed that data feeds were fairly simple and included routine information such as quantity, price, time, and the exchange in which each trade took place. The enriched feeds, however, had much more than that: information about our orders that we thought was hidden, as well as nuances that enabled HFT firms to backward-engineer how much investors were buying and selling, and in what manner.

The more we dug, the more convinced we became that something had gone awry. Most people believe the U.S. stock market is a duopoly controlled by NYSE and NASDAQ. We learned that the market had become one big conflicted, for-profit web of more than 50 trading destinations.

And it made us sick to our stomachs.

- If you are a retail investor, there's a reason why your online brokerage firm charges you only $8, or even nothing, for your orders. It's because they sell your orders to HFT firms that make money off of you.
- If you are a professional investor, there's a reason why your brokerage firm charges you only a half a penny a share if you use a volume weighted average price (VWAP) or percentage

of volume (POV) algorithm to execute your trades. (Algos slice a large order into hundreds of smaller orders and feed them into the market.) It's because your orders are fed to proprietary trading engines that make money off of you. Their algo figures out how your algo works, forcing you to pay more for buys and receive less for sells.

- And if you are an agency broker, like we are, there's a reason why some big brokerage firm salesmen offer their VWAP algo for free! It's because their firm has a way to make money by disadvantaging your orders all day long.

Our markets today are not about executing your trade and investment ideas in a way that is beneficial to you. It is about how dozens of HFT computers touch and manipulate your order so they can make money from your ideas—without you even knowing.

Explicitly, your transaction costs may have come down. Your commissions have declined, and spreads have narrowed. You think you're happy. Implicitly, you pay more for the stocks you buy or you receive less from those you sell. As a result, your assets, whether they are managed by you or by institutions, are slowly, but steadily, being whittled away.

The purpose of this chapter is to explain how and why the stock market has become an insanely complex mess of for-profit exchanges and dark pools. The more than 50 destinations on which your orders trade, and the complexity of this web of chaos, exists for two reasons:

- To maximize your interaction with HFT in a way that disadvantages you
- To maximize HFT ability to collect exchange rebates

To understand how we got to this point, you need to understand the history of stock exchanges in America.

NYSE and the Regionals

The public trading of shares of corporate ownership in America dates to 1790 when the first market center, the Philadelphia Stock Exchange, opened its doors. Two years later, it was followed by the New York Stock Exchange (NYSE), as well as other regional stock exchanges. You may have heard of them, such as the Boston Stock Exchange and the Pacific Stock Exchange, or the "P-coast." Other regionals included Baltimore, Buffalo, Cleveland, Detroit, Denver, Hartford, Louisville, New Orleans, Pittsburgh, Richmond, Seattle, Washington, DC, and even Wheeling, WV. Over the years, many of them closed, merged, and were swallowed up into the exchanges currently registered with the SEC.

The regionals played a key role in helping young American companies gain access to growth capital. The history of America can be broken down into the history of specific regions. A steel company in West Virginia wanting to expand capacity, to keep up with the demands of the growing automobile industry, benefited from a local market devoted to the trading and exchanging of capital in local companies. As the nation's infrastructure advanced (that is, trains, highways, phones, communications, computers, and even the Internet), the need for the regional exchanges diminished.

These regionals were member-owned by broker dealers, who bore the cost in exchange for the right to trade on them. These broker dealers were investment bankers, not trading shops. They brought companies public, issued research on them, and supported them with road shows and access to investors—all of course, at a profit. These broker dealers made money on trading, but that depended on their bringing companies public, which, in turn, generated their trading volume.

The consolidation of the regionals culminated in one major exchange, the New York Stock Exchange (NYSE); a handful of regionals, such as Boston, Philly and P-coast; and an over-the-counter (OTC) market, NASDAQ, for small growth issues.

NASDAQ

NASDAQ began trading as the world's first electronic stock market in 1971. NASDAQ was an acronym for National Association of Securities Dealers Automated Quotation system and was member-owned by the National Association of Securities Dealers (NASD). What started as a bulletin board quotation system grew into a full stock market, as the NASDAQ added volume reporting and automated trade systems. Due to less stringent listing requirements, small startups would raise money via initial public offerings (IPOs) on NAS-DAQ as opposed to the NYSE. It is hard to believe, but Intel Corp. started out as a $6.8 million IPO and Microsoft as a $60 million IPO.

Through NASDAQ, broker dealers competed with each other by providing two-sided quotes in each stock listed. Actual trades would predominantly be agreed to over the telephone. One broker, for example, Morgan Stanley, might quote a stock as

ABCD Corp. 1,000 17 1/4 bid, 17 3/4 1,000 offered

and another broker, for example, Alex Brown, might simultaneously quote the same stock as

ABCD Corp. 1,000 17 1/8 bid, 17 1/2 1,000 offered

As an investor, you would see that the "inside market" was

ABCD Corp. 1,000 17 1/4 bid, 17 1/2 1,000 offered

Your broker would get on the phone and buy your 1,000 shares from Alex Brown at 17 1/2 or sell your 1,000 shares to Morgan Stanley at 17 1/4.

NASDAQ flourished as an alternative to the NYSE, especially for the trading of smaller technology companies. It "out-listed" the NYSE dramatically in the 1990s, and its market share in trading U.S. companies exploded in the 1980s and 1990s. Trading was wildly profitable for its broker dealer members, as they made good money from wide, $0.25 bid-ask spreads.

Despite the dramatic increase in broker dealers joining the network and the competition that they brought, spreads remained wide. This became a source of contention. A 1994 academic paper by professors William Christie and Paul Schultz found substantial circumstantial evidence that market makers were colluding to keep spreads artificially wide.[2] The attention resulted in years of bad press for NASDAQ and its market makers, nearly a $1 billion class-action settlement, and a lot of scrutiny from the SEC.

While Washington spent years trying to make NASDAQ "more fair," the wide spreads resulted in innovative, free market solutions. That took the form of rapid volume growth on new electronic communication networks (ECNs), as well as opportunistic use of an automated execution system call the Small Order Execution System, otherwise known as SOES, that was put in place after the crash of 1987.

SOES

During the 508-point crash on October 19, 1987, when the Dow Jones Industrial Average dropped 22.6%,[3] many brokers did not answer their phones. Investors were livid. SOES, which was developed years prior, was mandated by NASDAQ in 1988 for broker dealers to redress the injustice. Using SOES, traders could automatically execute against the NASDAQ market maker quotes via computers and computer networks as opposed to using the telephone. The trades had to be for clients, and not broker proprietary accounts, and brokers had to wait a designated period of time after each execution before placing another SOES order on the same side of the market in the same stock.

SOES provided an efficient and liberating opportunity for small traders and retail investors to compete with the large brokers. And compete they did. SOES enabled day traders to buy and sell stock more frequently. Unfortunately, these traders often abused the waiting period and took advantage of slower-to-adjust market makers. Soon, SOES gave birth to a new breed of aggressive traders called, appropriately enough, SOES Bandits. Brokerage firms armed thousands of them with technology and momentum trading know-how.

The original SOES Bandits hit upon something—a way to use technology to make a lot of money by trimming a little money off a lot of traditional retail and institutional trades. Sheldon Maschler and Harvey Houtkin were two of the original and most famous SOES Bandits. Their business model and short-term, day-trading focus seeded the market structure we have today.

Maschler headed Datek Securities, a proprietary trading firm. With the help of two boy wonders, Jeff Citron and Josh Levine, Maschler in 1989 created Watcher. Watcher was a software program that enabled day traders to take advantage of a weakness in the SOES system—relatively slow updating of price quotes. While SOES was intended for small client orders, Datek used SOES, in combination with Watcher, to execute larger, proprietary trades, buying stocks and then selling them within seconds. Datek was very successful. By 1996, it had 500 traders, many of them fresh out of Ivy League schools, making as much as $750,000 a year each.[4]

Datek gurus Citron and Levine developed the Island electronic communication network (ECN) in 1997 to complement their usage of SOES. They did this to cut down on the commissions they were paying to other ECNs, such as Instinet. They also created a new pricing strategy to incentivize order flow away from the other ECNs. While Instinet charged a flat commission rate for all executions, Island paid traders for adding limit orders to its order book and charged traders only if they crossed the spread and executed against another limit order. For the first time, traders were paid just to bring their orders to a market center. Island grabbed 15% market share of NASDAQ trades by 1998 and was later bought by NASDAQ.[5]

Harvey Houtkin's brokerage firm, All-Tech, another proprietary trading firm, in 1998 created an ECN called Attain, for the same reason Datek created Island. In 2005, Attain was sold to Knight Trading, which renamed it Direct Edge. Knight then sold stakes in Direct Edge to Goldman Sachs, Citadel Investments, and the International Securities Exchange (ISE). Today, Direct Edge is one of the four major exchange families in the United States.

Instinet

Instinet is a firm near and dear to our hearts. It is our alma mater. It is where we cut our teeth learning the workings of institutional stock trading, market structure, and the electronic trading revolution. Instinet's green-screen terminal was the original off-exchange trading alternative. Founded in 1969, it didn't actually gain traction until Bill Lupien, a former P-coast specialist, took the helm in the mid-1980s and began marketing the platform to broker dealers, as well as its original, buy-side constituency.

Instinet flourished. Its terminals enabled subscribers, be they mutual funds or broker dealers, to enter orders to buy and sell stock in real time. Execution was automated and anonymous. The competition among orders was truly democratic. Highest bids were matched with lowest offers. As a result, in any given stock, the bid-offer spread on Instinet's closed system was tighter than what was quoted on NASDAQ's public system. It would be typical, for example, to see a NASDAQ stock quoted publicly by the broker dealers at

ABCD 17 1/4 1,000 bid, 17 3/4 1,000 offered (1/2 point spread)

while on Instinet the market was

ABCD 17 3/8 2,300 bid, 17 5/8 1,100 offered (1/4 point spread)

In the 1990s, a booming economy and new IPOs brought much price appreciation and wealth to retail and professional investors. More individuals became active in the stock market, and trading took off. Instinet's platform made trading more frictionless than ever. Volumes exploded, and we were in the thick of it as Instinet employees, constantly struggling to update our trading capacity, bandwidth, and technology.

Instinet was so successful that it attracted competition in the form of other ECNs, such as Bloomberg's Tradebook, Goldman's REDI, BRUT, Archipelago, and Island. It also attracted attention from NASDAQ, whose market share was decimated by these ECNs. In response, NASDAQ introduced SelectNet, the supposed "Instinet Killer," as well as SuperSOES, and eventually SuperMontage. By upping its technological game, NASDAQ hoped to stem its market share erosion.

Lobbyists for major NASD brokerage firms caused Instinet to attract the attention of regulators. The SEC expressed concern that private markets, such as Instinet, featured superior prices (that is, narrower spreads) than the publicly quoted NASDAQ.[6] The SEC was worried that mom-and-pop investors did not have access to the advantages Instinet provided. In response, the SEC implemented Regulation ATS (alternative trading systems) in the late 1990s. Reg ATS mandated that all orders, including orders in ECNs, such as Instinet, be displayed publicly in a consolidated quote accessible for all.

While many of us were concerned that Reg ATS was going to eliminate Instinet's advantage, we underestimated the increase in trading across the board that would result from narrower spreads and an even faster marketplace. Volumes took off again. Instinet, and the other new electronic trading venues, benefited dramatically. Venues competed based on speed and bandwidth. Automated trading firms bathed in the glory of lower friction and costs. Trading by mutual funds skyrocketed.

Problems for NYSE and NASDAQ

Instinet and the other ECNs continued to pose a problem for NASDAQ. However, NASDAQ's parent, the NASD, had the conflicting role of both regulating its members and protecting their interests. On one hand, NASDAQ the exchange had to get more automated and faster to compete for the growing volume of day traders. On the other, parent NASD had to protect its broker dealer membership from these same traders.

NASD broker dealers were getting their "behinds" handed to them by speedy short-term day traders. They were inundating NASD brokers via SOES and SelectNet simultaneously to execute against NASDAQ broker quotes. SOES was an *automated execution* platform, whereas SelectNet was an *order delivery system.* NASD members were risking double execution through the two versus any single given quotation. And they couldn't "back away" from their SelectNet obligations without regulatory ramifications. SOES traders were forcing NASD brokers to honor a commitment to transact at a posted quote—twice. For example, an NASD member brokerage firm that posted an offer to sell 1,000 shares of MSFT at 25 1/8 was made to honor that price for 2,000 shares.

The SOES Bandits were exploiting a market structure weakness at the expense of NASD brokers. In a July 1997 letter to the SEC, Mary Schapiro, then president of NASD Regulation (today, chair of the SEC), and Richard Ketchum, then executive vice president and chief operation officer (today, chairman and CEO of FINRA, the successor organization to the NASD), sought specific guidelines from the SEC to address the situation.[7] They were looking for help to clarify the application of the Firm Quote Rule. In layman's terms, they wanted the SEC to allow their member brokers to back away from honoring their quotes if it would result in double executions.

How could NASDAQ compete with the faster, less regulated ECNs that catered to short-term traders when its member owners were looking to be protected from those same traders, as well as looking to protect their spreads (and their large margins)? The answer was that NASDAQ could not serve two masters. Beginning in 2000, plans were set in motion to spin off NASDAQ into a shareholder-owned, for-profit company.

The ECNs also posed major problems for the NYSE. The NYSE was a physical location. Stocks traded at "posts" within the exchange, and "specialists" managed the orderly trading of each stock. The specialist was, of course, a member firm. He would trade for his own firm's proprietary account, as well as match customer buy and sell orders. Brokers would deliver buy and sell interest to the specialist post. Brokers would trade with each other, as well as with the specialist, or with limit orders on the specialist's book. The specialists were highly profitable; it wasn't that hard when you had the customer order tickets in your pocket.

But the specialist also made the market orderly. If a sell at the market order for 10,000 shares came through, and no buyers or crowd were around, the specialist would use his firm's capital and buy those shares within some proximity to the market price at the time of the order receipt. A seller might execute 2,000 shares at 30 3/8, 2,000 at 30 1/4, and 6,000 at 30 even. Contrast that to the situation we have today in which such an order can, and frequently does, cause a price drop of much greater magnitude. HFT market makers, who have replaced the specialists of yesteryear, yank their bids when they see that order coming, creating a short-term liquidity vacuum. The insider-jargon for such situations is mini-flash crash.

During the 1990s, the NYSE steadily watched NASDAQ take away market share, eventually eclipsing the NYSE in terms of size. The NYSE, however, was reluctant to change. It emphatically asserted that its model for trading, while slower, was more fair and orderly than NASDAQ's. Change, however, was banging on NYSE's door.

Four For-Profit Exchanges

While the leadership of the two big stock exchanges seemed resistant to change, the new trading centers, such as Instinet, Island, Attain, Redi, and Archipelago, were making their presence known on Wall Street, as well as in Washington. Industry leadership, such as Jerry Putnam, CEO of Archipelago, spent much time in DC lobbying to protect the ECN model.

Putnam testified in October 1999 before the Senate Banking Committee, advocating for-profit exchanges.[8] At the time, Putnam was awaiting approval from the SEC on Archipelago's application to become a national exchange. Here's some of what he said:

> Tomorrow's exchanges will be characterized by two distinguishing factors: for-profit corporate organization and technological expertise.

> ECNs are in the very uncomfortable position of being regulated by their competitors. For instance, Archipelago is a registered member of the National Association of Securities Dealers (NASD), which is the parent company of our competitor, NASDAQ. Exchange status is a remedy to this awkward and conflicted situation.

> Exchanges are able to collect listing and tape fees. Although Archipelago's business model would not rely heavily on these fees because we see them growing less significant over time, they still nonetheless would be a source of revenue.

> Fundamentally, exchanges serve three purposes: execute orders, aggregate information, and regulate exchange participants.

His comments were representative of the thinking at the other ECNs as well. What was particularly significant about Putnam's testimony was his new vision for a stock exchange. The founders of the NYSE recognized that the primary purpose of the stock market was helping businesses to access capital to expand and grow. Putnam saw it as a computer service to "execute orders, aggregate information, and regulate exchange participants."

It was war between business models. One side focused on speedy trading and efficiency. The other side focused on protecting wide spreads and the status quo. Politicians and regulators in Washington saw this war in the context of an investing public that was outraged over allegations of market maker collusion. NASDAQ had egg on its face from the 1994 Christie-Schultz paper. The end result was that Washington encouraged the concept of for-profit exchanges that were focused on technology and trading. A plethora of new regulations were enacted—new order-handling rules, Reg ATS, pricing to decimals, and ultimately Reg NMS—all with the goal of improving the efficiency of trading. This was the driving focus of the SEC from the mid-1990s until the Flash Crash of 2010.

A sea change engulfed the industry. NASDAQ and NYSE divested themselves from their member owners and converted to for-profit between 2000 and 2006. They also became publicly traded companies to access much needed capital to compete with the plethora of lightning-fast electronic trading venues. They invested heavily in data centers and technology. The NYSE bought Archipelago, NASDAQ bought BRUT, and Instinet merged with Island to form INET, which was eventually bought by NASDAQ and merged into BRUT.

Two other electronic trading powerhouses became for-profit exchanges: Direct Edge and BATS (an acronym for Better Alternative Trading System). Direct Edge was built on SOES Bandit Harry Houtkin's ECN platform, Attain. BATS was built by Dave Cummings, founder of Tradebot, a prominent HFT firm. As Archipelago's Putnam highlighted in his Senate testimony, being a for-profit exchange, as opposed to an ATS, had advantages, such as sharing the $500 million market data revenue pie.

Direct Edge initially was fueled by order flow from its owners, Knight Capital, Citadel, Goldman Sachs, and others. The flow tended to be retail, coming from online brokers who had developed their business model based on attracting $10/per trade (or less) orders and selling them to firms such as Knight and Citadel. Knight and Citadel would use that retail flow to trade against or fill institutional orders, whatever suited them best.

Cummings' computer/engineering academic background helped him seed Tradebot out of a spare bedroom in 1999. His creation of automated algorithmic trading strategies proved to be lucrative. He generated massive amounts of order flow and was a substantial customer of his own BATS exchange. His motivation to create BATS partially arose from his disappointment with NASDAQ's ECN consolidation. After NASDAQ bought INET and merged it with BRUT, NASDAQ increased fees, which was a source of contention for Cummings.[9]

In addition to Tradebot, BATS' initial order flow came from Cummings' business partners, which included HFT firms and Wall Street brokerages, such as GETCO, Wedbush, Lehman Brothers, Morgan Stanley, Merrill Lynch, and Credit Suisse. Cummings quickly signed on new subscribers, many of them also high frequency traders, as their order flow was substantial and sensitive to trading costs.

Conflicts of Interest

The rapid growth of Direct Edge and BATS was attributable to their ability to attract high volume HFT order flow, largely because they were majority owned by players with HFT interests. As a result, practices that clearly smacked of conflicts of interest began to creep into everyday trading that affects retail and institutional investors. Two good examples are how payment for order flow (PFOF) and flash orders are used.

For years some of the owners of Direct Edge understood the value of buying online brokerage account investor orders. These orders could be financially modeled to separate the "smart" orders from the "dumb" ones that could be traded against for profit. When you send an order to buy a stock through your online broker, most of the time that order is sold to such market makers.

In the split second it takes for these HFT market makers to handle your order, they can determine, based on all the orders they are "seeing," whether the stock you want to buy or sell will go higher or lower after your trade. They sell you the stock if it will move lower. Or they send your order to an exchange if it will move higher. You pay a higher price on buys or receive a lower price for sells. Often, your order is delayed if you are the buyer. Sometimes that delay results in you not getting the stock you were trying to buy, as someone beat you to it, perhaps even the market maker.

Direct Edge was the first major exchange to widely implement flash order types. NASDAQ soon followed. For a subsecond, Direct Edge and NASDAQ "flash" investor orders to HFT firms. The exchanges' public rationale was that sometimes these HFT firms would fill an investor order at a slightly better price, typically 1/100 of a penny less than the public quote. The reality was that those HFT players used information from flash orders to trade ahead of the investor and then turn around and fill the investor's order at an inferior price.

The SEC recognized the unfairness of these order types and proposed banning them in late 2009.[10] The NYSE criticized the practice as being patently unfair as well, as did numerous brokerage firms.[11] NASDAQ also spoke out against these orders as being wrong for markets and damaging for investors. Amazingly, however, it implemented its own version of flash orders so as not to lose market share to Direct Edge.[12] To date, the SEC's proposed ban has not been implemented, and the order type is alive and well, especially in the options markets. We write about the flash order controversy in more detail in Chapter 6, "The Arms Merchants."

Fragmentation

After the exchange landscape consolidated into the Big Four, the remaining exchanges gave birth to six registered subexchanges. Today, the United States has 13 exchanges, 10 of which are owned by the Big Four. It's like an alphabet soup:

- NYSE, NYSE Amex, and NYSE Arca (3)
- NASDAQ, NASDAQ PSX, and NASDAQ BX (3)
- BATS and BATS Y (2)
- EDGX and EDGA (Direct Edge) (2)

We also have seen a proliferation of dark pools and alternative trading systems. Why? Because it benefits HFT in four critical ways versus retail and institutional investors.

Exchange Arbitrage

Many industry experts like to call what so many of these HFT firms are doing "market making." At the dozens of industry conferences we attend annually, we often hear HFT experts describe it as follows:

> Say you have a stock, like IBM quoted at $185.00 by $185.02 in London, yet it is quoted in New York as $185.03 by $185.05 at the same time. HFT simply sells it on the higher market (say $185.03 or higher if it can sell higher than that London bid) and buys it back on the lower market (say $185.02 or lower if it can buy lower than the New York offer).
>
> HFT uses its low latency technology and algorithms to arbitrage these momentary differences in price. It is doing the market a service by keeping price discovery in check across markets.

There are always timing differences between different market centers. If an HFT firm is fast enough and colocates at each market center, it can capture those profits nearly risk free. Thus, HFTs benefit greatly from having more destinations to arbitrage.

Rebate Arbitrage

Exchanges have maker-taker pricing models to attract HFT players and brokerage firm members to trade on their venues. Recall that in this type of pricing model, firms receive rebates when they add liquidity and are charged fees when they remove it. Financial modeling by HFT market making firms tries to be the first in the queue of orders at a given price to collect those rebates and maximize their arbitrages. It is such a profitable game that it has attracted many firms.

As more HFT firms enter this game, however, it gets crowded competing to be at the top of the queue at any price level. As a result, the exchanges have been dividing into subexchanges to help their most profitable and volume-driven customers have more opportunities to get to the top of the order book.

Fragmentation

HFT firms also benefit from fragmentation, as do the exchanges that sell them the tools to be successful at it, such as colocation and enriched data feeds. Investors, on the other hand, do not benefit. To trade large orders, institutional investors need deep centralized order books. Retail investors are also harmed because they have an increasingly smaller chance to be at a reasonable spot in the order queue at any given limit price.

HFT firms are geared to beat everybody at that game; the rebate arbitrage form of HFT by itself has diminished the effectiveness of an investor limit order and has thus dis-incentivized investors from placing them. What is the point of entering a static limit order in any stock when your chances of having it executed in a reasonably timely fashion are diminished, and your order just creates a target for various kinds of HFT?

Dark Pools and ATSs

The number of dark pools and ATSs has also skyrocketed over the past decade. Today, nearly one in every three shares trades off-exchange.[13] There are currently approximately 40 such dark pools, where stocks trade without their orders displayed to the public.

The first few dark pools were wonderful complements to trading on the "lit" public exchanges. They helped large pension and mutual funds move sizable blocks of stocks in ways that the flickering, rapid-fire, smaller-quote-size public markets could not. However, a significant number of the dark pools that have been introduced in more recent years are nothing more than conduits through which investor orders can be internalized by brokerage firms.

These dark pools exist as a pit stop for investor orders, be they retail or institutional, to pass through for the benefit of the pool operator. Large brokerage firms operate dark pools that are populated with order flow from their own HFT prop trading models. Frequently, the same broker provides agency algorithms to automatically feed orders from institutional customers into these pools. This practice needlessly exposes investor orders to interaction with "high alpha" proprietary trading, as opposed to letting those orders get best execution by interacting with a wider variety of participants in larger, more centralized pools.

The Tale of the Aggregator

The policy of the SEC over the past 15 years in overseeing how stocks trade in the United States was best described by Erik Sirri, director of the agency's Division of Trading and Markets from 2006–2009. Asked to comment on the number of dark pools that has sprung up since the millennium, he replied, "I'm not sure we have any concerns right now; we really have let a thousand flowers bloom."[14]

Stated differently, the SEC has embraced a policy to encourage competition at all costs. We presume regulators believed that investors would benefit from narrower spreads from so many destinations competing for orders. We doubt they envisioned that this competition would become a competition to *trade around investor orders*, rather than execute them.

Our markets have changed from two centralized pools of liquidity—NYSE and NASDAQ—to a web of more than 50 destinations, where none of them possess healthy cross-sections of all types of investors and traders. Many are owned by HFT firms, large brokers who employ HFT strategies, or for-profit public entities that make most of their revenue from large HFT firms. Taking advantage of this situation, HFT shaves pennies, nickels, and dimes off your trades all day long.

While you might witness narrow spreads and cheap commissions in trading the 100 most active stocks in the United States, in the other 95% of our stocks, spreads have widened, with less size and liquidity than just a decade ago. Although HFT firms may have solved the problem of how to trade Bank of America for an $8 commission and a narrow spread, they have driven out all the many brokerage firms that supported smaller and mid cap stocks.

As the SEC has allowed ever-increasing shares of our stock trades to be executed in the dark, we also have become dangerously close to a threshold in which the public markets are not conveying enough information, and accurate price discovery is at risk. Investors buy risky assets, such as stocks, because they see a liquid secondary market that gives them confidence they can exit their investment when they want, at a reasonable cost. If the majority of that secondary market trades in the dark, will investors be confident the liquidity is there? If not, what effect will that have on capital formation?

To highlight this conflicted web of chaos, we close this chapter with an anecdote about our experience with an algorithmic provider. As a result of all the problems in our markets, we worked extensively with this firm to provide a tool that would enable us to access the liquidity in a great number of dark pools, but on our terms. The developers of this tool, which we'll call the Aggregator, worked with us closely so that we could avoid certain dark pools outright and safeguard our interaction with the remaining dark pools we wanted to hit.

Typically, we would use the Aggregator to buy 50,000 shares of a relatively thin, small or mid-cap stock. It would accumulate shares in dark pools in decent size without tipping our hand to the market. We loved it—and trusted it—because we had worked to exclude the more toxic, HFT-populated destinations that had been hurting our executions.

In February 2011, our salesman from the Aggregator firm gave us great news. Because we were such a good customer, the firm was going to lower our costs. Joe responded with a hearty thank-you and gave the rest of our desk the news: "Starting Monday, our commission rate for the Aggregator is cut in half." Times were tough, and this was going to save us money.

Monday came, but something was amiss. The stock prices of orders that we entered into the Aggregator were dancing away from us, a significant departure from our experience in the past. We called our salesman and asked whether something had changed.

"To lower your rate, we placed back some of the destinations you excluded," he explained. "Those destinations started trading with us for free. I thought it would be a great way to lower your commissions, since you have been busting my chops about it for months."

Subsequently, our rate increased as our destinations were returned to their prior settings. It is telling of how conflicted our market structure is when brokerage firms put their interests ahead of what they know to be the best interest for their investor clients.

Endnotes

1. Herb Greenberg, "Yes, Virginia, the Markets Are Broken," CNBC.com (Oct. 11, 2011), http://www.cnbc.com/id/44857612/Yes_Virginia_the_Markets_are_Broken.

2. William G. Christie and Paul H. Schultz, "Why Do NASDAQ Market Makers Avoid Odd-Eighth Quotes?" *Journal of Finance* vol. 49, no. 5 (Dec. 1994), Jstor website, http://www.jstor.org/pss/2329272.

3. To equal the 1987 crash, the Dow at approximately 12,000 would have to drop more than 2,700 points.

4. David Barboza, "Golden Boy?; He's Dazzled Wall Street, but the Ghosts of His Company May Haunt His Future," *The New York Times*, May 10, 1998, http://www.nytimes.com/1998/05/10/business/golden-boy-he-s-dazzled-wall-street-but-ghosts-his-company-may-haunt-his-future.html.

5. Funding Universe, company profile of Datek Online Holdings Corp., Funding Universe website, http://www.fundinguniverse.com/company-histories/Datek-Online-Holdings-Corp-company-History.html.

6. Securities and Exchange Commission, "Regulation of Exchanges and Alternative Trading Systems," 17 CFR parts 202, 240, 242, 249, rel. 34-40760, file S7-12-98, RIN 3235-AH41, Securities and Exchange Commission website, http://www.sec.gov/rules/final/34-40760.txt.

7. Mary L. Schapiro and Richard Ketchum (National Association of Securities Dealers), letter dated July 7, 1997 to Richard Lindsey (Director, Division of Market Regulation, Securities and Exchange Commission), Financial Industry Regulatory Authority website, http://www.finra.org/web/groups/industry/@ip/@reg/@notice/documents/notices/p004500.pdf.

8. Senate Banking Committee Subcommittee on Securities, "Prepared Testimony of Mr. Jerry Putnam, Chief Executive Officer, Archipelago ECN" Senate Banking Committee website (Oct. 27, 1999), http://banking.senate.gov/99_10hrg/102799/putnam.htm.

9. Liz Moyer, "Swinging at Nasdaq," Forbes.com, May 21, 2007, http://members.forbes.com/forbes/2007/0521/090.html.

10. Securities and Exchange Commission, "SEC Proposes Flash Order Ban," press release 2209-201 (Sept. 17, 2009), http://www.sec.gov/news/press/2009/2009-201.htm.

11. Jenny Anderson, "U.S. Proposes Ban on 'Flash' Trading on Wall Street," *New York Times,* Sept. 17, 2009, http://www.nytimes.com/2009/09/18/business/18regulate.html.

12. Nina Mehta, "2009 Review: The Past and Future of Flash Orders: Washington Strikes Back," Traders Magazine.com, Dec. 2009, http://www.tradersmagazine.com/issues/20_301/-104778-1.html.

13. Tom Steinert-Threlkeld, "New Year Not Happy: Stock Trading Down 18 Percent," TradeTech's Securities Technology Monitor, Jan. 18,2012, Securities Technology Monitor website, http://www.securitiestechnologymonitor.com/news/stock-trading-down-18-percent-january-2012-29871-1.html.

14. Gregory Bresiger and Nina Mehta, "No New Regs Will Be Coming to Dark Pool Land," Trader's Magazine.com, July 2007, http://www.tradersmagazine.com/issues/20070715/2863-1.html.

4

Regulatory Purgatory

In 1994, professors William Christie and Paul Schultz produced a research report that would become one of the biggest black eyes for the SEC up until that time. *Why Do NASDAQ Market Makers Avoid Odd-Eighth Quotes?* found that such quotes—think 1/8, 3/8, 5/8, or 7/8—were virtually nonexistent for 70% of the 100 most actively traded stocks. The minimum spread on many NASDAQ stocks was found not to be smaller than $0.25 in most instances.

Christie-Schultz stated, "We are unable to envision any scenario in which 40 to 60 dealers who are competing for order flow would simultaneously and consistently avoid using odd-eighth quotes without an implicit agreement to post quotes only on the even price fractions." Although they didn't explicitly allege collusion, many who read the paper believed market makers were in cahoots with each other. How could this be? How could one of the biggest stock markets in the world conduct business not much differently from the mafia? And where was the SEC?

The industry immediately came under intense political and media scrutiny. The SEC was put on the defensive and knew it had to act. It was about to embark on a series of regulations that would be the building blocks for our current fragmented equity market. Whether the SEC knew it at the time, the Commission was playing with the future of Wall Street. Its actions would cause thousands of lost jobs as trading systems run by people were replaced by computer systems that would eventually lead to the proliferation of algorithmic and high frequency trading (HFT).

Early 1990s Change in Regulations

One thing almost all these regulations had in common was that they were approved under the leadership of SEC Chairman Arthur Levitt, who ran the Commission from 1993 to 2001. Levitt, who arrived a year before the Christie-Schultz study, seemed like he was on a quest to "fix" the industry. In particular, we believed that Levitt wanted to crush Instinet.

In September 1995, the SEC proposed the Order Handling Rules.[1] This was an attempt to add more transparency. After receiving 152 comments, the rules were approved and then implemented in January 1997. The part called the Display Rule stated that market makers and specialists should display publicly the limit orders they receive from customers when the orders are better than the market maker's or the specialist's quote. The SEC hoped this rule would tighten spreads.

While the Display Rule was a bit of a change, the part called the Quote Rule was more so. This rule required specialists and market makers to publish "the best prices at which [they are] willing to trade. A specialist or market maker may still trade at better prices in certain private trading systems, or ECNs, without publishing an improved quote. This is true only when the ECN itself publishes the improved prices and makes those prices available to the investing public."

No longer could a market maker or specialist "hide" a quote on a private trading system. The SEC basically was shutting down the private market that brokers and institutions were using to trade with each other. The company that bore the biggest brunt of this rule was our former employer, Instinet, which would now need to display most of its quotes alongside all other market participants. Our bosses at the time knew this was going to hurt. A good portion of our orders was generated by broker dealers who didn't want to display them. Instinet organized what turned out to be an unsuccessful letter-writing campaign. The battle was lost, but the war was just beginning.

In May 1997, the SEC published a Concept Release that explored ways to deal with the rapid rise of alternative trading systems (ATS). Now that the Order Handling Rules were approved, electronic communications networks (ECNs) were starting to pop up everywhere to challenge the dominance of Instinet. Island, the ECN formed from Datek Securities, had been around since 1996, and Archipelago entered the game in 1997 (see Chapter 3, "Web of Chaos"). The SEC decided that it needed to get a grip on these new upstarts because they were not regulated like exchanges. So, in 1998, the SEC approved Regulation ATS.[2]

Reg ATS revised the definition of an exchange. ECNs had to submit to a self-regulatory organization or become an exchange, which would be costly and onerous, so that was not an option at the time. Reg ATS also paved the way for the eventual demutualization of the nation's stock exchanges, providing guidance on how they could meet the requirements of becoming for-profit companies.

The big thing Reg ATS did was force ECNs to display all their orders to the public. It required "alternative trading systems that trade 5 percent or more of the volume in national market system securities to be linked with a registered market in order to disseminate the best priced orders in those national market system securities displayed in their systems (including institutional orders) into the public quote stream."

Referring to the Order Handling Rules, the SEC said: "While these rules have helped integrate orders on certain alternative trading systems into the public quotation system, they only disclose the orders market makers and specialists enter into ECNs, unless the system voluntarily undertakes to disclose institutional prices. In many cases, institutional orders, as well as other nonmarket maker orders, remain undisclosed to the public."

We believed that the SEC was really going after I-Only orders, one of the most popular order types that Instinet offered and one that early high frequency traders could not see or model. On Instinet,

I-Only orders could be placed by either brokers or institutions, but only institutions could see them. Instinet clients relied on I-Only orders—and Reg ATS was about to take them away under the premise of "fairness." These orders were often much chunkier in size. They gave institutional traders an advantage and typically resulted in large trades that did not move the quote. They reduced the implicit cost of trading dramatically.

To give you a picture of how significant I-Only orders were, one day in 1997, Joe and some other Instinet employees visited a large broker dealer client after a new hardware and software release. The release changed the location of some of the keys on the Instinet terminal, and many of our broker clients did not like it.

Suddenly, the head of the broker's trading desk stood up and yelled, "Ya gotta help me!" He was having trouble entering an order to buy 25,000 shares of Intel so that only institutions would see it.

One of our reps ran over to assist. The next thing we heard was the head trader screaming as loud as he could, "Oh my God! No! I-Only! I-Only!"

Our rep had forgotten to hit the I-Only key. The order was now displayed to the entire world in the public quote. The stock immediately gapped up almost a half of dollar. The head of the desk was fuming.

Seeing orders like that was a major win for the high frequency traders. No longer would they have to worry about a real order trading between two investors without them knowing. They could model order books and predict prices with much greater certainty. This was the beginning of the algorithmic revolution. Up until this time, trading algos, which sliced up block orders and fed them piecemeal into the market, were primarily used by sophisticated quantitative traders. With Reg ATS and more quotes being displayed, algos were about to be used more widely by institutional investors. Most of these initial algos followed a simple volume weighted average price strategy that was easy to pick off by HFTs. To HFTs, it was like shooting ducks in a barrel and making millions of dollars. Over the next decade, thousands of traders would lose their jobs to the algos, and a countless number of institutional orders would fall victim to HFT machines.

The revolution had begun, but it was taking place only on the NASDAQ side of the stock market. Under the leadership of Richard Grasso, the NYSE was still protected and did not have to worry much about these new rules because most NYSE order flow was still directed to the floor of the exchange. While NASDAQ was under assault by the ECNs, the NYSE was protected behind their walls and under the umbrella of Rule 390, which prevented member firms from trading NYSE-listed stocks away from the floor of the exchange.

But in 2000, this changed. Levitt and the SEC were energized after their Order Handling Rules and Reg ATS victories. The SEC was now eyeing the NYSE. In a prescient September 1999 speech at Columbia Law School, Levitt telegraphed his next battle: "One way or another, Rule 390 should not be part of our future."[3]

With pressure mounting from the large brokerage houses, the NYSE heeded Levitt's threat and voluntarily removed the rule in May 2000. One brokerage house that was thrilled was Madoff Securities. Bernie Madoff commented, "This will very quickly change the landscape positively by giving [brokerages] more flexibility to execute orders most efficiently for their customers."[4] Another supporter was former SOES Bandit and Island ECN executive Josh Levine. "The elimination of Rule 390 is a good step toward competition in the listed-stock world," he said.[5] Both Madoff and Levine were chomping at the bit to access more NYSE order flow electronically.

Every time a regulation or rule change was proposed, it seemed that it was always "helping to improve competition." In his September 1999 speech, Levitt said, "But the perennial question has been, how can we further tap competition to augment market integrity and quality?" He then threatened, "We dare not allow any market structure to take hold that extinguishes the power of innovation."

It was clear that Levitt and the SEC were on a quest to change the once duopoly market into a multiple market center competitive landscape. If he succeeded, many would benefit, including the large brokerage houses and the high frequency traders, who were still in their infancy stage. But there was one large problem with his plan: fragmentation. Levitt tried to disarm the issue by saying, "Today, is there 'fragmentation' in the sense that there are separate, isolated markets with reduced liquidity in normal trading hours? I think not. But is there 'fragmentation' in terms of multiple pools of liquidity competing for orders based on transparent quotes and prices? Absolutely." Fragmentation would try to be dealt with at a later time with some rules the SEC had not even thought of yet.

Late 1990s Regulations—Decimalization, Reg NMS, and Demutualization

The Order Handling Rules, Reg ATS, and the elimination of Rule 390 were the SEC's air campaign, which softened the battlefield before the ground forces landed. The next stage was decimalization, demutualization of the exchanges, and the SEC's ultimate weapon, Reg NMS. Many have wondered whether these rule changes were part of a grand vision the SEC was formulating to change the way stocks trade. Or was the fragmented market that we have today an unintended consequence? Although we agree some effects were unintentional, we also believe that many of the inequalities that you see today were designed by the major exchanges that had input in to the rules.

The SEC wanted to get rid of the archaic notion of eighths and sixteenths and pushed for trading stocks in decimals in 1997. On the surface, this was tough to argue against. Almost everything we calculate in our lives is in decimals. Why did stocks still need to trade in fractions? After three years of pressure from the SEC, stocks began phasing in decimal pricing in August 2000. Instead of 8 or 16 price points per dollar, stocks now had 100.

A critical flaw in decimalization was that it did not mandate a minimum spread or price increment, regardless of the market cap of the stock. Thus, a $50 billion company that traded 100 million shares per day could now have the same spread as a $50 million company that traded 100,000 shares per day. The economics of market making were fast changing, because dealers were no longer compensated for their risk in the form of spreads. The SEC and proponents of decimalization pointed out that bid/ask spreads on stocks dropped dramatically after the conversion to decimals.

The collateral damage was high. Although spreads may have been reduced, so was displayed liquidity at the National Best Bid and Offer (NBBO). Because there were now 100 price points per dollar, limit orders were no longer clustered. Quotes at various price levels became thin. Market maker quotes of 1,000 shares were now replaced by 100 share orders that could easily be canceled. Before U.S. Senate Banking Sub-Committee in May 2001, Acting SEC Chair Laura Unger testified that the SEC "estimated that quote sizes in NYSE-listed securities have been reduced an average of 60% since the conversion to decimals and preliminary analyses of NASDAQ securities show a 68% reduction in quote sizes."

Pinging and sniffing for order flow became much easier. Limit orders that were displayed by retail and institutional investors could easily be stepped in front of now because it took only a penny to price improve. The short sale uptick rule became virtually useless because it, too, took only a penny to move a stock back into compliance.

The effect on small and mid-cap market maker economics was devastating. Margin compression drove many market makers out of business. The void would later be filled by high frequency traders who posed as market makers, but with none of the affirmative and negative obligations that specialists and NASDAQ market makers had. These obligations would require a NYSE specialist, for example, to step into the market when there was no liquidity, but step back when it was abundant. No such obligations exist for today's market makers.

Why did the SEC push so hard for decimalization? Was it in reaction to the Christie-Schultz study? Were self-interested, high frequency traders trying to create more price points to "arbitrage"? Or was it to fulfill grander visions of a more competitive marketplace?

In a June 2000 press release, Levitt said, "As the securities markets become more global, with many stocks traded in multiple jurisdictions, the U.S. securities markets must adopt the international convention of decimal pricing to remain competitive. The overall benefits of decimal pricing are likely to be significant. Investors may benefit from lower transaction costs due to narrower spreads, and prices will be easier to understand. It is time for the U.S. securities markets to make this change."[6]

No doubt Levitt was trying to tilt the playing field toward the individual investor and away from the mutual fund industry. Even though mutual funds represent the retail investor, Levitt apparently thought they had too much power. In his 2002 book, *Take on the Street*, he attacked the mutual fund industry on its fees and performance.

For NASDAQ, the pieces were now in place to demutualize. The industry was in the process of changing from net trading (where there was no explicit commission) to a transaction-based model. The exchanges would now get to charge a transaction fee similar to the ECNs for every share that was traded. Demutualization would allow these profits to get passed directly to the for-profit exchange owners. NASDAQ demutualized in 2000, but the NYSE waited until 2006, after Reg NMS was passed, because the rule changes up until that point hadn't affected the exchange as much.

Demutualization changed the ownership of the exchanges from a member-owned, nonprofit organization to a shareholder-owned, for-profit corporation. What was once thought of as a quasi-government utility-type organization would now be a bottom-line driven, publicly traded, shareholder-focused company. The old method of having members vote on proposals and rule changes would be abolished. Exchanges would now make decisions by executives who reported to the board of directors who served the shareholders. Unfortunately, as we have seen all too often, shareholder interests and investor interests are not always the same (see Chapter 6, "The Arms Merchants").

Concern, however, was growing around the world. In June 2001, the International Organization of Securities Commissions issued a report outlining how, "due to increased pressure to generate investment returns for shareholders, a for-profit exchange may be less likely to take enforcement action against customers or users who are a direct source of income for the exchange."[7]

In other words, a for-profit exchange is not likely to take any action against its highest-volume customers (the high frequency traders) because they generate the most amount of revenue. We believe this conflict of interest has sometimes led the exchanges to offer products that give their highest volume clients an edge over all other clients. This is evidenced in the flash orders that some exchanges unveiled in 2009. Flash orders gave a sub-second peek at an order to a subset of exchange clients who paid for this privilege. Clearly, financial motivations of the exchanges had caused one set of clients to be disadvantaged over another set (see Chapter 9, "Dude, Where's My Order?").

Where did the SEC stand on demutualization? In his September 1999 speech, Levitt explained, "In the wake of this heightened competition from ECNs, NASDAQ and the NYSE are pushing forward with their plans to demutualize. The Commission has no intention, whatsoever, of standing in the way of a movement toward for-profit status."

Early 2000s—Reg NMS

The next challenge the HFT community faced was breaking down the walls of the NYSE to enter the holy land of trading NYSE listed stocks. However, it had to get more rules changed. It had to hope a new SEC chairman would help, as Levitt left office in February 2001. And it had to deal with one other, really big problem: Richard Grasso, chairman of the NYSE from 1995 to 2004. He managed to keep the NYSE specialist system safe from the attacks of the regulators and high frequency traders for all those years. As a result, the NYSE maintained its 80% market share even after all the rule changes the SEC had passed.

The NYSE specialist system was both loved and hated. Institutions loved the ability to work an order on the floor and get blocks done but complained that specialists were "ripping them off." Even though Rule 390 was repealed, the NYSE still enjoyed the benefits of the Trade Though rule. The Trade Through rule required that when a stock is traded in more than one market, trades may not occur in one market if a better price is offered on another. The NYSE continued to maintain 80% market share primarily for the reason that clients "didn't want to miss stock." Because the floor of the exchange was the primary auction center, most investors wanted to be in the main liquidity pool and not tinker around in a smaller, regional exchanges or ECNs.

Many of you who read this who cover institutional accounts no doubt at one point missed participating in a block of stock that went up on the floor of the NYSE. Maybe you were trying to get your client a better price or had a "feeling" about the market. But after that block trade went up, your client was most likely calling and asking how much of that was his trade. You probably performed your best song and dance explaining why your client was shut out of the block trade. Nobody wanted to miss being part of a block trade, and that was one of the true magnetic forces of the NYSE.

While many predicted the demise of the NYSE, Grasso seemed to breathe new life into it. After the September 11, 2001 terrorist attacks on the World Trade Center four blocks away, Grasso worked around the clock to get the NYSE back up and running within a week. Many saw him as a national hero. *Fortune* called him "a reassuring— and ubiquitous—presence in the aftermath of the devastation." When the NYSE reopened, Grasso was quoted as saying, "Today, America goes back to business, and we do it as a signal to those criminals who inflicted this heinous crime on America and all Americans that they have lost."[8]

Grasso was the backbone of the NYSE. But then, in August 2003, news leaked of his $140 million pay package. It was considered astronomically high for a "nonprofit" company. He underwent a media assault culminating in his resignation in September 2003. The following year he would be sued by New York State Attorney General Elliot Spitzer, claiming that the NYSE board was misled. Eventually, Grasso was exonerated and Spitzer disgraced, but that's another story. With the boss gone, the NYSE was now open to attack from an even more devastating enemy—regulators and automated traders.

In February 2004, the SEC published for comment its most devastating regulation yet. The 500-page Regulation NMS was billed as a way to modernize and strengthen the existing national market system (NMS). Due to changes in technology and regulations over the previous decade, the SEC thought it was time for sweeping reform. The Commission was inundated with 1,691 comment letters from the industry. Many saw the rule as damaging to their business and were trying to protect themselves. Others saw it as a golden opportunity and were staking out their position.

The original Reg NMS proposal in February 2004 had four parts:[9]

- **Trade Through Proposal:** Market centers would be required to prevent trade-throughs, which are the execution of an order in its market at a price inferior to a price displayed in another market.

- **Market Access Proposal:** The goal was to modernize the terms of access to quotations and execution of orders in the NMS. The SEC wanted market centers to provide nondiscriminatory access to their quotes.

- **Sub-Penny Proposal:** Market participants would be prevented from accepting, ranking, or displaying orders, quotes, or indications of interest in a pricing increment finer than a penny, except for securities with a share price below $1.00.

- **Market Data Proposal:** Market data revenue rules would be modified to reward market centers for trades and quotes. The formula for the splitting of the estimated $500 million/year market data pot would now be based on 50% trades and 50% quotes at the national best bid and offer.

The most disruptive part of Reg NMS was the Trade Through proposal. The rule was intended to make sure that smaller orders that were priced better did not get bypassed when a block trade occurred. This rule was already in place for NYSE listed stocks, but Reg NMS would extend it to all market centers, including NASDAQ. In its original version, the Trade Through proposal had an exception that would have enabled a "fast" automated market to trade through a "slow" non-automated market, such as the NYSE, up to a certain level. The NYSE wouldn't need to convert to a "fast" market because the trade through exception enabled investors to trade through "slow" markets. The power of "being downstairs" and "in the crowd" was left intact. But now that Grasso was out of the way, the Trade Through exception faced an assault from automated traders that wanted full access to an all-electronic book.

On April 21, 2004, the SEC held a public hearing on Reg NMS. The attack on the Trade Through exception was about to begin. The witness list read like a who's who of Wall Street and included exchange executives, brokerage executives, specialists, and academics. Without Grasso to organize a coordinated defense, the NYSE auction market was dead. Tower Research, an automated trading firm, complained that Trade Through created "an unfair advantage for slower market centers."[10] Bernie Madoff stated at the hearing that the SEC should "require all 'quoting' market centers to employ an automated order execution facility for inter-market orders."[11] Professor Daniel Weaver of Rutgers, an associate of David Whitcomb, who was one of the original high frequency traders, demanded that "price priority should be established in all markets."[12]

In December 2004, the SEC relented to the pressure from the HFT community and submitted a new Reg NMS proposal that significantly altered the Trade Through proposal, which was renamed the Order Protection Rule. The Order Protection Rule would protect only quotations that were on top of the book and electronically accessible. If the NYSE wanted to be part of the NBBO, then it would have to change from a "slow" market to a "fast" market. Reg NMS was approved in June 2005. The Order Protection Rule was the death of the "slow" market...and of the status quo at the NYSE.

Reg NMS passed by a vote of 3 to 2 with commissioners Paul Atkins and Cynthia Glassman dissenting. Atkins and Glassman claimed the Trade Through rate in the market was much less than what the SEC had said it was and therefore was not a problem. In their dissent, they wrote:[13]

> We believe that Regulation NMS turns back Commission policy regarding competition and innovation and sets up road-blocks for our markets. The majority's statutory interpretations and policy changes are arbitrary, unreasonable and anticom-petitive.... Regulation NMS saddles the marketplace with anachronistic regulation that reduces investor choice and raises investor costs. Far from enhancing competition, we believe that Regulation NMS will have anticompetitive effects.

Reg NMS was fully implemented in July 2007, and the war was over. From 1997 to 2007, the SEC had fully changed how the equity market functioned. Volumes in listed stocks exploded as competing market centers began fragmenting liquidity. Because the NYSE was becoming obsolete, so was the block trade. Average trade sizes plummeted, as orders began to get chopped up by institutional traders seeking to cloak their larger orders from fast HFT traders. Spreads did shrink, but so did the amount of displayed liquidity in the best bid and offer.

The new equity market had arrived, and it was about to wreak havoc on every investor.

Endnotes

1. Securities and Exchange Commission, "Self-Regulatory Organizations; National Association of Securities Dealers, Inc.; Order Granting Partial Approval and Notice of Filing and Order Granting Accelerated Approval of Amendment No. 1 to Proposed Rule Change Relating to Implementation of the Commission's Order Handling Rules," release no. 34-38156, file SR-NASD-96-43, Securities and Exchange Commission website (Jan. 10, 1997) http://www.sec.gov/rules/other/34-38156.txt.

2. Securities and Exchange Commission, "Regulation of Exchanges and Alternative Trading Systems," 17 CFR parts 202, 240, 242, 249, rel. 34-40760, file S7-12-98, RIN 3235-AH41, Securities and Exchange Commission website, http://www.sec.gov/rules/final/34-40760.txt.

3. Arthur Levitt, speech titled "Dynamic Markets, Timeless Principles" given at Columbia Law School, New York, Sept. 23, 1999, SEC website, http://www.sec.gov/news/speech/speecharchive/1999/spch295.htm.

4. Thomas S. Mulligan, "NYSE to Repeal Rule Forbidding Off-Floor Trades," *Los Angeles Times*, Dec 2, 1999, http://articles.latimes.com/1999/dec/02/business/fi-39618.

5. Ibid.

6. Securities and Exchange Commission, "SEC Orders Securities markets to Phase In Decimal Pricing on September 5, 2000," Securities and Exchange Commission website, http://www.sec.gov/news/press/2000-79.txt.

7. Technical Committee of the International Organization of Securities Commissions, "Issues Paper on Exchange Demutualization," : 7, EXG.com (June, 2001), http://www.egx.com.eg/pdf/IOSCO_issues_on_exchange_demutualization.pdf.

8. Peter Elkind, "The Fall of the House of Grasso," *Fortune,* Oct. 18, 2004, CCN website, http://money.cnn.com/magazines/fortune/fortune_archive/2004/10/18/8188087/index.htm.

9. Securities and Exchange Commission, "Regulation NMS," 17 CFR Parts 200, 230, 240, 242, 249, rel. 34-49325, file S7-10-04, RIN 3235-AJ18, Securities and Exchange Commission website, http://www.sec.gov/rules/proposed/34-49325.htm.

10. John Martello (Managing Director, Tower Research Capital, LLC) letter dated June 30, 2004 to Jonathan Katz (Secretary, Securities and Exchange Commission), Securities and Exchange Commission website, http://www.sec.gov/rules/proposed/s71004/martello63004.pdf.

11. Bernard L Madoff, "Regulation NMS Public Hearings April 21, 2004," file S7-10-04, Securities and Exchange Commission website, http://www.sec.gov/rules/proposed/s71004/testimony/madoffs71004.pdf.

12. Daniel G. Weaver (Associate Professor of Finance, Rutgers Business School), letter to Jonathan G. Katz (Secretary, Securities and Exchange Commission), Securities and Exchange Commission website, http://www.sec.gov/rules/proposed/s71004/testimony/nmsweaver.pdf.

13. Cynthia A. Glassman and Paul S. Atkins, "Dissent of Commissioners Cynthia A. Glassman and Paul S. Atkins to the Adoption of Regulation NMS," Securities and Exchange Commission website (June 9, 2005), http://www.sec.gov/rules/final/34-51808-dissent.pdf.

5 — Regulatory Hangover

The changes were subtle at first, but then it felt like a new world on Wall Street.

- Volumes began to explode. In June 2007, just before Reg NMS was implemented, average daily volume across all exchanges was 5.6 billion shares per day. Two years later, in June 2009, it had increased more than 70%, to 9.6 billion.[1]

- Stocks were "flickering" more. Quotes were changing rapidly without any trades occurring. Bids or offers disappeared the instant an order was routed to them. Trading in any kind of size was becoming extremely difficult.

- The market was becoming less personal. Institutional orders were being fed into algorithmic trading systems, which broke up the orders into smaller pieces sent into the market throughout the day. As these algos replaced block trading, the floor of the NYSE was not as relevant. Brokers and clients were talking to each other less.

- HFTs were having a field day. While many institutional investors thought they were hiding their intentions behind the algos, they were leaving a big fat trail of data "cookie crumbs" that the HFTs were quick to identify and profit from.

The biggest changes were centered on the NYSE as it morphed from a slow, quote-driven market to a fast, automated computer service. Before Reg NMS, HFTs were largely confined to trading NASDAQ stocks because HFTs could work their strategies in only fully automated fast markets. Now, an entire new set of large, liquid stocks—perfect for HFT strategies—opened up for them.

We noticed these changes immediately and wrote a paper in 2008 titled "Toxic Equity Trading" to keep our clients informed:[2]

> Retail and institutional investors have been stunned at recent stock market volatility. The general thinking is that everything is related to the global financial crisis, starting, for the most part, in August 2007, when the Volatility Index, or VIX, started to climb.
>
> We believe, however, that there are more fundamental reasons behind the explosion in trading volume and the speed at which stock prices and indexes are changing. It has to do with the way electronic trading, the new for-profit exchanges and ECNs, and the SEC's Regulation NMS have all come together in unexpected ways, starting, coincidently, in late summer 2007.
>
> Little did we know.

The Flash Order Controversy

In summer 2009, the flash order controversy emerged. Flashing refers to the practice by exchanges of taking marketable orders and for a brief instant, showing those orders to the market centers' business partners (liquidity providers) to improve on the public quote, before the exchange sends the order to the National Best Bid and Offer (NBBO).[3]

While these business partners occasionally would provide sub-penny price improvement or trade ahead of the flashed order, in reality flash orders were giving some market participants a sneak peek at order flow. They were being used as a carrot by for-profit market centers to entice HFT firms to play in one exchange's sandbox over another's. Flash orders were created in 2006 when the SEC approved a rule filing by the CBOE for its equity trading platform. The Direct

Edge ECN soon began using them to gain market share on its competitors. In May 2009, NASDAQ and BATS both introduced their own version.

With the help of bloggers such as Zero Hedge, however, the public became aware that their orders were being "flashed" to a privileged few. Investors had trusted that their brokers send orders directly to the market. They didn't realize that their broker had an economic incentive to flash their order. Soon after the mainstream financial media exposed this practice, a firestorm erupted in Washington, DC. In July 2009, U.S. Senator Charles Schumer of New York sent a letter to SEC Chair Mary Schapiro demanding a ban:[4]

> This kind of unfair access seriously compromises the integrity of our markets and creates a two-tiered system where a privileged group of insiders receives preferential treatment, depriving others of a fair price for their transactions. If allowed to continue, these practices will undermine the confidence of ordinary investors and drive them away from our capital markets.

Something had gone horribly wrong with the regulation binge that the SEC had started in 1995. Rules that were enacted to help the small investor now seemed to be doing just the opposite. In addition to critics such as Themis Trading and Zero Hedge, politicians were becoming concerned about the state of the equity market. U.S. Senator Ted Kaufman took the lead in advocating for fairness and transparency.

The well-financed HFT community was not going to take this public attack lightly and started to trot out some big guns to defend its position. One such defender of the new status quo was Arthur Levitt. After masterminding the Order Handling Rules, Reg ATS, the elimination of Rule 390, and decimalization (see Chapter 4, "Regulatory Purgatory"), he stepped down as SEC chairman in 2001. Similar to many former regulators, he became an industry consultant. He is currently an advisor to GETCO and Goldman Sachs, two of the biggest high frequency traders on Wall Street. And he became a big defender of HFT. In a *Wall Street Journal* op-ed on August 17, 2009, titled "Don't Set Speed Limits on Trading," Levitt urged the public and regulators not to overreact and to ignore the HFT critics. HFT was simply using technology to get ahead of the competition, look for inefficiencies and, by exploiting them, correct them. "I see nothing sinister or unfair about the advantages that come out of their investments and efforts," he wrote.[5]

Two days later, Levitt went on Bloomberg radio. With his calming, grandfatherly tone, he once again claimed that HFT was "a net positive for the public" that was "squeezing down spreads and adding liquidity." But Levitt also admitted that regulations instituted while he was Chairman of the SEC had set the groundwork for the current fragmented stock market. Ultimately, he said, "As Chairman of the SEC, I instituted regulation specifically designed to foster today's competitive markets. Our markets today are a result of careful policies created to increase competition"[6]

After years of developing the current fragmented equity market, Levitt was now out front defending his work. No doubt his clients, including GETCO and Goldman Sachs, were happy to hear such reassuring words.

Under fire from the media and politicians, the SEC began to realize that it had to do something. In September 2009, the Commission proposed the elimination of flash orders. "Flash orders may create a two-tiered market by allowing only selected participants to access information about the best available prices for listed securities," current SEC Chair Schapiro explained. "These flash orders provide a momentary head-start in the trading arena that can produce inequities in the markets and create disincentives to display quotes."[7]

Then, in October 2009, the SEC proposed rules on the fast growing dark pool segment of the market. Since 2002, the number of dark pools had tripled to more than 40. The SEC defined dark pools as "private trading systems in which participants can transact their trades without displaying quotations to the public." The Commission found that too much volume was being conducted off-exchange. "Given this growth of dark pools, a lack of transparency could create a two-tiered market that deprives the public of information about stock prices and liquidity," the SEC explained. The proposals called for dark pool indications of interest to be treated like regular quotes and therefore required to be visible to all investors; real time disclosure of the identity of the dark pool that executed a trade; and any dark pool that traded more than 0.25% of a stock had to display those orders in the public quote.[8, 9]

Ironically, Reg ATS in 1998 was supposed to force more orders into the public quote to aid in the price discovery process. However, it resulted in almost one-third of orders being executed away from the public quote and in dark pools. With the flash order and dark pool proposals, it appeared that the SEC was serious about increasing transparency. The SEC received hundreds of comment letters, most by industry participants who wanted to maintain the status quo. Unfortunately, even though proposed in 2009, the SEC has yet to approve any parts of either proposal. Flash orders are still legal and dark pools are still gaining market share.

The two-tiered market that the SEC feared in 2009 is alive and well and growing every day.

The Concept Release on Market Structure...Interrupted

In January 2010, after a nonstop barrage of complaints from many different market participants, the SEC published its Concept Release on Market Structure. Regulators wanted to ask market participants what they thought of how the market was working after the regulatory binge over the past 15 years. The Concept Release sought comment on a broad range of issues, including HFT, colocation, and dark pools. As opposed to the SEC's flash order and dark pool proposals, the Concept Release asked questions but didn't make proposals.

We were happy to comment. We started our letter to the SEC, writing:[10]

> Regulations enacted by the Commission over the past decade, particularly Regulation NMS, have led to an enormous amount of unintended consequences, most notably fragmentation and the lack of transparency. The U.S. equity market is now a fragmented web of for-profit exchanges, ECNs, ATSs and dark pools connected by high speed, low latency lines.
>
> Visible liquidity in all but the top volume stocks has essentially disappeared as many market participants elect to hide in dark pools and piece their orders out in small slices throughout the day. One of the main goals of Reg NMS was to encourage displayed liquidity. It is now apparent that this goal was not accomplished.

We went on to detail the conflicts of interests of the for-profit exchange model, the timing issues that led to latency arbitrage, and the poorly designed market data revenue model (see the Appendix for the entire letter).

The SEC received hundreds of letters from many industry participants. Most were submitted by the April 21, 2010 deadline. Many stated that there was nothing wrong with the current market structure. Of course, many letters were written by participants who had a vested interest in the status quo. This comment from a high frequency trading firm was typical:[11]

> Our general view is the market structure that has evolved is effective and beneficial, especially with a view toward the public investor. The securities marketplace has witnessed a growth of technology in concert with regulatory reforms that have proven to equalize access to all investors, both professional and retail, reduce latency, narrow spreads and lower costs.

But before the SEC staff could read all the letters, something devastating happened on May 6, 2010—the Flash Crash. This one event would negate most of the comments trying to say there was nothing wrong. May 6 indeed proved something was horribly wrong. Here is how the SEC explained what happened that day:[12]

> The prices of many U.S.-based equity products experienced an extraordinarily rapid decline and recovery. That afternoon, major equity indices in both the futures and securities markets, each already down over 4% from their prior-day close, suddenly plummeted a further 5–6% in a matter of minutes before rebounding almost as quickly.
>
> Many of the almost 8,000 individual equity securities and exchange traded funds ("ETFs") traded that day suffered similar price declines and reversals within a short period of time, falling 5%, 10% or even 15% before recovering most, if not all, of their losses.
>
> However, some equities experienced even more severe price moves, both up and down. Over 20,000 trades across more than 300 securities were executed at prices more than 60% away from their values just moments before. Moreover, many of these trades were executed at prices of a penny or less, or as high as $100,000, before prices of those securities returned to their "pre-crash" levels.
>
> By the end of the day, major futures and equities indices "recovered" to close at losses of about 3% from the prior day.

We wrote a note to our clients the next day with our thoughts:[13]

> Today's price swings in a great number of stocks highlight the inherent and systemic risk of our automated stock market, which has few checks and balances in place. [When] the market sensed stress, the bids were canceled, and market sell orders chased prices down to the lowest possible point. Investors who thought they were protecting themselves with the prudent use of stop orders were left with fills that were far away from the closing price.
>
> Today's severe market drop should never have happened. The U.S. equity market had been hailed as the best, most

liquid market in the world. The market action of May 6 has demonstrated that our equity market has major systemic risks built into it. There was a time today when folks didn't know the true price and value of a stock. The price discovery process ceased to exist. High frequency firms have always insisted that their mini-scalping activities stabilized markets and provided liquidity, and on May 6 they just shut down.

Money began pouring out of the equity market, as nervous investors lost confidence. The SEC responded almost five months later, issuing a report titled "Findings Regarding Market Events of May 6, 2010." The report placed a good piece of blame on one midwestern money manager. Many HFT proponents felt vindicated.

Although the headlines of the SEC report seemed to exonerate HFT, many market observers believed there were more problems beneath the surface (see Chapters 10 and 11 for more detail on the Flash Crash). One of the biggest questions was why it took the SEC almost five months to produce a report on less than thirty minutes of trading. The SEC explained that most of the delay was because it did not have a consolidated data trail. The Commission needed to piece together what happened on May 6 from many different sources.

It was apparent that the SEC was lacking the tools necessary to police the new equity market that it had created.

The Band-Aid Fixes

Since the Flash Crash, rather than address the entire fragmented equity market, the SEC proposed and approved a number of short-term band-aid fixes.

Single Stock Circuit Breakers

In June 2010, single stock circuit breakers were approved by the SEC as an initial line of defense against another flash crash. They initiate a trading halt on moves of more than 10% within a five-minute window on Phase One or Phase Two securities (which include Russell 1000 stocks and some ETFs) and a halt on moves of 30% on all other stocks. Single stock circuit breakers are a supplement to existing marketwide circuit breakers, which activate when the Dow Jones Industrial Average drops by at least 10%.

Elimination of Stub Quotes

The SEC did eliminate stub quotes, which were essentially placeholders for market makers that wanted only to quote one side of a market. Typically, stub quotes were placed far away from the market, often as low as one penny for a bid. For example, if a market maker wanted to place an offer to only sell stock, he would have to place a stub quote as a bid to create a two-sided market. When Accenture traded at $0.01 during the Flash Crash, the bid that was hit was a stub quote. According to the SEC Flash Crash report, "Executions against stub quotes represented a significant proportion of broken trades on May 6."[14] Eliminating stub quotes was a no-brainer in our opinion.

What is needed, however, are more stringent market maker obligations. Currently, market makers need to quote within only 8% of the NBBO for most securities. There are even some securities where they are allowed to quote within 30% of the NBBO. How does quoting a stock at least 8% away from its NBBO help anybody? Does that build a stable, limit order book? This is not an obligation; it's just a way for the HFT market making firms and their exchange enablers to stand up at conferences and proclaim that they have quoting obligations. Today's automated market makers enjoy the benefits of seeing order flow first due to their colocated computers and access to direct data feeds. But they do not have meaningful quoting obligations to go along with these benefits. The slightest hiccup in the markets, and these new "market makers" will likely run for cover as many did on May 6, 2010.

Sponsored Access Rule

This rule, otherwise known as the market access rule, was fully implemented in November 2011. This was another no-brainer in our opinion. The rule requires brokers to screen all orders from their sponsored access clients before they are sent into the market and to perform credit and capital checks. When proposing the sponsored access rules, SEC Chair Schapiro said, "Unfiltered access is similar to giving your car keys to a friend who doesn't have a license and letting him drive unaccompanied...if a broker-dealer is going to loan his keys, he must not only remain in the car, but he must also see to it that the person driving observes the rules before the car is ever put into drive."[15] The rule was intended to prevent thinly capitalized HFT firms from entering orders directly into an exchange without first getting a pre-trade risk check. Smaller HFTs claimed this rule was unfair and would give their larger brethren a distinct advantage. They claimed additional latency would be introduced into their trading strategies now that pre-trade credit and risk checks are required. The jury is still out on this, but what also remains to be seen is how the regulators will enforce the rule.

Large Trader Reporting Rule

This rule was another way that the SEC was looking to get more knowledge on high frequency traders. The rule "requires large traders to register with the Commission and imposes record keeping, reporting, and limited monitoring requirements on certain registered broker-dealers through whom large traders execute their transactions."[16] Large traders will each have a unique I.D. number that the SEC believes will enable it "to promptly and efficiently identify significant market participants and collect data on their trading activity so that we can reconstruct market events, conduct investigations, and bring enforcement actions as appropriate." Although this rule may aid the SEC in identifying the culprits, it doesn't do anything to prevent the next flash crash. It also casts a wide net that captures many traditional money managers. Most traditional, long-only funds fall under the large trader reporting rule and have to register as well.

Consolidated Audit Trail

In addition, the SEC has also proposed capturing data across different asset classes. In its proposal, the SEC states:

> A consolidated audit trail would significantly aid in SRO [self-regulatory organization] efforts to detect and deter fraudulent and manipulative acts and practices in the marketplace, and generally to regulate their markets and members. In addition, such an audit trail would benefit the Commission in its market analysis efforts, such as investigating and preparing market reconstructions and understanding causes of unusual market activity....
>
> The proposed Rule would require the consolidated audit trail to capture certain information about each order for an NMS security, including the identity of the customer placing the order and the routing, modification, cancellation or execution of the order, in real time. In effect, the proposal would create a time-stamped "electronic audit trail record or report" for every order, and each market participant that touches the order would be required to report information about certain reportable events, such as routing or execution of the order.

To get an idea of how the current audit trail system works across different exchanges and asset classes, picture a bank vault. There are numerous exits to this vault. The security office at the bank has a camera trained on only a few of the exits. It is possible that it will catch a crook trying to rob the vault, but more than likely it will miss some key evidence because every exit door is not covered with a camera. By proposing a Consolidated Audit Trail, the SEC is trying to put a camera at every exit in the vault. Current audit trails do not include significant pieces of information. The SEC has acknowledged that "key pieces of information about the life of an order may not be captured, or easily tracked, if an order is routed from one exchange to another, or from one broker-dealer to an exchange."[17] Even with a consolidated audit trail, it still may be tough to catch the bad guys. But at least the security cameras at the vault should act as a deterrent.

While we applaud the SEC for taking steps to address the Franken-Market that they helped create, we wonder whether this piecemeal approach is the best way to address the problems. In a recent Reuters interview, SEC Chair Schapiro was quoted as saying, "The idea that the regulator of the largest capital markets in the world cannot easily reconstruct trading when there has been a problem, or when there is a suspicion of manipulation or misconduct, is not acceptable to me."[18]

Maybe a new approach that starts from scratch is a better idea.

Endnotes

1. Justin Schack and Joe Gawronski, "Rosenblatt's Monthly Dark Liquidity Tracker," Trading Talk, July 29, 2009, Rosenblatt website, http://rblt.com/lettherebelight_details.aspx?id=81.

2. Sal L. Arnuk and Joseph Saluzzi, "Toxic Equity Trading Order Flow on Wall Street: The Real Force Behind the Explosion in Volume and Volatility," Themis Trading website, http://www.themistrading.com/article_files/0000/0348/Toxic_Equity_Trading_on_Wall_Street_12-17-08.pdf.

3. Securities and Exchange Commission, "SEC Proposes Flash Order Ban" press release, Sept. 17, 2009, Securities and Exchange Commission website, http://www.sec.gov/news/press/2009/2009-201.htm.

4. Charles E. Schumer, "Schumer Urges Ban on So-Called 'Flash Orders' that Give Privileged Traders Sneak Peek at Stock Sales Before Other Investors," press release July 27, 2009, Schumer's website, http://schumer.senate.gov/new_website/record.cfm?id=316252.

5. Arthur Levitt, Jr., "Don't Set Speed Limits on Trading," *The Wall Street Journal*, Aug 17, 2009, Wall Street Journal website, http://online.wsj.com/article/SB10001424052970204409904574350522402379930.html.

6. Arthur Levitt, Bloomberg News radio interview (Aug. 19, 2009), YouTube website, http://www.youtube.com/watch?v=L5CN_YUcX5c.

7. Securities and Exchange Commission, "Elimination of Flash Order Exception from Rule 602 of Regulations NMS," 17 CFR part 242, rel. 34-60684, file S7-21-09, RIN 3235-AK40, Securities and Exchange Commission website, http://www.sec.gov/rules/proposed/2009/34-60684.pdf.

8. Securities and Exchange Commission, "Regulation of Non-Public Trading Interest," 17 CFR part 242, re. 34-60997, file S7-27-09, RIN 3235-AK46, Securities and Exchange Commission website, http://www.sec.gov/rules/proposed/2009/34-60997.pdf.

9. Securities and Exchange Commission, "SEC Issues Proposals to Shed Greater Light on Dark Pools," press release 2009-223, Oct 21,2009, Securities and Exchange Commission website, http://www.sec.gov/news/press/2009/2009-223.htm.

10. Securities and Exchange Commission, "Elimination of Flash Order Exception from Rule 602 of Regulations NMS," 17 CFR part 242, rel. 34-60684, file S7-21-09, RIN 3235-AK40, Securities and Exchange Commission website, http://www.sec.gov/rules/proposed/2009/34-60684.pdf.

11. Greg O'Connor (Compliance Manager, Wolverine Trading), letter dated April 21, 2010 to Elizabeth M. Murphy (Secretary, Securities and Exchange Commission), Securities and Exchange Commission website, http://www.sec.gov/comments/s7-02-10/s70210-143.pdf.

12. Commodity Futures Trading Commission and Securities and Exchange Commission, "Findings Regarding the Market Events of May 6, 2010," Executive Summary, Securities and Exchange Commission website (Sept. 30, 2010), http://www.sec.gov/news/studies/2010/marketevents-report.pdf.

13. Themis Trading, "The Emperor Has No Clothes; We Need a New Mousetrap," Themis Trading website (May 7, 2010), http://blog.themistrading.com/the-emperor-has-no-clothes-we-need-a-new-mousetrap.

14. Securities and Exchange Commission, "SEC Approves New Rules Prohibiting Market Maker Stub Quotes," press release 2010-216, Nov. 8, 2010, Securities and Exchange Commission website, http://www.sec.gov/news/press/2010/2010-216.htm.

15. Securities and Exchange Commission, "SEC Proposes New Rule to Effectively Prohibit Unfiltered Access and Maintain Market Access Controls," press release 2010-7, Jan. 13, 2010, Securities and Exchange Commission website, http://www.sec.gov/news/press/2010/2010-7.htm.

16. Securities and Exchange Commission, "SEC Adopts Large Trader Reporting Regime," press release 2011-154, July 26, 2010, Securities and Exchange Commission website, http://www.sec.gov/news/press/2011/2011-154.htm.

17. Securities and Exchange Commission, proposed rule 17 CFR, part 242, rel. 34-62174, file S7-11-10, RIN 3235-AK51, Government Printing Office website (June 8, 2010), http://www.gpo.gov/fdsys/pkg/FR-2010-06-08/html/2010-13129.htm.

18. Jonathan Spicer, Herbert Lash, and Sarah N. Lynch, "Insight: SEC Tightens Leash on Exchanges Post 'Flash Crash'," Reuters.com (Jan. 12, 2012), http://www.reuters.com/article/2012/01/12/us-sec-exchanges-leash-idUS-TRE80B1YA20120112.

6

The Arms Merchants

In the 2005 movie *Lord of War*, Nicholas Cage plays the role of Yuri Orlov, a ruthless international arms dealer who sells sophisticated weapons to dictators and tyrants all over the world. He is the unseen middleman responsible for arming any side that will pay. The weapons kill many, but because he never pulls the trigger, he's not the bad guy.

The Wall Street Yuri Orlovs are the stock exchanges. They provide and sell sophisticated tools to those willing to pay, tools that provide tremendous advantages over everybody else. In the movie, Orlov says, "The first and most important rule of gun-running is never get shot with your own merchandise." And that's exactly what the exchanges do. They provide the weapons but never get caught in the crossfire.

Over the past decade, the stock exchange business has undergone a radical transformation. What was once a nonprofit, quasi-utility, member-owned duopoly has turned into a for-profit, fragmented, and extremely competitive business with 13 exchanges and more than 40 dark pools, which enable traders to buy and sell large orders of stock, known as *blocks*, away from the "lit" or publicly quoted markets. To create additional arbitrage opportunities and sell more data products, exchanges also have created sub-exchanges, resulting in even more fragmentation. What was once a people-dominated business, where reputations were often a self-policing mechanism, is now a fully automated, anonymous, faceless business.

Normally, if a business model opened itself to competition, this would be viewed as a good thing. It would enable free markets to work. However, the stock exchange business has more responsibilities than profit. It has to help facilitate capital formation for companies and to protect individual investors. Unfortunately, the new for-profit landscape has caused the exchanges to forego these responsibilities in order to focus on the bottom line. To make matters worse, two of exchanges, NYSE and NASDAQ, are publicly traded companies that must answer to shareholders—investor protection be damned.

Most businesses follow the 80/20 rule, in which 80% of their business comes from 20% of their customers. This ratio is far different in the exchange business, in which nearly three-quarters of the volume comes from just 2% of the clients.[1] This distortion is the result of the exchanges catering to their biggest clients at the expense of average investors.

By attempting to level the playing field with all its new regulations, the SEC commoditized the stock exchange business. In turn, this led exchanges to supply high-value products and services to its highest volume clients. If they didn't, the exchanges feared these clients would move their volume to another market venue. This quest for profit has created significant conflicts of interests in the stock exchange business model. No longer do exchanges produce the majority of their revenue from corporate listings and services. Major revenue now comes from data services. In 2010, NYSE Technologies generated $475 million in revenue, or 20% of the parent company's overall revenue (less transaction-based expenses).[2] NYSE has stated that it expects to increase technology revenue to $1 billion annually by 2015.[3] When most new listing are ETFs and not IPOs (in 2011, 302 ETFs were listed vs. 125 IPOs), exchanges need to look elsewhere for profit.

This chapter talks about three exchange products and services that have distorted the true purpose of a stock exchange, demonstrating how the quest for profit is clouding the exchanges' judgment, with the equity market suffering as a result.

Colocation

The old saying that the three most important things in real estate are "location, location, location" is even truer for the stock exchanges. Due to simple physics, the exchanges' high frequency clients want to be as close as possible to the matching engine, the critical computer servers that execute the trades. It has been estimated that a one millisecond (that is one-thousandth of a second) advantage is worth up to $100 million a year to the bottom line of a large hedge fund.[4]

Exchanges realized they were literally sitting on a gold mine. What better place to locate your computer than in the same building as the matching engine? They decided to rent out computer rack space to clients who craved speed the most, and that space would not be cheap. Thus, colocation was born. The physical computer servers of the exchange's clients would sit in the same building as the computers that match trades with each other for the exchange.

Here is how NYSE explains its service:[5] "Being close to NYSE Euronext's trading engines can give your business model a competitive edge, and NYSE Technologies' colocation service provides unsurpassed value. By installing your trading systems in the NYSE Euronext US Liquidity Center, our new data center located in Mahwah, New Jersey, your firm can gain extremely low latency access to NYSE Euronext's markets."

NYSE uses the term "low latency," which is industry jargon for cutting out as much time from the trading process as possible. Although technically available to any investor, the NYSE's colocation service is extremely expensive.[6]

NYSE recently built two mammoth-sized colocation facilities at a combined cost of $500 million. One is in Mahwah, New Jersey just outside of New York City. The other in Basildon, United Kingdom, just outside of London. The Mahwah facility, located at 1600 MacArthur Blvd., has 400,000 square feet of space. That's the equivalent of seven NFL football fields, including the end zones.[7]

"Everything there is big," Bloomberg reporters Bob Ivry, Whitney Kisling, and Max Abelson wrote July 5, 2011. Twenty-inch pipes circulate water to cool the computers. Twenty surge protectors, each as big as a Hummer H4, guard against power outages. The facility consumes 28 megawatts of power, enough to run 4,500 residential homes. And if it loses outside power, generators on hand enable the facility to keep running.[8, 9] The facility, which is protected with state of the art security, has been classified as a "critical infrastructure" by the New Jersey's Office of Homeland Security. The U.S. Department of Homeland Security has given the Mahwah police department a grant of $125,000 to help pay for the facility's security.[10] So don't try to take any pictures.

NASDAQ describes its colocation service as follows: "NASDAQ OMX offers all customers the opportunity to colocate their servers and equipment within the NASDAQ OMX Data Center, providing proximity to the speed and liquidity of all of our U.S. markets. Through colocation (CoLo), participants are able to reduce latency and network complexity by utilizing high-density cabinets and a single hand-off for all NASDAQ OMX markets."[11]

NASDAQ doesn't own its data centers; it chooses to lease space from third parties. Its largest is housed in a Verizon business facility in Carteret, New Jersey. NASDAQ doesn't even view itself as a stock exchange anymore. "We really are a technology company," says Robert Waghorne, senior vice president of European Markets Technology, for NASDAQ. "It's the core engine for all of our business."[12]

The Direct Edge exchange houses one of its colocation facilities in a warehouse in a business park in New Jersey. "Few humans are present in this vast technological sanctum, known as New York Four," wrote Graham Bowley of *The New York Times* about his visit in 2011.[13] He described the facility as being three football fields long, filled with racks and racks of computer servers owned by major Wall Street firms.

This sure doesn't sound like a stock exchange. What happened to all the guys with different colored coats running around?

Colocation gives HFT firms the ability to see information a fraction of a second faster than other customers. And for this privilege, HFTs are willing to pay an enormous sum of money, which could range in the hundreds of thousands of dollars per year for a high-volume HFT firm. Large HFT firms colocate their servers with most of the major exchanges so that they can have the fastest access to every bit of trading data available.

Some have speculated where the optimal colocation facility should be located. Considering that exchanges are based around the world, a recent MIT study found that the ultimate site may be in the middle of the Atlantic Ocean.[14] Some exchanges make sure that each colocated customer receives equal amounts of connecting cable so that a server at the northeast corner of a facility has the same latency as one at the southwest.[15] It appears that "fairness" and the equalization of market data speed among colocated firms is a critical "must" for the exchanges, but not so when it comes to institutional and retail investors.

Private Data Feeds

In the 1987 movie *Wall Street*, insider trader Gordon Gekko tells aspiring broker Bud Fox that "the most valuable commodity I know of is information."[16] This is still true today, particularly for the stock exchanges. Private data feeds consolidate an enormous amount of information and transmit it at speeds faster than the consolidated quote system. Exchanges say they make these feeds available to everyone. Realistically, only those with the most sophisticated technology and programmers can use them. Some exchanges charge for this information. Others give it away for free to attract more order flow.

Information on private data feeds is much greater than what the public sees via the Securities Information Processor (SIP), which distributes public data feeds from the exchanges to Bloomberg, Dow Jones, Reuters, and Internet sites, such as Google and Yahoo. In a recent SEC filing, Direct Edge explained that its EDGX Book Feed contains "all displayed orders for listed securities trading on EDGX, order executions, order cancellations, order modifications, order identification numbers, and administrative messages."[17]

Private data feeds also supply information on revisions and cancellations. They can tell you what time an order was placed and whether it was revised. They can tell you whether an order had a partial fill and then canceled. They can tell you whether an order revised its price and how often. Most of this tracking is done by order identification numbers that monitor the life of an order. Think of it as if a video recorder attached to your favorite ATM. Every keystroke you make is captured. Then your bank sells or gives away the video to firms that can deconstruct what you did in your bank account to help predict the next time you will withdraw or deposit money and for how much.

This information is valuable because it enables high frequency traders to model the behavior of institutional and retail investor orders to predict the short-term price movements of stocks. Suppose you enter a buy order at $10 on NASDAQ in a stock currently quoted with a bid of $10 and an offer of $10.05. After the order is entered, it gets an identification number. Let's say your order doesn't get filled and you raise your bid to $10.02. Anybody monitoring the private data feed will know that you revised your order. This is what is happening millions of times per day.

The granddaddy of all data feeds is NASDAQ's ITCH, which was developed by the Island ECN, which, in turn, was developed by Datek Securities, a SOES Bandit brokerage firm. Island described ITCH as "one of Island's proprietary protocols. Through ITCH, Island provides a vendor-level data feed service that disseminates Island's order and trade information. This data feed contains information concerning buy and sell orders, last match price, and other information that is specific to Island's system. Island has entered into arrangements with data vendors that repackage this data feed and sell it to others."[18] Island was bought in 2002 by Instinet, which later sold the ITCH feed to NASDAQ. Many other exchanges and ATSs around the world, including the London Stock Exchange's Turquoise trading platform, offer private data feeds based on the ITCH protocol.

In an April 29, 2010 comment letter to the SEC, the Securities Industry and Financial Markets Association (SIFMA), which represents hundreds of securities firms, banks, and asset managers, summarized the benefits of private data feeds. "...Direct market data often is faster and more detailed than consolidated data," SIFMA wrote. "Also, direct data feed recipients generally are able to more easily trace orders they submit to an exchange or electronic communications network (ECN) using such feeds—facilitating, for example, their ability to analyze the implications of a particular trading strategy. But some SIFMA members believe that direct market data feeds may be used by third parties to generate more implicit information about the markets."[19]

Think of the data feeds as the high octane fuel that runs the HFT race car. With regular fuel (trades and quotes), the car would be fast. But with high octane fuel (orders, ID numbers, trades, cancellation times, revisions, and so on), the race car can get around the track in record time. No matter how many exchanges where an HFT colocates and how many programmers that an HFT hires, their trading programs would be useless without the enhanced private data feeds.

This is a major issue of concern for investors. But what if we told you that in addition to the information already described, private data feeds also supplied information on orders that you, the investor, thought was totally private? See Chapter 7, "It's the Data, Stupid," to find out how some exchanges were caught giving out hidden information, breaching the trust of some of their largest clients.

Rebates for Order Flow (The Maker/ Taker Model)

"Make-or-take pricing has significantly distorted trading." This was one of many conclusions by James Angel of Georgetown University in Washington, Lawrence Harris of the University of Southern California in Los Angeles, and Chester Spatt of Carnegie Mellon University in Pittsburgh in their paper, "Equity Trading in the 21st Century."[20]

Since 1997, when the Island ECN introduced rebate trading, the equity market has used a maker/taker model. Almost every major exchange, ECN and ATS has copied what Josh Levine invented in 1997. Back then, we were working at Instinet, which had the dominant share of the ECN business. New regulations approved by the SEC, however, started to break Instinet's control. Island, a competitor, wanted a bigger slice of the institutional block trading pie. Island decided to pay its clients, namely HFT firms, to bring it order flow. In turn, Island charged clients, namely traditional institutional firms, for removing order flow.

Today, maker/taker has become the standard pricing model for exchanges. Liquidity "makers" get paid a rebate, and liquidity "takers" pay a fee. Typically, the rebate is less than the take fee. Rebates can range from $0.0020 for lower volume exchange clients to $0.0034 for ultra-tier higher volume exchange clients. Few in the trading community question why a maker/taker model is necessary. This is probably because the rebates and take fees are largely invisible to institutional and retail investors. Institutional and retail investors pay a flat commission rate to their brokers regardless of whether they are making or taking liquidity. Therefore, they may not realize how the maker/taker model affects them. But they should care because their implicit trading costs are directly affected. The brokers who sponsor algorithmic trading systems have figured out a way for this model to be profitable. The exchanges are content with receiving the spread between the make/take rates. And both the exchanges and the brokers have a vested interest seeing this model continue.

The authors of *Equity Trading in the 21st Century* believe the maker/taker model has: "...distorted order routing decisions, aggravated agency problems among brokers and their clients, unleveled the playing field among dealers and exchange trading systems, produced fraudulent trades, and produced quoted spreads that do not represent actual trading costs."[21]

How could this be? How could a simple pricing model be distorting the execution of a trade? The maker/taker model is at the core of the equity market structure problem. It has influenced how most broker-sponsored smart order routers access liquidity. Institutional investors typically enter their algorithmic orders into a smart order router, or SOR, provided by their brokerage firm in exchange for a low commission rate. The "algo" chops up large block orders of 100,000 shares, for example, and doles out small slices of say 100–500 shares each that are routed to various market centers. The purpose is to minimize market impact. However, some orders are not routed to the destination where best execution would dictate, but to the destination where the broker receives the best rebate. While these SORs may be "smart" for the broker, they may be pretty dumb for the client.

The pecking order of these routers differs depending on which broker sponsors the algo. A common goal is to route to the least expensive destination that maximizes the brokerage firm's profit. Most of the time this means routing to a dark pool before routing to a displayed liquidity venue. Typically, dark pool fees are lower to attract more flow. Many dark pools, however, are filled with predatory traders, who are electronically hiding out so that they can watch for institutional algo footprints, to take advantage of these orders. See Chapter 8, "Heart of Darkness," for more about adverse selection issues with dark pools.

Institutional investors may think they are lowering their transaction costs because their brokers are supplying algos at a commission rate of a fraction of a penny per share. The real cost of a trade, however, is what you don't see. In our Instinet days, we referred to this as the *transaction iceberg*. Routers that have the goal to maximize economics due to the maker/taker model are a good reason why these implicit costs are so high. In a comment letter to the SEC on March 4, 2010, Morgan Stanley explained:[22]

> The real, underlying problem that needs to be addressed is the conduct of market participants...The economic incentives that exist in the market to reduce execution costs inevitably lead to a race for cheaper execution alternatives.

> The acceptance of the "free look for a free execution" mantra has [led] to many market participants, including broker-dealers and exchanges, routing their orders to various alternative liquidity providers in lieu of the traditional lit marketplace. Competition and advances in technology have not only permitted, but have encouraged participants to look for the most cost-effective execution, many times in conflict with the underlying customer whose order information is "leaked" to sophisticated market participants and who is not the ultimate recipient of the resulting economic benefit.

How much money is made by brokers and exchanges when they make these routing decisions, which are ultimately hurting their own clients and helping the HFT predators? Morgan Stanley wrote:[23]

> We estimate that the annual economic benefit for broker-dealers aggressively routing in this manner could amount to $63 million (based on a 100 million shares average daily trading volume). Similarly, exchanges that would have otherwise incurred a net loss of approximately $10 million from having to route to other exchanges could turn that loss in an annual economic

benefit of approximately $76 million (based on a 100 million shares average daily trading volume) through fiscal routing to alternative liquidity sources.

This money comes from somewhere. A good part of it is coming from the leakage of institutional algos because brokers and exchanges have an economic incentive to route their customers' trades to the cheapest and sometimes most adverse venue.

Not Your Father's Stock Exchange

Colocation, private data feeds, and the maker/taker model are all relatively new innovations for stock exchanges. To stay competitive, exchanges needed to change their business model from serving long-term investors and publicly traded companies to serving short-term, high frequency traders. No doubt the regulations that were approved by the SEC forced the exchanges to change in order to survive.

The exchanges realized that they must offer the fastest speed at the lowest price to their HFT clients because HFTs represented the majority of the exchanges' business. The exchanges also realized that the HFT community was willing to spend billions of dollars per year to get an edge on their competitors. The problem with arms races, however, is that they are zero sum games. In a 2009 blog post commenting about HFT, Rick Bookstaber, now a senior policy adviser at the SEC, wrote: "Like any arms race, the result is a cycle of spending [that] leaves everyone in the same relative position, only poorer... What is happening with high frequency trading is a net drain on social welfare."[24]

The stock exchange business is extremely competitive. The exchanges compete among themselves as well as the multitude of other market centers for order flow. Volumes are often dominated by just a small subset of their highest volume clients. For-profit exchanges have sacrificed their long-standing goals to help companies raise capital and investor protection so that they can increase their own bottom line. In a *New York Times* interview, Andrew Lo, director of the Laboratory for Financial Engineering at M.I.T., noted that regulators were "caught unaware of how quickly the technology has evolved. Sometimes, too much technology without the [cap]ability to manage it effectively can yield some unintended consequences....It is the Wild, Wild West in trading."[25]

Endnotes

1. Rob Iati, "The Real Story of Trading Software Espionage" (July 10, 2009), Advanced Trading website, http://www.advancedtrading.com/algorithms/218401501.

2. New York Stock Exchange Technologies, Listings page, U.S. Equities website, http://usequities.nyx.com/listings/leading-technology.

3. Ibid.

4. Matthew Vincent, "Speed Fails to Impress Long-Term Investors" (Jan. 1, 2011), *Financial Times*, Sept. 22, 2011, *Financial Times website*, http://www.ft.com/intl/cms/s/0/df141604-e070-11e0-bd01-00144feabdc0.html#axzz1n3cofl4o.

5. New York Stock Exchange, Service Description, New York Stock Exchange website, http://www.nyse.com/pdfs/Colocation-NYSE-Euronext-US-Liquidity-Center.pdf.

6. New York Stock Exchange, Price List 2012, U.S. Equities website, https://usequities.nyx.com/sites/usequities.nyx.com/files/nyse_price_list_01.01.12_0.pdf.

7. Peter Chapman, "A Buttonwood Tree Grows in Mahwah" (May, 2010), Traders Magazine.com, http://www.tradersmagazine.com/issues/23_308/buttonwood-nyse-mahwah-nyfix-colocation-data-center-105760-1.html.

8. Bob Ivry, Whitney Kisling, and Max Abelson, "How America Ceded Capitalism's Bastion to German Boerse Seizing Big Board" (July 5, 2011), Ethnic Cliques, Bloomberg website, http://www.bloomberg.com/news/2011-07-06/how-america-ceded-capitalism-s-bastion-to-germans.html.

9. Wall Street and Technology, "NYSE Datacenter," Exchanges page, Wall Street and Technology website, http://wallstreetandtech.com/exchanges/NYSE-Datacenter.

10. Jessica Mazzola, "PD Receives $124K to Buy Security Equipment for NYSE Data Center" (Sept. 2, 2011), MahwahPatch.com, http://Mahwah.patch.com/articles/pd-receives-124k-to-buy-security-equipment-for-nyse-data-center.

11. NASDAQ Trader, "NASDAQ OMX Co-Location (CoLo)," U.S. Market page, NASDAQTrader.com, http://www.nasdaqtrader.com/Trader.aspx?id=colo.

12. Rich Miller, "NASDAQ Steps Up Its Game in the Data Center" (March 15, 2011), Data Center Knowledge website, http://www.datacenterknowledge.com/archives/2011/03/15/nasdaq-steps-up-its-game-in-the-data-center/.

13. Graham Bowley, "The New Speed of Money, Reshaping Markets" (Jan. 1, 2011), *New York Times*, Jan. 2, 2011, New York Times website, http://www.nytimes.com/2011/01/02/business/02speed.html?pagewanted=all.

14. A. D. Wissner-Gross and C.E. Freer "Relativistic Statistical Arbitrage (Physical Review E 82, 056104 (2010)" (Nov. 5, 2010), Alexander Wissner-Gross website, http://www.alexwg.org/publications/PhysRevE_82-056104.pdf.

15. Ivy Schmerken, "Exchanges Say Colocation Is a Regulated Business" (Dec. 20, 2011), Wall Street and Technology website, http://wallstreetandtech.com/exchanges/232300847.

16. Oliver Stone, Wall Street (1987), IMDb website, http://www.imdb.com/title/tt0094291/quotes.

17. Securities and Exchange Commission, "Self-Regulatory Organizations; EDGA Exchange, Inc.; Notice of Filing and Immediate Effectiveness of Proposed Rule Change to Make Available Without Charge the EDGA Book Feed and to Add a Description of the EDGA Book Feed to New Rule 13.8: 2," rel. 34-64792, file SR-EDGA-2011-19 (no date provided), Securities and Exchange Commission website, http://www.sec.gov/rules/sro/edga/2011/34-64792.pdf.

18. Instinet Group, excerpt from SEC 8-K Filing (Sept. 23, 2002), Edgar-Online website, http://sec.edgar-online.com/instinet-group-inc/8-k-current-report-filing/2002/09/23/section11.aspx.

19. Securities Industry and Financial Markets Association, "SIFMA Submits Comments to the SEC Regarding Concept Release on Equity Market Structure" (April 29, 2010), Securities Industry and Financial Markets Association website, http://www.sifma.org/issues/item.aspx?id=897.

20. James Angel, Lawrence Harris, and Chester S. Spatt, "Equity Trading in the 21st Century" (Feb. 23, 2010), Social Science Research Network website, http://papers.ssrn.com/sol3/papers.cfm?abstract_id=1584026.

21. Ibid.

22. William P. Neuberger and Andrew F. Silverman (Managing Directors, Morgan Stanley Electronic Trading), letter dated March 4, 2010 to Elizabeth M. Murphy (Secretary, Securities and Exchange Commission): 2, Securities and Exchange Commission website, http://sec.gov/comments/s7-27-09/s72709-74.pdf.

23. Neuberger and Silverman, letter dated March 4, 2010 to Murphy.

24. Rick Bookstaber, "The Arms Race in High Frequency Trading" (April 21, 2009), Rick Bookstaber blogsite, http://rick.bookstaber.com/2009/04/arms-race-in-high-frequency-trading.html.

25. Bowley, "The New Speed of Money, Reshaping Markets."

7

It's the Data, Stupid

On a cold February morning in 2010, we received a short email that would shake up the HFT industry and question the credibility of some major exchanges. The email, which came in from an account that we didn't know, said simply, "Check out the data feeds. Information on hidden orders is being leaked."

Being deeply involved in the HFT debate, we had begun receiving quite a few emails from the public. Many encouraged support of our stance. Others were critical and questioned our motives. Occasionally, we would receive tips on how to find how HFTs were getting an official edge over retail and institutional investors.

We always respond to every email and follow up any clues. This email was a bit different, though. It was short and to the point. To us, it was obvious that the email came from someone who really did know something but did not want to reveal his or her identity.

We were familiar with the stock exchange private data feeds and the information that they provided to HFT clients. By early 2010, we had been analyzing the feeds for some time and believed that they contained the kind of data that fueled the HFT engine.

If true, the tip that we received could be extremely damaging to any client that was using a hidden order type. A hidden order is placed on an exchange or dark pool, but it is not publicly visible in the quote. Investors who use this type of order are willing to give up their place in the time/price priority sequence to be more discreet about their order. Hidden orders are often used by large institutional investors who are trying to cloak themselves to not get spotted by the HFTs. If the exchanges were providing information on hidden orders to HFTs, then the exchanges were violating a sacred trust with their clients.

We immediately downloaded the specifications of the NASDAQ TotalView-ITCH feed from the NASDAQ website. As mentioned in Chapter 6, "The Arms Merchants," the ITCH feed was created by the Island ECN and subsequently copied by almost every exchange, ECN, and ATS as the basis for their data feeds. The ITCH feed disseminated enhanced information about orders and trades from an exchange to clients who subscribed to the feed.

The information contained in ITCH was a lot more than just when a trade or quote happened. It contained information on cancellations, modifications, and executions. And it contained lots of cryptic flags and order identification numbers. To the average investor, looking at an ITCH is like looking at a message sent between two spies. You could never figure it out. But to an HFT computer, the information is like a gold mine, giving HFTs an advantage over retail and institutional investors.

The rationale that the exchanges give for selling this information is that it is public and available to any investor who wants to subscribe. Some exchanges give it away to lure new business. The lifeblood of an exchange is order flow, and an exchange will go to great lengths to please high-volume clients. Other exchanges see private data feeds as profit centers and charge monthly access fees. Although access is nondiscriminatory, for the private data feed to mean anything, it needs to be decrypted by sophisticated hardware and software.

The NASDAQ TotalView-ITCH protocol, however, is not something that the average investor would read. It is more than 30 pages of cryptic messages that include codes, flags, and values.[1] We dove into this document, picking it apart line by line. At first, we were not sure where to look. Section Four was titled "Message Formats" and stated: "The TotalView-ITCH feed is composed of a series of messages that describes orders added to, removed from, and executed on NASDAQ."

We must be getting close, we thought. There was information on system events, addition of orders, and cancellation of orders. And then, as clear as day, we spotted it in Section 4.6, "Trade Messages." It said, "The Trade Message is designed to provide execution details for normal match events involving non-displayable order types.... A Trade Message is transmitted each time a non-displayable order is executed in whole or in part. It is possible to receive multiple Trade Messages for the same order if that order is executed in several parts. Trade Messages for the same order are cumulative...." The non-display order on the book being matched also indicates whether the trade was a buy or sell.

Information for Sale on Hidden Customer Orders

They might as well just broadcast it in bright lights. Nondisplayable orders are hidden orders. Here's what the paragraph meant in layman's terms: Every time a hidden order is executed, NASDAQ sends a message on its private data feed that not only identified that a trade occurred, but also identified whether the order was a buy or sell. In addition, the ID number associated with that trade was "cumulative." This meant that every time a trade executes part of a hidden order, the same ID number is attached to that trade as the original trade. This enabled ITCH subscribers to determine how much of the stock in question that a hidden buyer or seller had accumulated or sold.

Suppose an institutional investor was looking to buy 100,000 shares of mid cap semiconductor stock Novellus Systems (NVLS). The stock has an average daily volume of three million shares. Although that might sound large, NVLS is not an active stock, such as Bank of America (BAC), which trades around 300 million shares per day. As a result, the institutional investor knows that her large order could move the stock, so she chooses to enter a hidden buy order on NAS-DAQ. The buy order resides on NASDAQ's order book and interacts with sell orders that match its price, but the buy order is not visible to the public markets.

Here is a hypothetical sequence of events. Say the bid price is $46.96 and the offer is $46.98.

1. The institutional trader enters one-quarter of her buy order (25,000 shares) as a hidden order on NASDAQ with a price of $46.96.

2. Seller enters order to sell 500 shares of NVLS on NASDAQ at $46.96.

3. The hidden order buys 500 shares at $46.96. This trade appears on the consolidated tape that all investors can see and also appears in the NASDAQ ITCH data feed. However, the NAS-DAQ ITCH data feed attaches two pieces of information to the trade: an order ID number and the flag of "B" because a buy was executed.

4. The seller enters an order to sell 300 shares of NVLS on NAS-DAQ at $46.96.

5. Again, the hidden order buys the 300 shares at $46.96. The trade appears on the consolidated tape and in the NASDAQ ITCH feed. Here is where NASDAQ reveals critical information about the trade to its data feed subscribers: The order ID number attached to this trade was the same ID number as the first 500 share trade.

6. Any subsequent trades that interact with the hidden order have the same order ID number.

Any market participant monitoring the ITCH data feed would know a hidden buy order was accumulating stock. If you were monitoring only the consolidated tape, you would not know this. Who benefits from this additional information? Predatory HFTs looking to take advantage of institutional order flow. These HFTs have sophisticated software and hardware that reengineers the order ID numbers to predict the short-term price movement of the stock to trade ahead, or front run, the institutional order. This has the effect of driving up the institution's transaction cost.

We could not believe that an exchange was selling such nonpublic information on its clients. We called NASDAQ, and people there confirmed that the exchange was providing information about hidden order flow. We wondered whether other market centers were doing the same thing. We quickly discovered something similar offered by the BATS exchange via its PITCH feed. In the PITCH protocol, we found: "If an order's Price or Display values change within the BATS matching engine, a Cancel Order Message will be immediately followed by a new Add Order Message with the same Order ID as the original order. An order that changes its Display value from 'N' to 'Y' will not lose its priority."

This was different from NASDAQ but equally as bad. BATS attached an ID number to each order submitted. The ID number was then sent out to subscribers of the PITCH feed. After a reserve book order (an order that displays only a portion of the entire order) was placed in BATS for execution, the ID number tracked cumulative trades over the life of the order. Any trade execution related to that order had the same ID number as the original order. HFTs who subscribed to PITCH could determine how much an order had traded and whether it was revising its price.

Data Theft on Wall Street

Now that we found out about exchanges selling or giving away data on hidden or reserve orders, the question became, what should we do with it? Our main priority has always been informing our clients immediately about significant market structure issues so that they could factor them into their trading decisions. But this was much bigger. We needed to let the public know.

It also opened our eyes to how, in a day and age of computer-dominated trading, the actual performance of a company whose stock is traded is not the most significant piece of information anymore. It's the data that feeds the HFT trading machines, and who owns, controls, and sells it, and why.

We decided to write a white paper titled "Exchanges and Data Feeds: Data Theft on Wall Street." We knew this paper would be explosive and could rock the industry. We spent months checking and double-checking our facts and writing and rewriting our paper. After speaking with our clients to make sure they understood the issue, we released the paper in PDF form on our blog May 11, 2010.

The paper circulated faster than we could have imagined. Within days, we were fielding calls from financial reporters around the world. Although the immediate response in the United States was tepid, the institutional trading community in Europe was outraged. Buy-side firms were shocked that information on what they thought was non-displayed order flow was distributed to the HFT community. They felt violated by the exchanges. On May 25, 2010, Jeremy Grant of the *Financial Times* reported "volumes on Chi-Delta—the Chi-X platform—and on the BATS platform plunged as so-called 'buyside' participants called their brokers with instructions to pull their orders, fearful their orders were being exploited." One unintended beneficiary of this mutiny was Turquoise, a multi-trading facility (MTF) owned by the London Stock Exchange, which saw order flow temporarily migrate to them.[2]

Within weeks after releasing our white paper, BATS and Chi-X changed their data feeds by randomizing the order IDs. Bloomberg reported May 21, 2010 that the move came "after customers said they are concerned that identification information could lead to others guessing their trading strategy and followed a May 11 report from

U.S. brokerage Themis Trading LLC titled 'Exchanges and Data Feeds: Data Theft on Wall Street.'"[3]

It took a little while longer for NASDAQ. Finally, in the fourth quarter of 2010, NASDAQ stopped revealing information about hidden orders. On October 8, 2010, *Dow Jones* reported: "While NASDAQ said the reference numbers could not be used by anyone trying to game the system, the exchange will replace them with zeros to ease any lingering worries."[4] NASDAQ, however, did not remove the trade message "B" (Buy) and "S" (Sell) attached to non-displayable orders. This means that as of this writing, NASDAQ is still leaking information on hidden order flow to clients who subscribe to its private data feeds.

The Heat Is On

The release of "Data Theft on Wall Street" also put the heat on brokers who supplied algorithmic trading systems to their clients. The institutional community demanded to know whether information on its hidden and reserve book orders was being leaked to the market. Brokers immediately ran for cover. Similar to the flash order controversy that exploded the year before in the summer of 2009, the brokerage community was quick to deny that it had anything to do with the information leakage. Clients sent tersely worded emails to their brokers. Brokers sent emails to clients trying to distance themselves. One major broker sent this note out:

> The Themis Trading article is quite accurate, however, this is something that we have always been aware of. A couple of years ago we asked both NASDAQ and BATS to change their feeds, and while BATS made some changes, both the problems mentioned in the article still remain. As a result, we do not send any cancel replace orders to any ECNs or exchanges. Whenever we

need to change any parameter of an order that we have sent to an ECN or exchange, we will completely cancel the original order and send in a new order resulting in a new order ID and eliminating the problems presented in the article.

We also took a lot of heat from the HFT industry. As we mentioned, one of the biggest beneficiaries of the paper was Turquoise trading facility. One of Turquoise's executives is Natan Tiefenbrun. We knew Tiefenbrun from our old Instinet days when he was brought in as a boy genius to help grow the business. In October 2010, he wrote an article for the Tabb Forum, a well-respected industry website, titled "HFT Bashing," in which he attacked those who questioned HFT. Sal wrote a comment back to Tiefenbrun on the Forum. Rather than responding to Sal, Tiefenbrun wrote a new piece for the website titled "Responding to HFT Bashers," which began:

> Let me start by responding to Sal Arnuk of Themis Trading, King of HFT Bashers, and champion of unsophisticated traders everywhere...
>
> Firstly, yes, I did read the Brogaard study.
>
> Secondly, given that market operators cannot discriminate between different types of flow originating from large broker dealers, it's somewhat unfair and disingenuous to lambast NASDAQ for doing its best to provide a representative sample.
>
> Thirdly, I note that the study conclusions undermine all of the unfounded arguments Sal and Joe have been making—but recognize that it's just one study.
>
> Lastly, Sal—where's your evidence? Aside from your commercial self-interest, how do you justify perpetuating a witch hunt against HFT when every piece of empirical evidence undermines your prejudices, and when the detailed study on the Flash Crash didn't produce the "proof" you were expecting?

The gloves were now off, and it was time to have some fun. Sal responded to Tiefenbrun on the Forum:

> Natan, King of HFT Bashers? I am flattered. And I thank you for giving us the credit for taking on the giant HFT billion-dollar lobby and industry. My mom thinks it's also pretty remarkable that two guys from New Jersey could force the logic-loving people of great nations to embark upon a witch hunt.
>
> Again, I am surprised at the venom, considering Joe and I single handedly are responsible for Turquoise's best quarter in years. Perhaps we will write another paper for you. We'll think about it.
>
> Regarding proof in studies, I just poked holes in the one that you held up in your "praise of HFT job-interview" and debunked it. It was not personal. If you want studies showing harm, I can refer you to our blog, and numerous studies by the likes of QSG, ITG, Jefferies, the NY Fed, Nanex (have you seen [its] analysis of the E-mini trades? Wowsa!), and of course the SEC's Flash Crash Study. If you would like Joe or [me] to take you through the liquidity provision statistics analyzed and cited by the SEC's Berman during the period before the Crash, and during, we will be happy to do so.
>
> Actually we take much more issue with the exchanges and for-profit arms merchants than we do the prop HFT firms. It was fun trading barbs with you; but I shall run. I guess I regret getting personal to begin with, although I think you will agree you one-upped me on the "getting personal" front. Regardless, I'll live, and I suppose so will you.
>
> Best of luck. I'll let you know when the paper comes out.

Actually, forget the paper, the book is now out.

Phantom Indexes

Another place where something funny may be going on with data on Wall Street is with the indexes. While generally not known by the public, many Wall Street professionals understand that the major market index values are not calculated dynamically and feature only a subset of all trade data available. We wrote a white paper about this in 2011 titled "Phantom Indexes," which was published in the *Journal of Indexes*.[5]

The investment world trusts and relies upon indexes such as Dow Jones Industrial Average, S&P 500, NASDAQ 100, and Russell 2000 for gauging market activity. In recent years, this emphasis has become even greater due to the explosion in popularity in tradable index-based products, such as ETFs, futures, and options. In addition, the market has become increasingly dominated by trading volume from arbitraging index, ETF, and other derivative movements versus the underlying equities.

Surprisingly, on an intraday basis, these widely watched indexes and possibly others are based on less than 30% of all shares traded. We confirmed in writing with representatives from Dow Jones Indexes, S&P, NASDAQ, and Russell that these indices are calculated using only primary market data. Nowadays, in a world of microsecond trading, these indexes have become phantoms—they reflect some trades involving their components, but not the majority of them.

Once again, fragmentation can be blamed. Prior to Reg NMS, more than 80% of NYSE listed stocks traded on the exchange. Now, NYSE has less than a 30% market share because of the proliferation of dark pools and competing exchanges. Since index values only use primary exchange trades for their calculation, the index is being calculated with only a subset of data and is therefore not accurate. The primary market alone is no longer a complete enough source since it represents only about one in four trades.

This problem can easily be fixed. Index suppliers simply need to adjust their methodology to accurately reflect all trades intraday in a timely manner. Since this would be relatively easy to do, we can't help but wonder why the exchanges haven't pressed for change. Do current indexes make exchange data feeds more valuable for HFT firms? By subscribing to all the exchange data feeds, HFT firms can calculate their own, much more accurate index values seconds faster than what the public sees. This could easily create valuable latency arbitrage opportunities in the trading of ETFs and other tradable products linked to indexes (see Chapter 2, "The Curtain Pulled Back on High Frequency Trading").

Machine-Readable News

Knowing how valuable the combination of colocation and data fees are to HFT firms, the exchanges also have begun entering the business of delivering news in a high-speed, "machine-readable" format, which can be easily used by computer-driven trading programs. In December 2011, NASDAQ acquired RapiData, a leading provider of machine-readable economic news to trading firms and financial institutions.[6] Two years earlier, Deutsche Borse acquired Need To Know News, another machine-readable news firm. Many of the major financial news services, including Thomson Reuters, Dow Jones, and Bloomberg, also have entered the business.

Machine-readable news data feeds enable HFT computers to react within microseconds to news events, beating out traditional institutional and retail investors. The instant a corporate news release runs on services such as PRNewswire or BusinessWire, it is parsed by machine-readable programs and sent to HFT firms' subscribers, who incorporate it into their algorithms to make instantaneous trading decisions. Not only are corporate news releases disseminated this way, but major economic news releases from Government and industry organizations, such as jobs numbers from the U.S. Bureau of Labor Statistics or the Chicago Purchasing Managers Index, are distributed in machine-readable format.

Firms such as RapiData market themselves by highlighting their low latency and sophisticated design, which enables news feeds to be integrated easily into trading programs. They also tout that some data is sent directly from government lockups, which allows it to be parsed the instant an embargo is lifted. They station their "reporters" in government press rooms to enter the data into their computers. When the embargo is lifted, the machine-readable news firm releases the news to subscribers.

The danger is that the machines can "interpret" the news incorrectly. On December 21, 2011, trading in Constellation Energy (CEG) demonstrated what could go wrong. Here is the sequence of events:

- **11:58 AM:** Headline crosses financial news service: "U.S. sues to block Excelon acquisition of Constellation Energy." CEG is trading at $38.93.
- **12:03 PM:** Trading in CEG is halted due to a circuit breaker after the stock drops 10%. CEG last trade was $35.03.
- **12:08 PM:** CEG trading reopens and the stock shoots back up to $38 on heavy volume.
- **12:10 PM:** Headline crosses financial news service: "U.S. settles with Excelon."

With 12 minutes, two distinctly different headlines ripped a stock up and down 10%. Some may say that the circuit breaker did what it was supposed to do and allowed cooler heads to prevail. They would be partially correct. But the question remains, how does a stock drop that quickly and spring back up that quickly? The news was barely disseminated. Bids disappeared almost instantaneously. Stop-loss orders kicked in. Volume soared in the five minutes of trading before the halt as volume-weighted participation algorithms chased the spike down.

Since the news was disseminated immediately in machine-readable format, there was no time for a human to intervene to try and make sense of the headlines. This example highlights how acting on news before properly digesting it can have devastating consequences. While HFT firms may want to trade news immediately, they risk destabilizing the markets. Rather than acquiring and potentially financing the growth of machine-readable news, perhaps exchanges should be more focused on investor protection.

Who Owns the Data?

Our Data Theft white paper revealed only one example of what is going on with data feeds on Wall Street. The bigger question is, who owns the data? We can understand an exchange claiming ownership of consolidated quote and trade information that compiles everything that is happening in a given stock. But what about all the other information in these feeds? This information is based in some manner on the data created by end customer orders.

Over the course of the past decade, the exchanges have truly developed this into a business. Is it appropriate or ethical for the exchanges to sell this data? How would you react if other types of financial institutions sold similar data? Would it be okay if a bank sold information about to whom you wrote checks? Would it be okay if Visa/MasterCard sold information about what you bought? Would it be okay if the telephone company sold information about who you called?

We don't think so. But in the securities business, it appears to be legal for the exchanges to sell information about the trades you executed so HFTs can develop strategies that would cause you to pay more if you want to buy or receive less if you want to sell a stock.

We believe that you, the retail and institutional investor, own the data. After all, it is information on your order that is sold and distributed to HFTs so that they can model your behavior. Exchanges have now given you the ability to opt out of certain order ID numbers. We believe that exchanges should also give you the ability to opt out of their private data feeds. Regardless of how fast an HFT computer is or how close it is colocated to an exchange server, it still needs access to private data feeds to fuel the HFT trading program.

Endnotes

1. NASDAQ Trader, "NASDAQ TotalView-ITCH 4.1, 4.1" (Nov. 1, 2011), NASDAQTrader.com, http://www.nasdaqtrader.com/content/technicalsupport/specifications/dataproducts/nqtv-itch-v4_1.pdf.

2. Jeremy Grant, "Trust in Dark Pools Is Dented" (May 25, 2010), *Financial Times*, May 25, 2010, Financial Times website, http://www.ft.com/intl/cms/s/0/d9d568e6-682b-11df-a52f-00144feab49a.html#axzz1n3CoFl4o.

3. Nandini Sukumar and Nina Mehta, "Bats Gives Stock Traders More Ability to Mask Their Identities" (May 28, 2010), Bloomberg website, http://www.bloomberg.co.jp/apps/news?pid=20670001&sid=aJngAEFFvVO8.

4. Kristina Peterson, "NASDAQ Will Remove Hidden Order Data to Assuage Worries" (October 8, 2010), Dow Jones Newswires, Chicago Tribune Breaking News website, http://archive.chicagobreakingbusiness.com/2010/10/nasdaq-to-further-secure-trade-reference-numbers.html#more-16180.

5. Joseph Saluzzi and Sal Arnuk, "Phantom Indexes," *Journal of Indexes* (November/December 2011), Index Universe website, http://www.indexuniverse.com/publications/journalofindexes/joi-articles/10097-phantom-indexes.html.

6. NASDAQ OMX, "NASDAQ OMX Acquires the Business of RapiData LLC" (December 19, 2011), NASDAQ OMX website, http://ir.nasdaqomx.com/releasedetail.cfm?ReleaseID=634230.

8

Heart of Darkness

On October 24, 2011, while working a few trades for Themis clients, Sal noticed a news headline scroll across his Bloomberg terminal: "Alternative Trading System Agrees to Settle Charges That It Failed to Disclose Trading by an Affiliate."

"Hey Joe, check this out," Sal said. "The SEC is charging an ATS with wrong-doing...whoa, it's the Pipe!"

"What?" Joe asked. "You're joking, right?"

We went to the SEC website to get the details. Pipeline, a dark pool that most of Wall Street used to trade large orders, was fined for engaging in proprietary trading in its agency crossing network, unbeknown to its clients. The SEC had been looking into allegations of misconduct for a period of time, most likely due to a whistle-blowing tip coming from someone at Pipeline. A settlement was reached, without admitting or denying the SEC's allegations. Pipeline agreed to pay a $1 million fine. Its CEO, Fred Federspiel, and its chairman and former CEO, Al Berkeley, who was a former president and vice chairman of NASDAQ, also agreed to pay $100,000 each, without admitting or denying any wrong-doing.

According to the SEC, Pipeline was billed as a crossing network that matched customer buys and sells anonymously. Yet behind the scenes, a trading firm that it owned was actually *trading against investor orders entered into the system.* The SEC's administrative order highlighted the following:[1]

- Pipeline actively advertised that it had no prop trading, the trading opportunities in its dark pool were "natural," it would never reveal customer order information, and it denied arbitrageurs and HFT firms any information about order flow.

- In reality, Pipeline owned and completely funded a trading firm—Milstream—that it set up a few months before its public ATS launch in September 2004. Milstream employed high frequency tactics and traded in the Pipeline dark pool.

- Milstream had two major purposes. One, enter order flow so that Pipeline could show subscribers that there was "natural" activity in its dark pool to make them confident in Pipeline's liquidity. Two, make money. Milstream was on the other side of more than 90% of Pipeline trades.

- Milstream was provided information about the customer orders in Pipeline and encouraged to "pre-position" and then sell back to the investors in the pool at an inferior price. If a mutual fund client of Pipeline entered an order to buy 100,000 shares of stock, Milstream would buy the 100,000 shares in other dark pools and exchanges outside of Pipeline and then sell it back to the mutual fund at a higher price in Pipeline.

- Customers not only knew nothing about how they were misled and stolen from, but Pipeline was communicating to them repeatedly that it was a refuge from all that was wrong on Wall Street.

We were floored. Were we harmed when we occasionally used Pipeline? Who at Pipeline knew of this malfeasance? Would Pipeline stay in business? If this pilferage and breach of trust was going on at one of the larger, more successful and reputable dark pools, was it going on in any of the other 40 dark pools?

The reaction was swift. Institutions stopped trading with Pipeline virtually overnight. Many unknowing Pipeline employees lost their jobs. Federspiel and Berkeley stepped down. Pipeline's board brought in ex-Liquidnet executive Jay Biancamano as CEO and gave him the weighty task of reinstilling customer trust. Biancamano has an uphill battle. On Wall Street—and Main Street—trust takes years and even generations to build, and only a day to collapse.

Dark pool is the industry term given to ATSs that enable traders to buy and sell large orders of stock, otherwise known as *blocks*, away from the "lit" or publicly quoted markets. Dark pools are so named because trades supposedly take place "blind." Another definition of a dark pool is any execution venue that does not display its orders to the public quote. Originally, these pools were fixed-price "blind" auctions; other names were *crossing networks* and *call markets*. These original pools held auctions at predetermined times, like end-of-day using the closing price, or every hour on the hour at the prevailing midpoint between each stock's bid and ask. The main reason why mutual and pension funds and money managers use dark pools is to find the "natural" other side of larger orders, the perfect complement if you will in order to trade without moving the price of the stock.

Unfortunately, over the years, the original spirit of dark pools has been violated, as the Pipeline story illustrates. What started out as a tool to help large institutional funds move in and out of stock positions, with minimal information leakage and price impact, has morphed into a tool that often helps dark pool owners to extract money from institutional and retail investors.

The Birth of Dark Pools

In the 1980s the "institutional market" in the U.S. began growing faster than the infrastructure of the exchange duopoly. Mutual funds were mushrooming in number much the same way exchange traded funds (ETFs) have been exploding in number in recent years. Mutual funds pooled and managed money from individual investors, using economies of scale to minimize commission and friction costs.

Mutual fund growth necessitated trading large blocks of stock. Institutional investors quickly learned that exposing their size and intentions to floor brokers and specialists on the NYSE, or market makers on the NASDAQ, resulted in adverse stock movement before they got a chance to buy the size they needed. It was next to impossible for a brokerage firm's trading desk to assemble a large block of shares without "calling around" or explicitly or implicitly communicating their intentions. Hence, the need for mechanisms to enable institutions to interact in size with minimum information leakage.

In the 1990s, when we worked at Instinet, we had the Instinet Crossing Network. At the end of each trading day, our institutional customers would enter their buy and sell orders (that is, buy 150,000 IBM, sell 500,000 AT&T, and so on) into the system. No one would see their sizes or know their identities. The cross would "run" and buy orders would be matched with sell orders, using that day's closing price. The trades would print to the consolidated tape in bulk at 8:00 a.m. the next morning when clients would receive their execution reports. The Instinet Crossing Network filled a large institutional need to trade with each other in a way that achieved sizable liquidity, in a no-lose, no-information-given-up way.

The Instinet Crossing Network was not the only original dark pool. Jefferies, an institutional investment banking-brokerage firm, operated a "fourth market" electronic trading system called Portfolio System for Institutional Trading (POSIT), run by its ITG unit, which was spun off in 1999 and today is a publicly traded company. POSIT ran blind auctions at specified times intraday. It was common to see customers pull their orders out of Instinet's real time trading system just before each of POSIT's "crosses."

Also innovative in the 1990s were Steve Wunsch's Arizona Stock Exchange (AZX) and Bill Lupien's Optimark. AZX was a fixed-time crossing platform for institutions, similar to Instinet Crossing Network and POSIT. However, AZX set a clearing price for each security; its matching engine calculated the price at which the auction would take place, as opposed to a reference price observed in the market, such as each stock's closing price on that day. Optimark similarly set clearing match prices for each security based on participants' entering an optimal matrix listing prices they would pay for different share sizes. Optimark was ahead of its time, as it attempted to formulaically attach value to liquidity based on size demanded. If this sounds complicated to you, it was complicated to Wall Street traders, too. Optimark had a hard time gaining traction.

Instinet Crossing Network, POSIT, AZX, and Optimark were soon joined by another notable platform. Liquidnet gained great traction as its system "read" clients' electronic trade blotters, automatically alerting buyers and sellers to potential matches. Clearly, Liquidnet learned from Optimark's brief tenure. Dark pools must be easy to use and intuitive to increase usage and value. Where Optimark was brilliant in its conception, it was clunky and tough to use. By contrast, Liquidnet was simple. The trader didn't have to do hardly anything.

For the most part, these early dark pools were a great complement to our more traditional "lit" markets. We have learned in our 20-plus years in the business that there is no such thing as one perfect market or way to transact for all participants. The combination of these early block crossing pools with the technologically rich exchanges served retail, institutional, and the public's interest. Large orders had a means to be transacted in ways beneficial to mutual fund holders. Small retail orders had a means to be transacted on the exchanges, as had always been the case. And there was a nice balance between public "lit" and nonpublic "dark" transactions.

This is a significant point. Transparent stock markets need to convey accurate information about asset pricing. When you open your account statement, you need to be confident that the pricing for the securities you own reflects reality and your wealth. Stated another way, most investors would prefer to have 10% of all trading done in the dark and priced off of the 90% of trading that takes place in the open rather than the other way around. We can only hope that the SEC has given this serious thought, because today nearly one of every three shares is traded off of the public markets.[2]

Dark Pools Cross Over...to the Dark Side

Somewhere along the way we went from the handful of dark pools used to trade large blocks of stock to more than 40 in 2011. Why? What differentiates all these platforms from each other? Is the reason for the proliferation of these pools to aid institutions in moving sizable chunks of stock? Empirical data on the average trade size in the majority of these newer pools suggest that the answer is a resounding "No." Liquidnet's average trade size, as of July 2011, was approximately 52,000 shares.[3] In contrast, Morgan Stanley's dark pool, MS Pool, exhibited the second smallest average trade size for a dark pool in July 2011—approximately 200 shares.[4]

The earlier dark pools were designed to fill a market need. However, brokerage firms saw an opportunity to exploit this need by launching their own dark pools. The purpose was to keep "in house" as much as possible of the brokerage firms' institutional algorithmic trading. By "internalizing" this order flow, brokerage firms would simultaneously increase their trading revenue and lower their costs because they would not need to incur the fees charged by external trading venues, such as exchanges and other dark pools. As a result, virtually all major brokerage houses today operate at least one dark pool.

Independent HFT firms, such as GETCO, Citadel, and Automated Trading Desk (ATD), have also launched dark pools. When investor orders pass through these firms' dark pools, they are mostly interacting with their owners' HFT flow as opposed to other investor orders. Although your order is sometimes filled, that happens only when the HFT firm decides it is in its economic interest to do so.

Why should all this matter to you? If you understand what type of players and trading is done in the pools, you can make informed decisions on which pools to allow your orders to swim in.

ITG, which owns POSIT, has assembled much research on dark pools, such as its 2008 report "Are You Playing in a Toxic Dark Pool? A Guide to Preventing Information Leakage"[5] and its 2009 report "Understanding and Avoiding Adverse Selection in Dark Pools."[6] The reports break down the dark pool industry into five groups:

- Public crossing networks, such as Instinet, Liquidnet, and POSIT
- Internalization pools, such as Goldman's SigmaX and Credit Suisse's Crossfinder
- Ping destinations, such as dark pools operated by GETCO and Citadel (these orders do not rest in the pool but give the prop-trading owners of the pool the option to trade with you)
- Exchange-based pools, such as ARCA Hidden and BATS Hidden
- Consortium-based pools, such as BIDS

ITG highlights how adverse selection in these pools varies greatly. Stated another way, due to the varied degree of investor order flow interaction with HFT prop trading, some pools exhibit substantially more toxicity than others. Investor orders in these pools are routinely disadvantaged and gamed, resulting in inferior prices for trade executions.

Clearly, dark pools have evolved into many different types of models. The original purpose—facilitating large institutional trades, anonymously, and without market impact—has been bastardized in our current structure, in which most of the newer pools feed their owners' desires for internalizing customer orders for greater revenue, cost reduction, and most damaging to investors—prop trading.

How HFT Internalization in Dark Pools Hurts Investors

We referred to internalization when discussing why brokerage firms launch their own dark pools. They want to match customer buy and sell orders within the firm without routing those orders out to other trading venues. However, there is another type of internalization that is more damaging to you: HFT internalization. HFT internalization occurs when an HFT firm hides in the dark, steps in front of your displayed limit order, and takes away fills and execution opportunities that belong to you.

Say you want to sell 3,000 shares of stock in a mid or small cap name characterized by wider spreads and lower daily trade volume, for example Select Comfort (SCSS), the air mattress manufacturer, where the stock is bid at $25.92 and you are the lone offer at $26.00. A buyer comes in to take your 3,000 shares at $26.00. Pre HFT-internalization, a trade would have occurred of 3,000 shares at $26.00, and you would have sold your stock. Not so in today's market structure. Today, the buyer's buy order first travels through his brokerage firm's smart order router and then often through an HFT-owned dark pool. It passes through this pool because it is a free execution for the buyer's brokerage firm, should one take place. The buyer is filled in that dark pool at $25.9999 by an HFT firm, instead of by you at $26.00. The buyer was theoretically price-improved by $0.30 on an order valued at about $78,000, an insignificant savings, while you are left with no execution and a selling opportunity lost.

Dennis Dick of Bright Trading LLC has been outspoken on the unfairness of internalization, the proliferation of these sub-penny tactics employed by HFT firms, and the damage it does to traders. He has written comment letters to the SEC and compiled a great presentation demonstrating how investors are harmed. In his "Undisplayed Trading Centers Compromising the NBBO," which has appeared on the Zero Hedge website,[7] Dick details example after example. He also calls on the SEC to review the implementation of Rule 612, its sub-penny rule, and the exceptions it provides to brokerage and HFT firms:

> It is our belief that Broker-Dealers and Algorithmic programs are circumventing the current rule by stepping ahead of the NBBO through the use of dark pools, and broker-dealer internalization. We request that the Commission review Rule 612, and make amendments to better regulate the Broker-Dealer price improvement process, and to stop algorithmic systems from hiding orders in front of the NBBO.

Dick highlights that investors are not allowed to use sub-penny prices to enter orders, such as $25.9999, yet brokerage and HFT firms can. The damage to investors is not only missed trading opportunities due to an uneven playing field, but harm to the integrity of public markets and quoting. What incentive is there for investors to display their quotes when those quotes can be used, in turn, to disadvantage them?

How Latency Arbitrage in Dark Pools Hurts Investors

Another way HFTs hurt investors in dark pools is through *latency arbitrage*. Latency arbitrage arises from the two speeds in the markets. On one hand, HFT firms, who colocate at the exchanges and buy their private data feeds, can construct the National Best Bid and

Offer (NBBO) of any stock milliseconds before the investing public sees stock prices via the Securities Information Processor feed (SIP). On the other hand, most dark pools use the slower SIP to calculate reference prices (the prices that stocks will trade in their dark pool at any moment in time, such as the NBBO midpoint).

As a result, dark pool pricing is 10 to 15 milliseconds behind the real-time prices that HFT firms use.[8] This provides HFT firms with a real time arbitrage opportunity built into our market structure. They take advantage of it by employing automated algorithms to "pick off" investor orders based on slower dark pool pricing.

The Wall Street Journal published two articles detailing this practice: "Measuring Arbitrage in Milliseconds" by David Gaffen and Rob Curran in March 2009 and "Fast Traders' New Edge: Investment Firms Grab Stock Data First and Use It Seconds Before Others" by Scott Patterson in June 2010.[9, 10] "You have tomorrow's newspaper today," said Richard Gates, a portfolio manager for the TFS Market Neutral Fund in West Chester, PA., in the 2009 article, describing the HFT advantage, while everybody else is "looking at stale prices."

The 2010 article reported how Gates set about to prove how latency arbitrage damaged his firm and its clients. Gates sent an order to buy Nordson Corp (NDSN) into a midpoint priced dark pool, with a limit not to pay above $70.49. Then, he sent a sell order into another destination in order to push the midpoint of the NBBO for NDSN down to $70.47. Nordson was sold to TFS for $70.49—the old, higher midpoint—in broker pool No. 2, which didn't reflect the new sell order. "TFS got stuck paying two cents more than it should have," wrote Patterson. Gates has apparently tested the arbitrage numerous times, across a plethora of dark pools, with consistent results.

Goldman Sachs, which operates Sigma X, one of the largest dark pools by volume, has recently undertaken the services of Redline Inc. and its InRush Ticker Plant product to speed up Sigma X's NBBO calculation.[11] To us, this is an acknowledgment of the harm latency arbitrage causes investors.

In a white paper we published in December 2009, "Latency Arbitrage: The Real Power Behind Predatory High Frequency Trading," we raised three serious questions about market integrity surrounding Latency Arbitrage:[12]

1. The primary response from HFTs or market centers is typically "a penny or two should not matter to long-term investors; this is much ado about nothing," to paraphrase the CEO of a major ATS who was addressing a financial industry conference in New York City in early November. We disagree completely. It isn't $0.01–$0.02. It's $1.5–$3 billion. Which leads us to question number one: *Do HFT firms have an unfair advantage?* Most professionals on Wall Street have taken a standard from our past for granted; that everyone sees the same quote and market data at the same time. What if the time differential between what the HFTs see and what everybody else sees was five minutes instead of five milliseconds? Would that be acceptable? It is not the amount of time that matters. *It's that a differential exists at all.* Who would bet on a horse race if a select group already knew who won?

2. Latency Arbitrage has created a two-tiered market of technology-enhanced insiders (composed of a handful of large banks, brokerage firms, and hedge funds) and the rest of us. To be clear, HFTs enjoy this advantage only because market centers are selling them the right to colocate and access raw data feeds. For-profit market centers are incentivized to do this. This leads us to question number two: *Is it fair to sell these rights to the highest bidders when market centers are supposed to be protecting all participants' interests equally?* At the end of the day, aren't market centers charging HFTs a higher fee in exchange for giving them an advance look at the NBBO?

3. When a market center provides an HFT with the ability to out-maneuver institutional orders, isn't the exchange putting institutions and their brokers in breach of their fiduciary responsibilities, especially those institutions managing pension funds governed by Employee Retirement Income Security Act (ERISA)?

What Else Is Being Done to Stop Dark Pool Abuse?

In December 2010, SEC Chair Mary Schapiro testified before Congress that the Commission was looking into "abusive colocation and data latency arbitrage activity in potential violation of Regulation NMS."[13] At the close of 2011, however, there had been no action on this subject, and the SEC's own 2009 Dark Pool Proposal is still sitting in limbo.

Today we have more than 40 pools adding to market fragmentation, where the majority of them feed/benefit proprietary trading as their predominant intention. Although institutions initially made a conscious choice to participate in dark pools as a way to limit market impact, today they mostly participate by default because the algorithms they use to divide up their orders and execute in small pieces throughout the day automatically pass though most of them.

Ironically, where institutions originally traded in the dark to avoid the toxicity of HFT order flow on the exchanges, institutions are currently interacting with HFT flow in dark pools in the same proportion as they do in the public lit markets. In other words, the dark markets have become much lighter, and the lit markets have become much darker.

We speak daily with institutions managing long-term investor money. They are all baffled with the complexity, lack of transparency, and conflicts in today's dark pool environment. We frequently consult with them to help them think through how to protect their order flow. In the wake of the Pipeline scandal, they asked us to prepare a list of questions to ask their brokers, which follows:

1. Does your firm or any of its affiliates engage in prop trading? If so, how does that trading interact with your dark pool? Does it engage blindly? Or can it see the order flow? Can it execute against the order flow at its discretion?

2. What is the matching logic in your dark pool (that is, time/ price, size/price, and so on)? Is your pool using pricing from the slower SIP or faster colocated feeds? Is there any preferencing among participants? Can you disclose statistics on where executions take place within the NBBO in your pool and their share sizes, including odd lots?

3. Is your dark pool completely dark? Or does it transmit information around your orders to other destinations, including your own prop trading, in the form of Indications of Interest (IOIs), Solicitations of Interest (SOIs), Ping-for-a-Fill messages (PFAF), or Conditional Orders (COs)?

4. Does any part of your firm, including your dark pool, order routers, prop desk, or affiliates, collect and keep information about our order flow for any reason, such as financial modeling? If so, why? Have you asked us permission to do so?

5. Does any part of your firm transmit information about our dark pool orders to other destinations? Can we opt out of them easily? Can we set minimum execution quantities or transmission sizes (that is, do not IOI under 1,000 shares)? Do the recipients of that information retransmit it to other destinations or keep the information?

One final comment. Doesn't it speak volumes about how treacherous our public markets have become if so many institutional investors are willing to use these dark pools? We hope our regulators at the SEC chew on that question a bit.

Endnotes

1. Securities and Exchange Commission, "Order Instituting Administrative and Cease-and-Desist Proceedings Pursuant to Section 8a of the Securities Act of 1933 and Sections 15(b) and 21c of the Securities Exchange Act of 1934, Making Findings, and Imposing a Cease-and-Desist Order," Securities Act of 1933, rel. 9271, Oct. 24, 2011/Securities Exchange Act of 1934," rel. 65609, Oct. 24, 2011/ Administrative Proceeding, file 3-14600, Securities and Exchange Commission website, http://www.sec.gov/litigation/admin/2011/33-9271.pdf.

2. Steinert-Threlkeld, "New Year Not Happy."

3. Tom Steinert-Threlkeld, "Market Volatility Means Spike in Institutional Volume" (April 10, 2011), Securities Technology Monitor website, http://www.securitiestechnologymonitor.com/news/liquidnet-institutional-volume-market-volatility-28624-1.html.

4. Nina Mehta, "Morgan Stanley Changing Dark Pool to Attract Bigger Orders" (Sept. 21, 2011), Businessweek website, http://www.businessweek.com/news/2011-09-21/morgan-stanley-changing-dark-pool-to-attract-bigger-orders.html.

5. Hitesh Mittal, "Are You Playing in a Toxic Dark Pool? A Guide to Preventing Information Leakage" (June 2008), Investment Technology Group website, http://www.itg.com/news_events/papers/ITGResearch_Toxic_Dark_Pool_070208.pdf.

6. Nigam Saralya and Hitesh Mittal, "Understanding and Avoiding Adverse Selection in Dark Pools" (Nov. 2009), Investment Technology Group website, http://www.itg.com/news_events/papers/AdverseSelectionDarkPools_113009F.pdf.

7. Dennis Dick, "Undisplayed Trading Centers Compromising the NBBO" (April 8, 2010), Zero Hedge website, http://www.zerohedge.com/sites/default/files/SubPennying%20Summary%20Prez.pdf.

8. David Gaffen and Rob Curran, "Measuring Arbitrage in Milliseconds" (March 9, 2009), Wall Street Journal MarketBeat blog, Wall Street Journal website, http://blogs.wsj.com/marketbeat/2009/03/09/measuring-arbitrage-in-milliseconds.

9. Ibid.

10. Scott Patterson, "Fast Traders' New Edge: Investment Firms Grab Stock Data First and Use It Seconds Before Others," *The Wall Street Journal* (June 4, 2010), Yahoo! Finance website, http://finance.yahoo.com/news/pf_article_109725.html.

11. A-Team Group, "Q&A: Redline's Mark Skalabrin on Goldman, and Why Cell Is Better" (Sept. 25, 2011), Low-Latency website, http://low-latency.com/article/qa-redlines-mark-skalabrin-goldman-and-why-cell-better.

12. Sal Arnuk and Joseph Saluzzi, "Latency Arbitrage: The Real Power Behind Predatory High Frequency Trading" (Dec. 4, 2009), Themis Trading website, http://www.themistrading.com/article_files/0000/0519/THEMIS_TRADING_White_Paper_--_Latency_Arbitrage_--_December_4__2009.pdf.

13. Mary Schapiro, "Testimony on U.S. Equity Market Structure by the U.S. Securities and Exchange Commission" (Dec. 8, 2010), Securities and Exchange Commission website, http://www.sec.gov/news/testimony/2010/ts120810mls.htm.

9

Dude, Where's My Order?

It was summer 1999, and the NASDAQ was rocking. It was the dot-com era, the time of "irrational exuberance." Our best institutional customer at Instinet was a large mutual fund company, with an army of traders executing large mutual fund orders. We would spend significant time each morning strategizing with one of its traders, who we called "Major."

Major was always inundated with large orders from his portfolio managers, especially in volatile NASDAQ technology stocks, such as PMC Sierra, which could go up $20 a day in the late 1990s. We were one of his "go-to brokers," and we worked many of his orders in the Instinet system. In that time period, stock quotes changed so rapidly and the markets moved so swiftly that waves of SOES Bandits would flow into and out of stocks, like ocean tides in fast-forward. Major needed allies he could trust to look after his interests, and we were happy to have his confidence and business.

Each morning, our conversations with Major reminded us of the "show me the money" scene in the movie *Jerry Maguire*, when Tom Cruise is on the phone with Cuba Gooding:

> Major: "Morning, hero. Are you ready?"
>
> Sal: "Yes"
>
> "I mean are you ready, hero?"
>
> "Yes...shoot Major."
>
> "A-game today. Focus. No sorry. No buts. We got wood to chop. Are you ready, hero?"

"READY MAJOR!"

"Better grasshopper. Be up man. Remember...the heaviest thing on a man's chest is his chin. Let's go: QCOM. Seller. Me. Take a hundred with a figure limit. Stock gets there...I lose. No cutesy bootsy, fellah. Say it back to me."

"QCOM selling 100,000 shares with a figure limit you would."

"That's right mister. Next. MCLD. Call is out in the name. They are gonna gun it early. Be there. Take half a hun. Get a third done in the first 15 minutes; then call me. You with me, hero?"

"Got it. Next."

"WCOM. Buyer. Me. Take 100k to buy and nibble. Don't chase. Nibble don't chase. But if the stock comes in to 50 cents I own. No cutesy bootsy. You with me hero?"

"Yes. WCOM buying 100k carefully."

Major likely had similar conversations with his other institutional brokers. He picked brokers who would act as he would, working orders directly in the destination that would give him and his clients the best prices. Instinet was "The ECN" if you were trafficking in NASDAQ names, which is why he traded so much with us. Similarly, Major used direct floor brokers for his NYSE-listed names because NYSE had an 82.5% market share in NYSE-listed stocks.[1] If any portfolio manager (PM) at Major's firm asked him where he was trading his WCOM order, he had an easy answer: "My WCOM order is in Instinet." If a PM asked him where his IBM order was, Major would answer, "It's being worked on the NYSE."

If only institutional traders had it that simple today. There is no "place to be" for any given stock. Liquidity is fragmented among more than 50 destinations. The best an institutional trader can do is try to guess where the deepest liquidity will reside on an individual name basis and try to concentrate on those pools, while making sure not to exclude all the other pools. If a trader can't engage in the labor-intensive guesswork and manual finessing required to do that, he can hope that the trading algorithms he chooses will.

Today, an institutional order goes through many steps on the way to getting executed. The process is remarkably more complicated than it was in 1999. This is a notable step backward for best execution. The gauntlet of complexity is an example of how technology has been leveraged in a way that doesn't serve the best interests as investors so much as it leverages conflicted interests.

How Algorithms Work: Making the Sausage

A portfolio manager (PM) generates the order, which then shows up on his trader's order management system (OMS). The PM explains his game plan to his trader. He can tell the trader he is passive and just quietly adding to a position, or that he is aggressive and wants to buy his stock quickly. The trader decides whether to allow the order to be seen by electronically connected "scraping" dark pools, such as Liquidnet. If he does allow such a dark pool to see his order, his order may trade with a large order on the opposite side of his. Having "blocked" a portion of his order, or not, he can next choose among several options. He can send the order to a broker whose capabilities he trusts, such as Themis Trading, after explaining his game plan. He also can choose to work an order manually, feeding portions to exchanges and dark pools of his choosing. Or he can send an order into any number of the broker-sponsored algorithmic suites at his disposal.

Typically, within each broker's suite are several variations of the following types of algos:

- **Volume weighted average price (VWAP):** Breaks the parent order into smaller child orders that are sent into the markets throughout the day at a rate based on the stock's historical intra-day volume dispersion.

- **Time weighted average price (TWAP):** Breaks the parent order into smaller child orders that are fed into the market at equal time increments throughout the day.

- **Percentage of volume (POV):** Delivers child orders into the market at trader-defined volume participation rates, such as a "10% of the trading volume order."

- **Close-targeting-algos:** Seeks to "beat" the day's closing price.

- **Arrival-targeting-algos:** Seeks to beat the price of the stock when the algo first starts working.

- **Dark liquidity seeking algos:** Looks for liquidity away from the public stock exchanges.

- **"Next Generation" algos:** Typically a variation of the above algos, using what's billed as "anti-HFT methodology."

If the trader chooses to send the order to an algorithm himself, the algo selected depends on the PM's goal for that specific order. For example, if there is a conference at which a company's management will be speaking midday, the PM might believe that management will make positive comments on business prospects. The trader might want to buy all the stock quickly, so he might use an algo focused on arrival price or one that targets a high percentage of volume. Conversely, if the PM expects no news in the short term and just wants to add quietly to his position, his trader might use a less aggressive option, such as a low POV algo or a constrained VWAP algo with price limits.

After the trader chooses an algorithm, he loses control over the process. Every broker's algorithms interact differently with the more than 50 exchanges and dark pools. Algos vary widely in where they route, in what order, and with what specific constraints. What happens to the institutional trader's order can be visually described in the diagram in Figure 9.1.

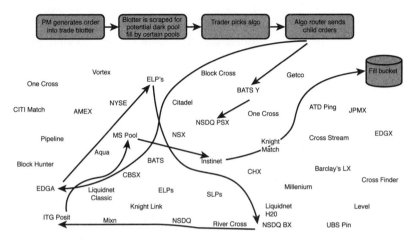

Figure 9.1 Today's convoluted buy-side order: the wandering path from order-generation to execution

How a Smart Order Router (SOR) Works: Regrinding the Sausage

When a trader chooses an algorithm, it breaks up the larger "parent" order, say 500,000 shares, into smaller "child" orders, which are fed into the marketplace. What trading venues each child order travels to is governed by the decisions of a computerized smart order router (SOR) created by the brokerage firm. Although the brokerage firm tells its institutional customers that its SOR is choosing destinations in a "smart" way—ostensibly to get each child order "best execution"—SORs are more typically optimized to benefit the cost structure and prop trading interests of the brokers. According to a study conducted by Woodbine Associates, a capital markets research and advisory firm, suboptimal order routing decisions cost institutional investors as much as $4.5 billion per year.[2]

We frequently appear at industry conferences to speak on topics ranging from market fragmentation to conflicts of interest built into our market structure. In November 2011, Sal spoke at one such panel in New York City on the topic of SOR. *Buy Side Technology*, an industry publication, reported on the event in a story titled "Smart Order Routing: Dancing with the Devil."[3] The article's author, Jake Thomases, recounted the back and forth between Sal and fellow panelist, Val Shlivko, an executive at Nomura Securities.

Sal told the audience of several hundred industry insiders that brokerage firms, in providing their algorithmic tools to their buy-side clients, placed their clients, best-execution needs behind the brokerage firms' economic interests. "There's no such thing as a free lunch," Sal said. Yes, you may pay very low commissions, he explained, but you've given up control. "You've placed the economics of your routing decisions in the hands of your broker."

Shlivko told the audience to ignore what Sal said with regard to Nomura's dark pool. "We absolutely don't do any of that." The audience laughed, a sign that the industry was "in on the joke," Thomases reported. Shlivko stressed that should a customer want his router tweaked, in terms of where and when it is sending orders, all the customer has to do is ask. Most firms would be happy to accommodate institutional customizations, Shlivko said.

We take issue with that. Why should institutions have to call up their algo provider and specifically ask that they do the right thing? Shouldn't the onus of sending an order to the place where it will receive the best execution go to the provider by default? Shouldn't the economic interests of the provider—be it based on a cheap execution or worse, the feeding of a prop trading model—take a backseat to best execution? Although traders on the buy-side should be educated on the inner plumbing of the marketplace, why should they have to play "gotcha" with their algo providers?

To make matters worse, after institutional child orders are sent by the brokerage firm algo to a stock exchange, the orders are subject to a new round of conflicted routing by the stock exchanges. This routing is based on low-cost logic that passes those orders through another gauntlet of dark pools and stock exchange liquidity partners. In a note to clients in 2011, we referred to two orders—"Bill" and "Bob"—as we described their routing through the Direct Edge and NASDAQ stock exchanges:

> The Direct Edge ROUC order is promoted as a cost-effective routing strategy. While it may be cost effective for the broker to use this order type in the algorithm that they supply to the institutional investor, the ROUC order leaves a lot of footprints in its path.

> Let's trace the path of this order. We are going to name this order "Bill." Before sweeping to the displayed public quote, Bill will go through a long journey. Bill first stops at dark pools that are his "best friends" (ones that have a special deal with Direct Edge). Next, Bill travels to dark pools that do not have a special deal with the exchange. Then, Bill makes a stop at the inverted fee structure exchange of NASDAQ BX. Along goes Bill and he moves to his friend DOT at the NYSE. After being sniffed by all of these destinations, if Bill is still alive, he returns back to Direct Edge and is converted to a ROUX order type that makes its way finally to the displayed liquidity available in the public quote. Poor Bill. What a long journey he takes for such a simple task.

> The NASDAQ TFTY order is another so-called low cost routing strategy. Let's take a walk through the maze that this order takes. We will name this TFTY order "Bob." First, Bob stops at NASDAQ BX, which offers a rebate for orders that remove liquidity. (Of course, brokers who supply algorithms to institutions would like to earn a rebate instead of paying a take fee.) Then, Bob travels to other "low priced liquidity venues." These venues, however, are not named, but if executed here, the fee is only $0.0005, which is substantially lower than the normal $0.0030 take fee that NASDAQ charges to most subscribers. If Bob is still not filled, then he travels to another NAS-DAQ exchange, the PSX. Still nothing [is] done and poor Bob

is starting to get tired as he leaves an increasingly long path of footprints in his order trail. Now, Bob heads over to Mahwah, New Jersey, where he attempts to match with the NYSE. Finally, after his long journey visiting many different exchanges and dark pools, Bob arrives at the NASDAQ order book where he will either get filled or post to the book.

While the journey that Bill and Bob take may seem long, it's important to note that the actual trip still takes far less than one second. But today's technology allows Bill and Bob to visit many different places in a very short amount of time before they arrive at their ultimate destination.

Bill and Bob are just two examples of the many conflicted order types that now exist in the market.

Brokerage firm algorithms know each exchange's schedule of rebates and take fees, as well as each dark pool's costs, and are designed to hit the lowest cost destinations first. HFT prop trading firms know the same things, too. At one point, CBSX, the CBOE's stock exchange, had rebates that were stock specific—the exchange was trying to entice order flow in certain high volume stocks and ETFs—which increased the predictability of where these securities would trade.[4]

Complex by Design: What Would Major Do?

Most PMs are unaware of all the pit stops their investment idea makes on its way to getting executed. Their trader probably has some idea, but little more. Buy-side trader regulatory responsibilities have grown significantly in the last decade. At the same time there are fewer traders working to get investment ideas executed. Although technology facilitates more order flow per trader, traders also must make sure they receive the best execution and generate enough commissions at brokerage firms to pay for stock research. Since the implementation of Reg NMS, nearly all buy-side traders will tell you that they spend a lot more time policing and protecting their order flow from the marketplace—a marketplace designed specifically to prey on that order flow.

The simpler market structure of 15 years ago was not only more intuitive to understand, but much less conflicted. Whether market participants had time horizons measured in seconds or in years, they all came together in centralized pools of liquidity. The most aggressive buyers traded with the most aggressive sellers, nearly all the time. This was a naturally intuitive and fair feature of markets at that time. In hindsight, we took it for granted. Today our market structure is highly fragmented, and order routing is highly conflicted. As a result, we have an environment in which those same aggressive buy and sell orders do not necessarily meet. Instead, today's market structure maximizes the insertion of intermediaries between natural buyers and sellers.

We believe institutional order routing has become complex by design. Today, large orders enter a sausage grinder that cuts them up, shreds them into tiny pieces, and delivers them to a nebulous cloud of exchanges and dark pools throughout the day, using a mind numbing array of "routes." Time/price priority means nothing in this cloud. And when the order finally gets to the public markets, or the 65% of it that hasn't been executed by dark pools and internalizers, colocated HFT firms beat the order to its intended price by a few microseconds.

What would a morning strategy session with Major be like today? We imagine it would go something like this:

> WCOM. Buyer. Me. Take 100k to buy. On one-third of it be between 5% and 7% of the volume. Be careful so that HFTs aren't sniffing you and predicting our participation rate. If that's the case, then throttle back and vary the rate. Also make sure you are not getting sniffed with odd lot dark-pool-sniffing

pings. Make sure you are playing in the deepest pool and not the cheapest pool. I need to know you are working for me and not for you, hero. Capiche? Stay away from the predictable VWAP curve if you can. We want to fly under the radar. And should the stock come in 50 cents, I want to own it. At that point enter it into your SuperBlast algo and soak up as much liquidity as you can. You with me, hero? Read it back to me....

Endnotes

1. New York Stock Exchange, "Market Share of Consolidated Tape Volume by Year (1976–2003)," Factbook, NYSE Data website, http://www.nyxdata.com/nysedata/asp/factbook/viewer_edition.asp?mode=table&key=128&category=4.

2. Woodbine Associates, "New Report: U.S. Exchange Performance, 2010," press release dated April 13, 2011, Woodbine Associates website, http://woodbineassociates.com/uploads/Woodbine_Press_Release_-_Exchange_Performance_2010_-_4-13-2010.pdf.

3. Jake Thomases, "Smart Order Routing: Dancing with the Devil," Sell-Side Technology (December 7, 2011), Waters Technology website, http://www.waterstechnology.com/sell-side-technology/analysis/2130628/waters-usa-smart-routing-fees-replace-commissions.

4. Chicago Board Operations Exchange, "CBOE Stock Exchange (CBSX) Offers New Taker Rebates on Select Group of Securities," press release dated Aug. 13, 2010, CBSX website, http://www.cbsx.com/aboutcbsx/ShowDocument.aspx?DIR=ACNews&FILE=cboe_cbsx_08_13_2010_1.ascx&CreateDate=13.08.2010&Title=CBOE%2BSTOCK%2BEXCHANGE%2B(CB.

10

The Flash Crash

Guest Chapter by R.T. Leuchtkafer

Introduction by Sal and Joe: *It was May 6, 2010. We had just finished yet another earnings season, where publicly traded corporations release their quarterly reports, and investors adjust their valuation expectations and trade accordingly. Wall Street had quieted down and shifted its focus to worldwide macro events. Greece's economic problems were front and center. CNBC was showing footage of civilians rioting in Athens. The market was sharply lower, but it was quiet at Themis. Sal went home early to mow the lawn. At 2:45 p.m., he received a frantic call. "Get back in here, farmer boy," Joe said. "The market is crazy." Sal shut down the mower and jumped in his truck. Five minutes later he walked into the office. "Grab my orders and man the phones," Joe ordered. "I'm on the line with Bloomberg." The rest of the afternoon was a blur. Joe described the crazy volatility going on to Carol Massar and Matt Miller live on Bloomberg TV. Rumors ranging from terrorist acts to a "fat finger" errant basket trade by a major brokerage firm made the rounds. The Street desperately tried to get to the bottom of how and why the market could drop 700 points and rebound within minutes.*

Sal and Joe saw May 6, 2010, which came to be known as the Flash Crash, as the poster child for the nation's broken market structure. That evening Joe went on CNBC to explain how HFT trading strategies created liquidity vacuums.[1] Sal examined the data and wrote a post mortem for Themis clients.[2] The weeks that followed were frantic as well. We spent a lot of time with financial journalists and academics explaining what we thought had happened and why it was a market structural problem.

We were not alone, which brings us to R.T. Leuchtkafer. He wrote this chapter and the next. Together, they represent the most thorough and understandable accounting of the failures of that day that we have seen. We started communicating with Leuchtkafer a month before the Flash Crash. He has written numerous editorials in financial publications, such as The Financial Times Trading Room *on* FT.com, *that have been critical of the darker effects of HFT on investors. He has also penned many excellent comment letters to the SEC, all publicly available, including his April 16, 2010 letter on the SEC's Concept Release on Equity Market Structure.[3] He is a friend of long-term investors and an avid proponent of an even playing field where all market participants can interact together fairly.*

On the morning of May 6, 2010, Mary Schapiro, chairman of the Securities and Exchange Commission (SEC), took to a podium to deliver the keynote address at a meeting of securities industry regulators and compliance professionals. It was a beautiful spring day in suburban Washington, DC, where the meeting was held, and Schapiro clearly felt good. The audience before her was filled with friends and acquaintances, people she had known for years during her decades-long career as a government and private sector regulator, and she was happy to be in front of what was certainly a friendly group.

She needed friends. Appointed chairman of the SEC just over a year earlier, Schapiro was trying to reform a government agency reeling from one spectacular failure after another, especially the Madoff and Stanford Ponzi schemes and the SEC's own role in the 2008 financial crisis. Madoff was an exceptionally deep wound. The SEC's Inspector General had recently issued a scathing report on the agency's failure to detect the scam. The report showed that despite many tips and warnings, some of them very detailed, and despite sending several teams of SEC examiners to Madoff's offices over the years to look for fraud, Madoff swindled clients for 20 years under the SEC's nose. Sworn depositions in the Inspector General's report portrayed senior staff who appeared more interested in each other's love affairs than in getting to the bottom of Madoff. Members of Congress were even calling for the SEC to be disbanded. The SEC was coming off of its most difficult year since 1934, the year it was created, and though few could imagine it, by the end of the day things would get worse.

After reaching new highs for the year just two weeks earlier, the stock market started to sell off as an economic crisis in Europe unfolded, and investors were in a sour mood that morning. In a press release from London, the credit rating agency Moody's warned of banking system risks in several European countries. Just the day before, protesters stormed the Greek parliament, and Moody's put Portugal's government bonds on review for a possible downgrade. There was talk of major European banks failing if Greece defaulted on its debt, as seemed likely if Greece wasn't bailed out. And if European banks were at risk, American banks could be next.

Even with all of the pessimism about Europe, by lunchtime the stock market was almost unchanged from the day before, though selling pressure was building. That selling pressure steadily increased into the early afternoon as buyers became more and more scarce. By 2:00 p.m. the market was down well more than 1%, and buyers headed for the exits. The market then quickly became very negative, falling more than another 1% by 2:30 p.m., altogether down about 3% for the day.

What happened next depends on who you believe. According to the SEC, "at 2:32 p.m., a large Fundamental Seller (a mutual fund complex) initiated a program to sell a total of 75,000 E-Mini contracts (valued at approximately $4.1 billion)"[4] and this order kicked off a disastrous chain of events. According to the Chicago Mercantile Exchange (CME), a big futures exchange which trades the E-Mini, a stock market derivative meant to track the performance of a large group of stocks, the Fundamental Seller had little to do with it. According to Nanex, a market data firm near Chicago, a giant burst of computer message traffic clogged up the systems that send out stock market information to investors around the world, and about a half-second later sizable and perhaps coordinated sell orders hit the markets, driving prices lower.

What is clear is that in the next few minutes more people lost more money, faster, than ever happened before in the history of financial markets. Suddenly the Dow Jones Industrials Average was off 1,000 points from the day before, about 9%. Jeremy Grant of *The Financial Times* called it "a fall unprecedented in its depth and speed."[5] And then, within about five minutes after that, investors made most of their money back, assuming they weren't unlucky enough to sell into the free fall—and many were that unlucky. In a short 10-minute span from 2:41 p.m. until about 2:50 p.m., the stock market first lost and then regained approximately $700 billion each way, a roundtrip worth $1.4 trillion. It's become known as the Flash Crash.

Mary Schapiro concluded that morning's speech to her fellow regulators by saying, "In the wake of the financial crisis, it has become a cliché that regulators cannot keep up with innovators in a market as dynamic as finance. I don't think that's true."[6]

Five hours later, the Flash Crash proved her wrong.

Deregulation

Beginning in the late 1990s, the stock market underwent a radical transformation. Only two stock markets then dominated the landscape—the New York Stock Exchange (NYSE) and NASDAQ. Between them, these two markets accounted for nearly all stock market trading. They seemed a virtually unassailable duopoly. As non-profit companies, they said they were in business to serve investors and publicly listed companies, but critics accused them of using their market power to fend off competitors, keep trading costs high, and protect their owner-members.

In 1997, alternative markets called *electronic crossing networks*, or *ECNs*, sprang up, encouraged by the SEC to compete with the established exchanges. The new ECNs were for-profit companies that, unlike the NYSE and NASDAQ, relied exclusively on computerized trading to do business. They also introduced a low-cost business model that was relatively new to the United States. Unlike NASDAQ and the NYSE, the ECNs didn't have middlemen called "specialists" or "market makers," regulated firms that were obligated to be in the market at all times, ready to buy and sell stock with investors. Instead, ECNs let investors trade directly with each other, cutting out the middlemen and in theory lowering costs, but also exposing their markets to the whims of whoever did or didn't show up.

Specialists and market makers belong to a class of firms called *liquidity providers. Liquidity* is simply the ability to buy and sell in a market. When a market has a lot of liquidity, it's not a problem to buy and sell because there are enough buyers and sellers in the market to make it easy to do business. When a market doesn't have a lot of liquidity, it's more difficult to buy and sell, and prices can jerk up and down depending on supply and demand at the moment. In the stock market, liquidity providers are firms that make a business out of buying and selling to everyone else. It is a vitally important role because, at their best, these firms can smooth out supply and demand so prices don't jerk around so much. In return for this service, these firms are entitled to earn a profit. To make it profitable for these firms, stock markets gave them certain privileges, such as exclusive rights to be middlemen as well as information about incoming orders no one else got to see. But because of those privileges, middlemen sometimes found it too tempting to take advantage of investors, with, some said, a blind eye from the stock markets themselves. The SEC was determined to change that.

The thinking behind this transformation was plain and well supported by market reformers at the time. In the 1990s, NASDAQ was embroiled in one of the largest stock market scandals in generations, a market maker quote-rigging scandal discovered by two academic researchers. Because of it, market maker firms eventually paid nearly $1 billion in fines, and NASDAQ and its parent company at the time, the National Association of Securities Dealers (now called the Financial Industry Regulatory Authority, or FINRA), were forced to implement changes allowing ECNs into the market. Reformers judged that if market makers were cheating their investor customers, then investors should just trade directly with one another, bypassing the market makers altogether. ECNs offered that service. Investors don't always come to the market at the same time, however. A buyer might have to wait quite a while for a seller to show up. The ECNs quickly discovered they too needed middlemen to provide liquidity to their markets. With an emphasis on blazing-fast computerized trading, and with an emerging technology base that supported vast amounts of computer transactions, in an ironic twist the ECNs soon became a food plot for a new kind of firm, one that looked like a middleman but wasn't regulated like one. Sharp-eyed traders figured out there was a good business in being a middleman on the ECNs if they didn't have to obey the same rules as the NYSE specialists or the NASDAQ market makers, and they didn't.

Several of these new firms were started by pit traders from the futures markets, particularly the futures markets in Chicago. These traders, called *locals* or *scalpers* in the futures markets, were usually small-time outfits that made their living rapidly buying and selling futures contracts all day long in the trading pits, making sure never to hold on to any contract for long—studies showed the average holding period was about two minutes—and making sure never to hold positions overnight because they couldn't afford the risk. *Scalper* is not a term of endearment, so these firms gussied up by calling themselves *liquidity providers* or *market makers* or *principal traders* instead.

Scalpers were long-established in the futures pits. The Federal Trade Commission published a book-length study on scalpers in the futures markets in 1926, but the modern-day stock market was an entirely new arena for them. In their infancy and hungry for business, ECNs courted these unregulated middlemen, and a symbiotic business model was born. The ECNs changed pricing to incent them, developed products and services to serve their needs, and sold them equity stakes. With their help, ECNs grew quickly and even began to crowd the established stock markets, particularly NASDAQ. Then the ECNs took a natural next step in their evolution. They decided to become formal stock exchanges rather than remain as alternative markets, so they merged with existing exchanges—by this time stock exchanges were rapidly converting from nonprofits to for-profit companies—or filed their own paperwork to become stock exchanges, and they brought unregulated market maker scalpers with them into the heart of the American stock market.

The hallmarks of these market maker scalpers are that they trade rapidly, they try not to hold on to a position for long, and they never hold a position overnight. In 1926, the Federal Trade Commission observed that a scalper "typically buys and sells in large quantities, expecting to hold the trade open only a very short time"[7] and that he "intends to be even as to quantities bought and sold at the close of the business day and is reluctant to carry a trade overnight,"[8] almost word-for-word what these firms would say about themselves 80 years later. Along with high-speed arbitrage traders and other firms with short-term investment models, they soon became known as *High Frequency Traders* (HFT) because their strategy was to use computers to trade often (thousands of trades a day) and quickly (in and out of the market in seconds).

Having helped ECNs grow into established exchanges, scalpers were in the catbird seat. Unlike traditional stock market middlemen, they didn't have many duties to the market, such as always being ready to buy and sell stock at a competitive price. They also didn't have to yield to public investor orders, as traditional middlemen did. One of the biggest differences was that these HFT scalpers could trade aggressively whenever they liked, regardless of the effect they might have on prices. Though they claimed they were passive traders, trying to make profits as simple middlemen, that wasn't always true.

Like traditional middlemen, though, they had several advantages over the public. They helped new ECN-exchanges design special data feeds to give them an edge, and though the exchanges offered these data feeds to anyone who paid for them, typical investors couldn't afford them and wouldn't have the necessary skills to use them even if they could afford them. HFT scalpers also convinced the exchanges to place their computers in the same room as the exchanges' own computers for a fee, a practice known as *colocation*. That made sure they had the fastest access of anyone. HFT scalpers who went ahead and registered as formal market makers got even more advantages, such as relaxed or waived rules on short sales. Because the new ECN-exchanges imposed few rules on their middlemen, all the HFT scalpers had to do was promise to post a quote, and any quote at all was good enough—even offering to buy only at a penny and offering to sell only at $100,000—to keep their privileges. These types of buy and sell quotes became known as *stub quotes*. Some exchanges submitted stub quotes for the scalpers as a service. The SEC approved all this.

Deregulation and technology gave HFT scalpers the latitude and the tools to scale their businesses to reach the entire stock market, a completely new phenomenon. Because an HFT scalper typically trades as much as it can as quickly as possible and likes to do its trades in small sizes, stock market volume skyrocketed even while the average size of a trade shrank. In 2003, average trade size was about 500 shares. By 2009, it was less than 200 shares. In the meantime, stock market volume doubled. High frequency traders overall were only 20% of stock market volume in 2003 but as much as 75% in 2009, much of that volume from HFT market maker scalpers. Certain HFT scalper firms were estimated to trade more than 10% of total U.S. stock market volume, or almost as much volume as the NYSE traded.

All this took some time to work its way through, but soon enough it was clear that HFT scalpers were a dominant force in the stock market and traditional middlemen were doomed. Traditional middlemen had to post competitive prices. HFT scalpers didn't—they quit the market if they thought it was too risky. Traditional middlemen were prevented from destabilizing prices and from trading in front of the public. HFT scalpers weren't. Traditional middlemen couldn't trade with the public unless they did it to keep prices stable. HFT scalpers could. Traditional middlemen kept inventory on hand, often for weeks, to maintain orderly markets. HFT scalpers rarely kept inventory more than a few minutes and never kept any overnight. By the end of 2008, stock exchanges had torn up the last of the old rulebooks, and traditional middlemen were out of business.

In a little more than 10 years, stock exchanges turned from nonprofit companies into for-profit, publicly traded businesses and eliminated almost all the restraints on middlemen but kept or even improved many of their advantages. Just in time for the greatest world economic crisis since the 1930s, the HFT scalper market structure and business model replaced 20th century stock exchanges.

Critics

As the financial crisis unfolded in the autumn of 2008, stock markets turned the most volatile in history, especially so relative to their size. Quite naturally, stock markets are volatile during crises. As almost daily crashes and surges terrified investors that fall, some tried to reassure the public by noting that though markets were as volatile as they had ever been, they were also volatile through the long economic crisis of the 1930s, so there was nothing unexpected about volatility in the 2008 crisis.

Historians will judge how dangerous and disruptive the current financial crisis is compared to the Great Depression, and the story is not over, but despite the tremendous pain caused by the financial crisis, it seems difficult to draw an equivalence between today's 9% unemployment rate and the Great Depression's 25% rate, or between today's hundreds of failed but insured banks and the thousands of failed and uninsured banks back then. It also seems willfully illiterate to ignore the many crises since the Great Depression when the market was not as volatile as it was in 2008. It wasn't as volatile during the Vietnam War, or the Cuban Missile Crisis, or the Korean War, or World War II, or the Berlin Crisis, or after 9/11, and more, a series of events that plainly included serious risks to life on Earth itself. The market in the 1930s was also tiny compared to modern-day markets. In the 1930s, average daily volume per stock was less than 2,000 shares a day, making it easy to knock prices around. Today, average daily volume per stock is about a million shares, 500 times more. Relative to the overall economy, the Depression-era stock market was also small. By any metric, the stock market today is titanic. Nevertheless, as the financial crisis took hold, the stock market started to wash around like a row boat in a typhoon. The world's largest companies routinely traded up and down 5% or 10% a day, even several times a day, on hundreds of millions of shares traded each. This extraordinary volatility fed the sense of crisis, which in turn created more volatility. There is obviously no doubt that economic fundamentals triggered sustained panic selling and monstrous volatility on the exchanges. To an emerging circle of critics, there was also no doubt that recent regulatory changes in the stock market exacerbated that volatility.

Sal Arnuk and Joe Saluzzi, founders of Themis Trading in New Jersey, were among the first to speak out. They published a white paper called "Toxic Equity Trading Order Flow on Wall Street" in December 2008 to call attention to how the architecture of the whole national market system had changed and to how those changes worsened volatility during the crisis. Changes to the national market system "resulted in the proliferation of a new generation of very profitable, high-speed, computerized trading firms and methods that are causing retail and institutional investors to chase artificial prices,"[9] they wrote. After detailing several ways in which they believed the public was at a disadvantage to these firms, they went on to say that "High frequency trading strategies have become a stealth tax on retail and institutional investors." According to Google Trends, the phrase "high frequency trading" barely existed in the world's consciousness until they published their white paper. There were HFT critics before Themis published it, but the topic was about to get hot.

A few weeks later in January 2009, an outspoken economics and financial industry blogger writing under the name Tyler Durden at ZeroHedge.com appeared. He soon started writing critically about HFT strategies and firms. In April he wrote, "What retail investors fail to acknowledge is that the quants [HFT firms] close out a majority of their ultra-short term positions at the end of each trading day, meaning that the vanilla money is stuck as a hot potato bag holder to what can only be classified as an unprecedented Ponzi scheme."[10] In July, after a former Goldman Sachs programmer was arrested on charges he stole Goldman's proprietary trading software, Tyler Durden wrote almost daily about the dominance and risks of hyperactive computer-driven trading strategies, drawing more attention to the practice than ever before. The mainstream press noticed, and stories about high-speed, computerized traders started appearing in *The New York Times* and *The Wall Street Journal*. Congress noticed, too. In August, United States Senator Ted Kaufman wrote a letter to Mary Schapiro to urge the SEC to "undertake a comprehensive, independent 'zero-based regulatory review' of a broad range of market structure issues," and noted that "Actions by the SEC over recent decades have, perhaps unintentionally, encouraged the development of markets which seem to favor the most technologically sophisticated traders."[11]

Collectively, Themis, Zero Hedge, and Ted Kaufman kept up a drumbeat about high frequency trading throughout 2009 and into 2010. Here the cliché would be to add "but they couldn't have predicted the Flash Crash," yet they did, in fact, predict it.

This Is the New Marketplace

No one knows who coined the term, but it was already being called the Flash Crash on the evening of May 6, when, in the wake of widespread shock and disbelief at what just happened, the SEC issued a short press release[12]:

> The SEC and CFTC are working closely with the other financial regulators, as well as the exchanges, to review the unusual trading activity that took place briefly this afternoon. We are also working with the exchanges to take appropriate steps to protect investors pursuant to market rules.
>
> We will make public the findings of our review along with recommendations for appropriate action.

Almost immediately attention turned to the futures markets in Chicago. Rumors said that a large seller there crushed the market. But there were other rumors. Some had it that a trader in New York entered a large sell order by mistake, selling billions of dollars worth of stock when he meant to sell only a few million. Whatever the cause, investors and listed company executives were horrified. At the depths of the crash, the value of Exxon Mobil, the world's largest corporation, fell by $35 billion. Procter & Gamble, the 170-year-old consumer goods company, lost more than one-third of its value, more than $60 billion. They were the lucky ones. The unluckiest companies, such as Accenture, a worldwide consulting company worth more than $30 billion that morning, briefly became almost worthless when its shares fell to a penny that afternoon. Some stocks bolted in the opposite direction. The auction house Sotheby's saw its shares zoom from $34 to $100,000 a share, and for an instant the company was worth more than $6 trillion, roughly equal to the annual nominal GDP of China or Japan.

Later in the day, *CNN Money's* Poppy Harlow asked Duncan Niederauer, CEO of the NYSE, "What kind of damage could this do to investors?"

He replied that "A lot of times what happens is these trades will be canceled. People will say 'Oh, we didn't realize what was going on.' The fact is, these electronic markets realize full well what's going on. They have policies to deal with these kinds of things. The last time this happened frequently was during the crisis, where there were thousands of trades canceled on a daily basis at the electronic venues because it's a different market model."

Harlow answered, "You said it's a different market model. It's what the traders told me: 'This is the new marketplace.'"[13]

Regulators canceled trades at the most outrageous prices, but thousands of ridiculous trades were allowed to stand. For no apparent reason, regulators canceled only those trades more than 60% away from prevailing prices just before the crash. So if someone sold Procter & Gamble at the lows of the day, he was out of luck because Procter & Gamble never traded more than 60% down. If someone else bought Procter & Gamble stock at those absurd prices, though, he was lucky indeed and got a bargain. Lots of ordinary investors were unlucky, but lots of HFT scalpers were lucky enough. Mary Schapiro would later say, "High-frequency traders turned what was a very down day for many investors into a very profitable one for themselves...."[14]

After the market closed, many traders noted that prices started tumbling when exchange order books emptied out as firms fled the market. In what quickly became an iconic narrative of the Flash Crash, Scott Patterson of *The Wall Street Journal* spoke to Dave Cummings, the founder of Tradebot, one of the largest of the new HFT firms. Cummings told Patterson that Tradebot shut down its trading when the Dow Jones Industrial Average was off by approximately 500 points, just as it was programmed to do. "That's what we do for safety," Cummings said. He blamed the sellers and claimed he didn't accelerate the crash at all by fleeing the market.[15]

The picture of HFT firms shutting down was fixed when Mary Schapiro appeared before Congress on May 11. In her testimony, Schapiro said, "Most significantly, it appears that some professional liquidity providers temporarily did not participate in the market on the buy-side in many stocks that suffered particularly egregious price declines, whether because of an intentional decision to withdraw or because of specific market practices," a more decorous way of saying that HFT scalpers cut and ran when the market started selling off. She went on to say, "Many of the most active and sophisticated traders in today's market structure are not subject to any obligations with respect to the nature of their trading. If active trading firms exploited their superior trading resources and significantly contributed to the severe price swings on May 6, we must consider whether regulatory action is needed to address the problem."[16]

That same day the SEC and the Commodity Futures Trading Commission (CFTC) announced they were forming a special committee called the Joint CFTC-SEC Advisory Committee on Emerging Regulatory Issues. The two agencies wrote a report in 2009 that recommended creating the Joint Committee, giving it the job to identify regulatory risks and figure out what to do about them. Headed by Mary Schapiro and Gary Gensler, the chairman of the CFTC, the Joint Committee included current and former regulators and a retired mutual fund executive. It also included two Nobel laureates and other prominent academics, some with significant ties to the financial industry. Among those ties were well-paid board seats—one professor earned more than $1 million from a single firm in recent years—research funding, and a patent application. The government knew at least some of this but didn't think to mention any of it.

The Joint Committee's inaugural public meeting was on May 24, and its first order of business was to investigate the Flash Crash. SEC and CFTC staffs were on hand to give a preliminary report about what they knew so far. Though the government was later criticized for taking too long to understand the dynamics of the crash, it was almost unheard of for federal agencies to move as quickly as the SEC and CFTC had to give a preliminary report, in public, on such a consequential event. The federal government is an institution in which it might take months to requisition a note pad, and yet in two weeks the SEC and CFTC collected and analyzed billions of pieces of information in enough detail to come to some preliminary conclusions about the Flash Crash and report them publicly.

Most important, terrorists or hackers didn't cause the crash. It also didn't look like a "fat finger" error of the kind where a trader mistakenly entered a massive sell order. After going through the events of the day and showing a variety of data about what happened, Gregg Berman, a deputy director in the SEC's new Division of Risk Strategy and Financial Innovation, offered up the money shot. He put up a slide in the presentation, slide 48, that illustrated how selling could ripple in the markets and cause more selling. He then used two deadly words that would come to define the frenzy on May 6, *feedback* and *cascade*.[17] Berman didn't say this, but others soon would—the Flash Crash happened because it was designed to happen.

Its next meeting was a month later, on June 22. At this session, the Joint Committee invited two panels of financial industry notables to make statements and answer questions. Dave Cummings of Tradebot was on the second panel, appearing alongside representatives from other trading firms. In his one-page statement, he wrote, "Forty-seven days after the Flash Crash, the market is still broken,"[18] and public confidence was destroyed by canceled trades and by trades at unreasonable prices, apparently still unbelieving that his firm's withdrawal on May 6 might have had anything to do with it. Tom Peterffy, chairman and founder of Timber Hill, a legendary and long-time market maker, said in a written statement that "HFTs operate without the significant regulatory burdens and costs borne by registered broker-dealer market makers.... HFTs have elbowed out market makers by copying or even bettering market makers' quotes but for very small sizes.... Since they have low regulatory overhead, no market making obligations, and few restrictions on their trading, they are free to take market share from registered broker-dealer market makers in placid markets and then withdraw or disappear entirely in times of increased volatility or serious market breaks."[19]

Peterffy came to Wall Street when he immigrated to the United States from Hungary in the 1960s. After a few years working in the ranks, he started a firm that became one of the most successful options market makers in the world and made him a billionaire. During the Q&A that followed the panel's prepared statements, Peterffy said, "Today, high frequency traders can do whatever they want, and I ask you, what is their purpose? What is the social or economic purpose for somebody to come in and try to make a penny here and make a penny there? I think they normally provide a lot of liquidity, usually, but not always. So, let us transfer them into a state where they always provide liquidity."[20] Skeptics could say that Peterffy was just complaining about a new class of competitors. Certainly he would complain—anyone would—if competitors copied his core liquidity provider business model but didn't have to shoulder all his costs.

Another panelist, David Weild of Grant Thornton and a former vice chairman of NASDAQ, tried to relate the erratic workings of the stock market back to the real economy and the average investor. Weild had been speaking out about problems in the stock markets for years and was especially worried about the decline in new companies going public; if fewer companies were going public, fewer companies were raising capital for their businesses, creating jobs, and growing the economy. Talking directly to Dave Cummings, Weild said, "Dave, take the ma and pa investor test. Ask your parents whether or not they think there's excessive volatility in the market. I sit around with 80-year-old parents who had their retirement fund somewhat decimated, and there's a lot of discomfort in the market."[21]

The Joint Committee met once more that summer. The most significant moment at its August 11 session came when Pamela Craig, Accenture's chief financial officer, described how the crash affected the company, its employees, and its investors. She began by calmly walking the committee through exactly what happened to Accenture's stock during the crash. Between 2:40 p.m. and 2:46 p.m. its stock price fell from $41.01 to $38 as buyers fled the stock market. That rapid price change caused the NYSE to slow trading down, as it was designed to do by rule, in the hope buyers would return and stabilize Accenture's price. But other stock exchanges, including a subsidiary owned by NYSE, continued to trade the stock. A few sell market orders, totaling only about 10,000 shares—which should be trivial to a $30 billion global company like Accenture—hit the exchanges still trading Accenture. There were few or no buyers on those markets, and Accenture's share price instantly collapsed. In 10 seconds or less, Accenture's share price crashed all the way down to penny per share stub quotes.

Craig said that the "erratic trading rattled overall investor confidence in the market" but specifically struck Accenture's investors, including Accenture's many employees who own stock in the company. Why was Accenture so affected by the crash versus other large companies, they wondered. While trades below $16.40 were canceled—Craig rightly called it an "arbitrary pricing threshold" for busted trades—because other low-ball trades stood, Accenture's stock price statistics for the year included trades that were plainly wrong. Investors looking at Accenture's stock price statistics would see that its 52-week low was $17.74, which, she said, "obviously reflects the malfunctioning of the market making process on May 6, and *not* the true 52 week low." (Emphasis hers.) Craig also said, "Based on what we've all witnessed that day and since then, there is every reason to expect that this will happen again."[22]

During all the Joint Committee's meetings that summer, much of the securities industry agreed there were problems with the stock markets, though people differed over exactly what they thought was wrong. What was remarkable about all this is that, with the exception of a few such as David Weild and the HFT critics, as recently as the morning of May 6 most people in the industry thought the market was in good shape. We know that because they said so. They said so in 175 or so letters they sent to the SEC before May 6 to comment on a think piece the SEC published earlier that year called the "Concept Release on Equity Market Structure."

Senator Ted Kaufman's August 2009 letter to Mary Schapiro called for the SEC to conduct a wide-ranging review of the nation's stock markets. A week or so after Kaufman wrote the letter, Schapiro was asked about it in an interview. She said the SEC was already working on such a review, and in January 2010 the SEC published the 74-page Concept Release. The document began by saying, "The secondary market for U.S.-listed equities has changed dramatically in recent years" and went on to describe those changes.[23] The SEC then solicited comments from the industry and the public about how the stock market worked and how to improve it.

Over the years, an informal protocol has evolved for responding to an SEC solicitation like this. Typically, the authors of a comment letter to the SEC identify themselves, praise the insight and leadership of the SEC, talk about what good citizens their own firms are, and then argue for regulations favorable to their business. Lots of people do it that way.

On April 30, 2010, NASDAQ sent a letter to the SEC to respond to the Concept Release, saying it "applauds the Commission for working to optimize market structure and to achieve Congress' directive to facilitate a national market system, promote investor protection, and maintain fair and orderly markets."[24] That's in just the first paragraph. In its conclusion to the letter, NASDAQ wrote, "U.S. equities markets are the fairest, deepest, and most efficient in the world" because of five factors, the first of which was "effective regulation." Nobody pays much attention when firms write this kind of boilerplate flattery, unless of course a week later the industry they helped deregulate suddenly loses close to $1 trillion in five minutes and their CEO is on ABC News saying, "The people who are assigned the responsibility of providing liquidity into the markets, especially in times of stress, did not do that. It's as if you walked up to the teller, and the teller shut the booth."[25] In those circumstances, what they said a week earlier can be quite interesting.

Other organizations praised the then-current state of the markets in their comment letters as well. In its letter dated April 27, 2010, one of the biggest HFT firms, GETCO, wrote "the current national market system is performing extremely well" and the stock market is "resilient and robust even during times of stress and dislocation."[26] On April 23, 2010, several HFT firms jointly signed a letter saying they believed "the quality of the markets has never been better." They also wrote, "The equity markets have also proven to be remarkably resilient" and "U.S. equity markets have never been healthier" and markets were "fair, open and competitive" and "the risk of automated professional trading firms creating instability in the markets is unlikely...."[27] Other HFT firms echoed these comments as a string of them lined up in April 2010 to tell the SEC how much they improved liquidity, even during volatile markets. One wrote "the particular aspects of professional trading that seem to be of concern to the Commission (for example, high frequency trading, colocation, and so on) are exactly what enable professional traders to provide liquidity to long-term investors during periods of market disruption."[28] Academics had much praise, too. Though they cautioned about the need for marketwide circuit breakers, James Angel of Georgetown University, Lawrence Harris of the University of Southern California (a former SEC chief economist), and Chester Spatt of Carnegie Mellon University (also a former SEC chief economist) together wrote on February 23, 2010, that "Virtually every dimension of U.S. equity market quality is now better than ever."[29] Under a Georgetown logo, Angel later wrote separately on April 30, 2010, a week before the crash, "The equity market structure is working better than ever" and "Most high frequency technology has not led to high frequency volatility."[30] Angel also repeated a call for circuit breakers because "eventually there will be some big glitch"; more on that later. He didn't mention that four days earlier, Direct Edge, an ECN that had just won approval from the SEC to launch two new stock exchanges, announced Angel was joining the board of directors of each of its new exchanges.

Much of this is reminiscent of one of the most famous bloopers in academic economics, when a truly distinguished economist named Irving Fisher remarked that "Stock prices have reached what looks like a permanently high plateau" just a few days before Black Thursday, the beginning of the infamous 1929 stock market crash. Fisher might have preserved his popular reputation if he changed his opinion after the market crash. He didn't. After the Flash Crash, though, HFT firms began to acknowledge flaws in the market. Chicago-based GETCO co-signed a letter to the SEC saying "the market events of May 6, 2010 have raised important questions about the operation of our market structure."[31] As for academics, James Angel wrote to remind the SEC of the several times in the past when he had called for circuit breakers, and concluded his letter by saying "Our market structure still works better than ever—most of the time."[32]

A few firms remained steadfast. In an interview, the founder of one well-known and successful firm said the immediate rebound after the crash showed that the market worked beautifully compared to how it used to work, which would be like saying a commercial airliner worked beautifully when, after mysteriously plunging 10,000 feet straight down in a mid-flight nosedive, the plane suddenly rocketed back to its original altitude. What the heck, at least you still got to Cleveland.

Most firms agreed there were some problems. They usually mentioned two. The first was uncertainty around when trades get canceled in a volatile market. The other was the lack of automated trading stops like circuit breakers or trade limits. Unsurprisingly, few said problems went deeper. Trade cancel policies and automated trading stops are important but small-bore reforms that don't threaten the status quo. A circuit breaker stops trading after a stock or index value falls (or rises) by a certain percentage. A trade limit sets a price band for a stock beyond which the market can't go, although the stock can continue to trade within the price band. Over time, market participants have been divided about these kinds of trading restraints, with some believing they stop markets from doing their job as price-setting mechanisms and some worrying about their unknown risks in a market as complicated as the modern stock market. Hundreds of stocks trading at a penny per share in the crash were persuasive enough, however, and the SEC made the exchanges implement circuit breakers and then start discussions about trade limits. The SEC also got the exchanges to clarify their trade cancel policies and to ban stub quotes. Even with circuit breakers and trade cancel policies, business still largely goes on as usual, though, and we know from the bulk of those 175 comment letters a lot of firms were happy enough with business as usual. Even the ban on stub quotes was little more than regulatory theater because firms could still quote as much as 8% away from current prices and still obey the new rules.

There were some critics who challenged business as usual, especially Themis Trading, Zero Hedge, and Ted Kaufman. Before the crash, each of them predicted disaster unless there were substantial market reforms. Joe Saluzzi of Themis Trading said in an interview in summer 2009, "I have a feeling one day the door is going to close, everyone is going to be running for the exits, there is going to be a major move in the market and everyone is going to wonder 'what happened?'"[33] Kaufman was eerily prescient when he said in early autumn 2009, "Moreover, unlike specialists and traditional market-makers that are regulated, some of these new high frequency traders are unregulated, though they are acting in a market-maker capacity. They have no requirements to 'maintain a fair and orderly' market. They trade when it benefits them. If we experience another shock to the financial system, will this new (and dominant) type of pseudo market maker act in the interest of the markets when we really need them? Will they step up and maintain a two-sided market, or will they simply shut off the machines and walk away? Even worse, will they seek even further profit and exacerbate the downside?"[34] Zero Hedge was relentless, publishing scores if not hundreds of posts in the year leading up to the crash criticizing HFT and the stock market and predicting a high-speed market meltdown.

A few weeks before the crash, on April 16, 2010, I submitted a comment letter on the SEC's Concept Release.[35] I wrote that "Formal and informal market makers in the equities markets today have few or none of the responsibilities of the old dealers...firms shed responsibility for price continuity, quote size, meaningful quote continuity or quote depth...[and] are free to trade as aggressively or passively as they like or to disappear from the market altogether. They still get valuable privileges if they register as market makers, and they promise in return to merely post any quote, and a penny bid can count as a valid quote...." I noted that when HFT firms "spot opportunities or need to rebalance, they remove liquidity by pulling their quotes and fire off marketable orders and become liquidity demanders. With no restraint on their behavior, they have a significant effect on prices and volatility" and "they cartwheel from being liquidity suppliers to liquidity demanders as their models rebalance. This sometimes rapid rebalancing sent volatility to unprecedented highs during the financial crisis and contributed to the chaos of the last two years...." I outlined a simple example of how this worked. "Imagine a stock under stress from sellers such [as] was the case in fall 2008. There is a sell imbalance unfolding over some period of time. Any HFT market making firm is being hit repeatedly and ends up long the stock and wants to readjust its position. The firm times its entrance into the market as an aggressive seller and then cancels its bid and starts selling its inventory, exacerbating the stock's decline." As we would soon find out, that's exactly what happened in the crash.

Endnotes

1. Joseph Saluzzi, interview on CNBC on May 7, 2010, YouTube website, http://www.youtube.com/watch?v=d_CHwBugl1A.

2. Themis Trading, "The Emperor Has No Clothes."

3. R. T. Leuchtkafer, Securities and Exchange Commission file S7-02-10 (April 16, 2010), Securities and Exchange Commission website, http://www.sec.gov/comments/s7-02-10/s70210-107.htm.

4. CFTC and SEC, "Findings Regarding the Market Events of May 6, 2010": 10.

5. Jeremy Grant, "High Frequency Trading: Up against a bandsaw," *Financial Times*, September 2, 2010.

6. Mary Schapiro, "Keynote Address at the Compliance and Legal Society of the Securities Industry and Financial Markets Association 2010 Annual Seminar" (May 6, 2010), Securities and Exchange Commission website, http://www.sec.gov/news/speech/2010/spch050610mls.htm.

7. Federal Trade Commission, "Report of the Federal Trade Commission on the Grain Trade," vol. 7: 4 (1926).

8. Ibid., p. 70.

9. Arnuk and Saluzzi, "Toxic Equity Trading Order Flow on Wall Street."

10. Tyler Durden, "The Incredibly Shrinking Market Liquidity, or the Upcoming Black Swan of Black Swans" (April 10, 2009), Zero Hedge website, http://zerohedge.blogspot.com/2009_04_05_archive.html.

11. Edward E. Kaufman letter dated August 21, 2009 to Mary L. Schapiro (Chairman, Securities and Exchange Commission), Senate Banking website, http://banking.senate.gov/public/index.cfm?FuseAction=Files.View&FileStore_id=e9898882-33e2-4269-890a-7ee021537084.

12. Securities and Exchange Commission, "Statement from SEC and CFTC" press release 2010-72 dated May, 2010, Securities and Exchange Commission website, www.sec.gov/news/press/2010/2010-72.htm.

13. Duncan Niederauer (CEO, NYSE) interview with Poppy Harlow (CNNMoney), "NYSE CEO Explains Selloff" (May 6, 2010), CNNMoney website, http://money.cnn.com/video/markets/2010/05/06/mkts_nyse_ceo.cnnmoney.

14. Mary L. Schapiro, "Speech by SEC Chairman: Remarks Before the Investment Company Institute's General Membership Meeting" (May 6, 2011), Securities and Exchange Commission website, http://www.sec.gov/news/speech/2011/spch050611mls.htm.

15. Scott Patterson, "Did Shutdowns Make Plunge Worse?" *The Wall Street Journal*, May 7, 2010.

16. Mary L. Schapiro, "Testimony Concerning the Severe Market Disruption on May 6, 2010" (May 11, 2010), Securities and Exchange Commission website, http://www.sec.gov/news/testimony/2010/ts051110mls.htm.

17. Mary Schapiro, "Meeting of the Joint CFTC-SEC Advisory Committee on Emerging Regulatory Issues, Monday, May 24, 2010," Securities and Exchange Commission website, http://www.sec.gov/news/openmeetings/2010/052410sec-cftcjointmeeting.shtml.

18. Dave Cummings, "Summary of Views" (June 22, 2010), Securities and Exchange Commission website, www.sec.gov/comments/265-26/265-26-16.pdf.

19. Thomas Peterffy, "Before the Joint CFTC-SEC Advisory Committee on Emerging Regulatory Issues/Comments of Thomas Peterffy, Chairman and CEO, Interactive Brokers Group, June 22, 2010," Securities and Exchange Commission website, www.sec.gov/comments/265-26/265-26-23.pdf.

20. Thomas Peterffy, "Joint CFTC-SEC Advisory Committee on Emerging Regulatory Issues Meeting, Wednesday, June 22, 2010," Securities and Exchange Commission website, http://www.sec.gov/news/openmeetings/2010/jac062210.shtml.

21. David Weild, "Joint CFTC-SEC Advisory Committee on Emerging Regulatory Issues Meeting, Wednesday, June 22, 2010," Securities and Exchange Commission website, http://www.sec.gov/news/openmeetings/2010/jac062210.shtml.

22. Pamela Craig, "Prepared Statement of Pamela J. Craig, Chief Financial Officer, Accenture, Before the Joint CFTC-SEC Advisory Committee on Emerging Regulatory Issues, August 11, 2010." Securities and Exchange Commission website, www.sec.gov/comments/265-26/265-26-29.pdf.

23. Securities and Exchange Commission, "Concept Release on Equity Market Structure," 17 CFR part 242, rel. 34-61358, file S7-02-10, RIN 3235-AK47 (Jan. 14, 2010), Securities and Exchange Commission website, www.sec.gov/rules/concept/2010/34-61358.pdf.

24. Joan C. Conley (Senior Vice President and Corporate Secretary, NASDAQ), letter dated April 30, 2010 to Elizabeth M. Murphy (Secretary, Securities and Exchange Commission): 1, Securities and Exchange Commission website, www.sec.gov/comments/s7-02-10/s70210-168.pdf.

25. Jake Tapper et al., "Wall Street Nervous after 'Flash Crash' Thursday," ABC News (May 7, 2010), ABC News website, http://abcnews.go.com/GMA/Business/wall-street-nervous-flash-crash-thursday/story?id=10581615.

26. John A. McCarthy (General Counsel, GETCO), letter dated April 27, 2010 to Elizabeth M. Murphy (Secretary, Securities and Exchange Commission), Securities and Exchange Commission website, www.sec.gov/comments/s7-02-10/s70210-158.pdf.

27. Liam Connell (CEO, Allston Trading), Richard B. Gorelick (CEO, RGM Advisors), Adam Nunes (President, Hudson River Trading), Cameron Smith (General Counsel, Quantlabs), letter dated April 23, 2010 to Elizabeth M. Murphy (Secretary, Securities and Exchange Commission), Securities and Exchange Commission website, www.sec.gov/comments/s7-02-10/s70210-155.pdf.

28. Donald R. Wilson, Jr. (DRW Trading Group), letter dated April 21, 2010 to Elizabeth M. Murphy (Secretary, Securities and Exchange Commission), Securities and Exchange Commission website, www.sec.gov/comments/s7-02-10/s70210-149.pdf.

29. Angel, Harris, and Spatt, "Equity Trading in the 21st Century," 5.

30. James J. Angel, letter dated April 30, 2010 to the Securities and Exchange Commission, Securities and Exchange Commission website, www.sec.gov/comments/s7-02-10/s70210-172.pdf.

31. John A. McCarthy and Christopher R. Concannon (Virtu Financial), letter dated July 9, 2010 to Robert Cook (Director, Division of Trading and Markets, Securities and Exchange Commission), Securities and Exchange Commission website, www.sec.gov/comments/s7-02-10/s70210-255.pdf.

32. James J. Angel, letter dated May 11, 2010 to Securities and Exchange Commission, Securities and Exchange Commission website, www.sec.gov/comments/s7-02-10/s70210-181.pdf.

33. Joseph Saluzzi, interview "Joe Saluzzi, Themis Trading, Bloomberg TV, 06-30-09," YouTube website, http://www.youtube.com/watch?v=g0U1vMUa2sc

34. Edward E. Kaufman, speech before the Senate on Sept. 14, 2009, C-Span website, http://www.c-spanvideo.org/appearance/595126357.

35. Leuchtkafer, SEC file S7-02-10.

11

The Aftermath

Guest Chapter by R.T. Leuchtkafer

SEC and CFTC staff issued a final report on the Flash Crash to the Joint Committee on September 30, 2010.[1] The report began, "On May 6, 2010, the prices of many U.S.-based equity products experienced an extraordinarily rapid decline and recovery" and said that many of the 8,000 stocks traded in the stock market dropped 5%, 10%, or even 15% or more before recovering, and how "Over 20,000 trades across more than 300 securities were executed at prices more than 60% away from their values just moments before. Moreover, many of these trades were executed at prices of a penny or less, or as high as $100,000, before prices of those securities returned to their 'pre-crash' levels." In 104 pages of careful analysis, the report described how on an already gloomy day in the markets a single large seller of futures, together with other sellers, exhausted what few remaining buyers there were, including HFT firms. High-frequency traders then hit their risk limits and immediately turned around and started selling frantically, competing with investors for any remaining buyers. But the only remaining buyers were other high-frequency traders, who themselves quickly hit their risk limits and cartwheeled to start selling aggressively. The futures market turned into a high-frequency cascading fratricide, a fratricide the report called "hot potato" trading, as high-frequency firms dumped inventory onto one another at lower and lower prices. In the final moments, the original large futures seller had mainly quit the market, or couldn't keep up with it, but events were already irretrievably out of control. The mayhem in the futures market instantly spread to the stock market as cross-market arbitrageurs started selling into the stock market, and the stock market collapsed. As the report put it:

> The combined selling pressure from the Sell Algorithm, HFTs and other traders drove the price of the E-Mini S&P 500 down approximately 3% in just four minutes from the beginning of 2:41 p.m. through the end of 2:44 p.m. During this same time cross-market arbitrageurs who did buy the E-Mini S&P 500, simultaneously sold equivalent amounts in the equities markets, driving the price of SPY (an exchange-traded fund [that] represents the S&P 500 index) also down approximately 3%.
>
> Still lacking sufficient demand from fundamental buyers or cross-market arbitrageurs, HFTs began to quickly buy and then resell contracts to each other—generating a "hot-potato" volume effect as the same positions were rapidly passed back and forth. Between 2:45:13 and 2:45:27, HFTs traded over 27,000 contracts, which accounted for about 49 percent of the total trading volume, while buying only about 200 additional contracts net.

In the face of all this selling, many HFT firms simply withdrew from the market. As he told *The Wall Street Journal* immediately after the crash, Dave Cummings' Tradebot withdrew when the Dow Jones Industrial Average was down approximately 500 points. *The New York Times* reported that at one firm, Tradeworx, someone walked up to a computer terminal "and typed the command HF STOP: sell everything, and shutdown."[2] As the SEC and CFTC staff final report put it, "Some market makers and other liquidity providers widened their quote spreads, others reduced offered liquidity, and a significant number withdrew completely from the markets.... HFTs in the equity markets, who normally both provide and take liquidity as part of their strategies, traded proportionally more as volume increased, and overall were net sellers in the rapidly declining broad market along with most other participants." Selling snowballed even more when "inter-nalizers"—firms that normally buy and sell with their own customers instead of sending customer orders to the exchanges—"began rout-ing most, if not all, of these orders directly to the public exchanges where they competed with other orders for immediately available, but dwindling, liquidity...orders that were part of this surge account for about half of the trades that were executed at the most depressed and extreme prices."

The frenzy continued until "At 2:45:28 p.m., trading on the E-Mini was paused for five seconds when the Chicago Mercantile Exchange (CME) Stop Logic Functionality was triggered in order to prevent a cascade of further price declines. In that short period of time, sell-side pressure in the E-Mini was partly alleviated and buy-side interest increased. When trading resumed at 2:45:33 p.m., prices stabilized and shortly thereafter, the E-Mini began to recover, fol-lowed by the SPY." After this trading pause in the futures market, the final report said, firms had "time to react and verify the integrity of their data and systems, buy-side and sell-side interest returned and an orderly price discovery process began to function." Within minutes, most stocks "had reverted back to trading at prices reflecting true consensus values."

The report also makes it clear that whatever else happened, there was no "big glitch," no fat-finger error or unforeseen computer error that triggered the crash. Instead, nearly every firm in the market at the time did precisely what it thought was rational according to current regulations. The rules allowed privileged HFT market maker firms, paid for providing liquidity, to aggressively sell everything at lower and lower prices, withdraw from the market, and post stub quotes—so they did. The rules allowed even unregistered firms to pose like liquidity providers and get paid for it but still aggressively dump their entire inventory whenever they wanted to, at lower and lower prices—so they did. The rules allowed internalizers to decide when to trade against their customers or just throw their orders overboard to the exchanges—so they did. The rules allowed HFT market makers to exacerbate price declines—so they did. The rules allowed HFT market makers to sell alongside the very same investors they had just bought from—so they did. In this sense, the Flash Crash was designed to happen—it was even predicted to happen—and all we needed for it to actually happen was the right combination of circumstances, the perfect storm of selling into a feedback loop that created more selling as prices cascaded downward. The crash wasn't a bug or a glitch. It was a *feature* of the newly deregulated stock market, of privileged but substantially lawless HFT market makers. A paper later coauthored by a member of the Joint Committee said "...the 'Flash Crash' is better understood as a liquidity event arising from structural features of the new high frequency world of trading."[3]

Within a few days of the SEC and CFTC staff final report, Andrei Kirilenko, the Chief Economist of the CFTC, and several academic economists released their own working paper called "The Flash Crash: The Impact of High Frequency Trading on an Electronic Market."[4] One of the most significant empirical market structure studies ever published, Kirilenko and his coauthors concluded that "High Frequency Traders exhibit trading patterns inconsistent with the traditional definition of market making," directly contradicting long-standing HFT scalper claims that they are nothing more than simple market makers or liquidity providers. He went on, "Specifically, High Frequency Traders aggressively trade in the direction of price changes," contradicting frequent HFT market maker claims that they dampen volatility. And more, "This activity comprises a large percentage of total trading volume but does not result in a significant accumulation of inventory. As a result, whether under normal market conditions or during periods of high volatility, High Frequency Traders are not willing to accumulate large positions or absorb large losses." As for signaling behavior, that is, whether all that HFT scalper trading volume tells investors anything useful at all, Kirilenko wrote,

"Moreover, their contribution to higher trading volumes may be mistaken for liquidity by Fundamental Traders [investors]."

To the heart of the matter, whether HFT scalper firms are healthy for the market, the policy point HFT scalpers and their academic and regulatory coreligionists cite as justification for a decade's worth of regulatory free-for-alls in the U.S., Kirilenko wrote "when rebalancing their positions, High Frequency Traders may compete for liquidity and amplify price volatility."

In quiet markets, HFT firms do contribute liquidity and improve standard market quality metrics. Several academics have published studies showing a gradual improvement in several of these metrics in recent years, at least for high-volume stocks. But their statistics are measured over months or years, and the disruptive and destabilizing trading practices of these firms are usually detectable only in episodes of transitory volatility, volatility that averages out in longer-term studies. As an example of this kind of statistical artifact, fatalities from a plane crash will not move national mortality statistics a jot, but that is no consolation to the many victims. Academic statistical studies to date are simply not sharp enough to detect most of these episodes. If you look at some of these statistics for 2010, the Flash Crash itself isn't even noticeable.

Nanex, the market data company with its own theories about the crash, did an analysis that looked at stocks using finely tuned statistics.[5] Nanex discovered hundreds—thousands—of "mini" flash crashes over the years. The worst year for them so far was 2008, but there were still more than a thousand of them in each of 2009 and 2010. There are several ways to define a mini flash crash. Nanex's analysis looked at the general case where a stock has an extreme short-term price movement and then an immediate rebound, and counted all these. Some would sort these instances into at least two categories: one in which a large order instantaneously clears out an exchange's order book down to (or up to) nonsense prices, and the other in which

HFT market makers empty a book by withdrawing, or by dumping inventory and withdrawing as on May 6, 2010, but the effect on investors is the same—ricocheting stock prices simply because of structural or regulatory defects in the stock market.

The Joint Committee Weighs In

With the SEC and CFTC staff final report in hand, the Joint CFTC-SEC Advisory Committee on Emerging Regulatory Issues wrote its conclusions and 14 regulatory reform proposals in February 2011.[6] Several of the Joint Committee's proposals expanded or refined volatility firebreaks, like circuit breakers, that the SEC had already put in place. Another set of proposals highlighted the SEC's recently enacted risk control rules for certain unsupervised firms and encouraged both the SEC and CFTC to supervise computer trading algorithms more closely. The last group of its proposals spoke to exchange fees, modest market maker rules, order routing practices, and more order book information for market participants.

Three recommendations from the last group were particularly promising. First, the Joint Committee said high frequency traders should pay for their high-speed antics, perhaps as a small order cancellation fee. In today's markets, it doesn't cost anything to submit and cancel orders, so these firms send and cancel millions of orders every day, looking for the tiniest advantage. More than 90% of their orders are canceled nearly instantaneously. HFT scalpers say they do it to manage risk, and that we all benefit because they can give us better prices. It distorts market prices, though, and can be predatory in nature. At best, it delivers fleeting liquidity while imposing huge technology costs on the industry as a whole. Second, the committee recommended that regulators reform internalizers, the firms that trade with their own customer orders, but can also throw their orders to the exchanges in volatile markets, adding even more volatility to an already rocky marketplace. Though regulators have fretted about internalizers for decades, the Joint Committee's imprimatur is the kind of muscle regulators need to overhaul this segment of the stock market. Requiring internalizers to keep at least some portion of their customer orders during volatile periods will relieve pressure on markets. Finally, the Joint Committee recommended expanding regulations to always guarantee investors the best available price, regardless of which exchange has it. This "trade-at" rule would protect the public's orders at every price, on all exchange order books, all the time. Today, only the best price on exchange order books is protected, and a large order is free to rip through a single exchange's book below the best price, causing a mini flash crash.

The Joint Committee's most grave point, though, boiled down to a handful of words in its introduction, a bleak commentary on a decade's worth of change: "In the present environment, where high frequency and algorithmic trading predominate and where exchange competition has essentially eliminated rule-based market maker obligations...even in the absence of extraordinary market events, limit order books can quickly empty and prices can crash...." They tell of how profoundly our recently deregulated stock markets have changed and of how stock exchanges can't seem to control even their own order books any more. In other words, a flash crash can happen again, at any time, even in quiet markets, even in the absence of extraordinary events. Do you feel lucky? It was surprising, then, that the Joint Committee didn't come out with stronger recommendations about HFT market maker scalpers than it did. Especially so given the 80 or so years of government and academic research into their behavior and their effect on markets.

In its 1926 report on futures market scalpers, the Federal Trade Commission said quite a bit that was later echoed in the SEC and CFTC staff final report and in Kirilenko's paper. The FTC wrote, "Because the pit scalper is not inclined to take a loss...he closes out his trades when the market goes against him, and this practice can but tend to accentuate the swing." Also, "the allegation that he is consistently a stabilizing factor is more open to question...they themselves often create the [volatility] with which they are most concerned." Finally, "when the market turns they run with it, and they may accentuate an upward or downward movement that is already considerable."

Although they can have a destabilizing effect on futures markets, their effect on the stock market is especially pronounced. Unlike the futures markets, prices in the stock market aren't disciplined by prices in the spot or cash market—it is the spot market. Unlike the futures pit markets, the public stock markets for the most part trade in fixed time order at a price, with no choice over who you trade with and no way to avoid HFT scalpers who might turn to compete for the liquidity they just extended. This is the main reason HFT scalpers are so time-sensitive, paying millions to get their computers as physically close as possible to exchange systems. The stock and futures markets differ in other ways, too, if only because of the public confidence required of them. Whether the public invests in stocks has much to do with its confidence in the stability and integrity of the stock market. Whether the public buys orange juice has little to do with its confidence in the stability and integrity of the orange juice futures market. As important as the futures markets are, they aren't forums for long-term, even generational capital commitments, and the public doesn't directly invest its nest-eggs and retirement savings in them. Companies don't rely on them to raise capital for new plants, equipment, and jobs.

There is, of course, more recent evidence than the Federal Trade Commission's report. In 1967, a professor named Holbrook Working published a paper describing how scalpers on the futures markets don't simply provide liquidity; they trade with the price trend and accelerate price movements. In 1985, a professor named Seymour Smidt wrote that while futures market scalpers can provide liquidity, they can also "'consume' liquidity and may cause temporary instability."[7] Smidt also described what he called "scalper inventory liquidation," a term he defined as "a situation in which scalpers as a group seek to reduce their inventories aggressively." Smidt wrote that when scalper inventories rise to levels the market maker scalpers are uncomfortable with, such as they might in the face of a large order, "the market becomes potentially unstable. Relatively small imbalances in order flows or minor news may lead to a scalper inventory liquidation, which will cause price changes that are likely to be large in relation to the imbalance that served as the immediate trigger." No doubt this is how a $4 billion order, one that had worked before without difficulty, and barely half of which actually traded on the way down, helped trigger $700 billion in losses in the Flash Crash. It unwittingly started a market maker-to-market maker panic, something which had never happened before in the stock market.

In 1996, two professors named Steven Manaster and Steven Mann published a paper on scalpers in the futures market and said that scalpers who aggressively manage inventory are "active profit-seeking" traders and that they have much shorter inventory lifetimes than market makers in the stock market. (This was back when market makers in the stock market still had meaningful rules.)[8] In 1997, a professor named Richard Lyons published a paper describing hot potato trading in the foreign exchange markets, where market makers liquidate inventory imbalances by dumping unwanted inventory on to each other, repeatedly, as prices become less informative because of it.[9] Lyons actually called it "hot potato trading," just as did the SEC and CFTC staff final report and Kirilenko. In another paper published around the same time, Lyons pointed out that this kind of behavior would not happen with the then better regulated stock market specialists. In 2003, two academics named Joon Chae and Albert Wang wrote a paper that looked at an overseas stock exchange and concluded that privileges alone don't induce market makers to provide liquidity. They also wrote that while market makers "may be meant to perform the socially beneficial function of liquidity provision, the institutional advantages granted to them also give the ability to act as super-efficient proprietary traders if they choose to."[10]

There's much more, but it should be clear we have known for a long time that market maker scalpers destabilize markets and do it in markets ranging from corn and financial futures to foreign exchange to, for the first time, the stock markets. Combined with the tools of modern technology, the business model's potential for disruption now reaches into almost every corner of the financial and commodity markets, just as individual HFT firms themselves trade in almost every market from commodities to stocks to currencies, in the United States and overseas. A senior official of the Bank of England said recently, "Far from solving the liquidity problem in situations of stress, HFT firms appear to have added to it. And far from mitigating market stress, HFT appears to have amplified it. HFT liquidity, evident in sharply lower peacetime bid-ask spreads, may be illusory. In wartime, it disappears. This disappearing act, and the resulting liquidity void, is widely believed to have amplified the price discontinuities evident during the Flash Crash. HFT liquidity proved fickle under stress, as flood turned to drought."[11] And as Mary Schapiro said on the first anniversary of the Flash Crash, "High frequency traders turned what was a very down day for many investors into a very profitable one for themselves by taking liquidity rather than providing it. I think their activity that day should cause us to thoroughly examine their current role."[12]

Several of the Joint Committee's recommendations addressed the behavior of high frequency traders, but to some critics few of them went far enough. The Joint Committee even seemed to rule out meaningful market maker rules from the outset, writing that increased competition and regulatory changes in recent years "have effectively eliminated much of the profitability of the registered market maker function and therefore, eliminated the ability for the Exchanges to impose significant quoting or trading obligations." But in a remarkable example of either intellectual incoherence or, more likely, divisions within the Joint Committee, just five sentences later it wrote, "As has been widely reported, such high frequency market making is a significantly profitable activity."

Which is it? Estimates of HFT revenues in the stock market vary widely, ranging from about $3 billion a year in one study to about $6 billion in others. What's useful to understand is that by at least one measure, HFT market making is more lucrative today than old-school market making, and precisely so because of recent regulatory changes. To see this, imagine an investor who wants to buy 1,000 shares of stock. A 2004 SEC filing from a large old-school market maker helps us understand how much money a middleman back then earned, on average, from those 1,000 shares.[13] Because of now-defunct regulations that limited when the firm could trade with the public, on average the firm traded with only about 23% of the volume it saw. In 2004, the old-school market maker earned a little less than seven-tenths of a cent per share it traded, so against 230 shares—23% of that 1,000 share order—the firm would earn about $1.54. One recent and widely cited study estimated HFT revenues at a little more than a quarter of a cent per share,[14] but because on average HFT firms trade with as much as 75% of volume, today's middlemen can earn $1.99 from that 1,000 share order—or 30% more than before. Inadvertently, the Joint Committee might be right after all. Per share, market maker profit margins are down because of deregulation. But because there are no rules today, they trade more than they ever could before and make it up on volume, so HFT market making is indeed a significantly profitable activity. As Tradebot says on its website, "In the 'good old days' the specialist margins were much, much fatter (and the public footed the bill). With these ultra-slim margins, the only way to stay in business is to make it up on volume—huge volume."[15] Of course, the public still foots the bill, and by these calculations investors pay middlemen quite a bit more today than they did just a few years ago.

The Abyss of Destruction

As of this writing, more than a year after the Joint Committee finished, there are few if any signs the SEC is working on any of the

Joint Committee's recommendations beyond the smattering the SEC had already proposed or implemented by February 2011, when the Joint Committee released its work. There is considerable evidence the SEC needs to go further, that what little the SEC has done since the Flash Crash won't prevent another crash.

Shortly after the crash the SEC forced the stock exchanges to implement circuit breakers for the largest stocks. It later proposed tight trading limits. Nanex exhaustively tested the SEC's trade limit proposals against data from the Flash Crash and persuasively argued they would not have stopped it.[16] Nanex also argued the SEC's proposals could easily have made the crash worse. The SEC didn't publish any analyses of its own, so for the time being the only public evidence we have shows that the SEC's ideas won't work. Going back to our nose-diving aircraft, it's as if to fix the problem the Federal Aviation Administration required engineering changes to all commercial aircraft, didn't release any test results showing the fixes actually worked, was handed evidence they didn't work, but insisted on them anyway. In the meantime, market volatility is still extreme. Within one week in August 2011, the Dow Jones Industrials Average went up or down by 400 points four days in a row, something it had never done before, ever. *Crain's New York* called it the "wildest week on record," and this after at least some of the SEC's fixes were already implemented. As a point of comparison, President Kennedy first told the nation about the Cuban Missile Crisis on the evening of October 22, 1962, and warned the entire world was at "the abyss of destruction." The next day the front page of *The New York Times* screamed "Kennedy Ready for Soviet Showdown." The stock market's reaction? The Dow Jones Industrials Average fell about 200 points, after adjusting for different baselines between 1962 and 2011. It may well be that Standard and Poor's downgrade of U.S. debt from AAA to AA+, which kicked off that wild week in August, was a greater cataclysm than imminent all-out nuclear war between the United States and the Soviet Union, but it's difficult to believe.

By some metrics, 5 of the 10 most volatile years since 1929 have been just since ECNs were introduced—the other 5 were 1929 through 1933—and the public is turning away from these markets. CNBC's "All-America Economic Survey" in December 2011 showed that affluent Americans, the ones most likely to invest in the market, were negative about investing in stocks, and by a large margin said volatility was the main reason why.[17] Steve Liesman of CNBC said, "This group of people, the investor class, the financial elite, they have become down on stocks.... These are the people that are worried about volatility, so it's really interesting to us to see those people who are aware of what's going on, all this volatility in stocks seems to be turning off some critical demographics to the stock market." According to the Investment Company Institute, from the Flash Crash until the end of March 2012, investors pulled nearly $250 billion from domestic stock funds, or 5% of domestic stock fund assets. Aside from a similar exodus at the depths of the financial crisis in autumn 2008, nothing like it has happened in modern memory. Again, there is no doubt economic fundamentals drive markets. There is also no doubt HFT scalpers exacerbate volatility, day in and day out. As Andrei Kirilenko wrote in his paper, there was nothing special about May 6, 2010: "HFTs did not change their trading behavior during the Flash Crash." Instead, HFT scalpers liquidated inventory as a flock, and $700 billion disappeared in five minutes.

A particularly ironic example of a flash crash happened in the spring of 2012, when a company called BATS Global Markets attempted to go public. BATS Global Markets owns the BATS Exchange, one of the latest ECN-exchanges. Founded as an ECN in 2005 by Dave Cummings of Tradebot, the SEC granted BATS an exchange license in 2008. The company planned to list its shares on its own stock exchange and go public on March 23, 2012. What happened instead was a disaster. Though BATS has a well-deserved reputation for high quality computer systems, it ran into a bug during its initial public offering. The bug delayed trading as the company tried to sort through the problem. After it finally posted its first trade, NASDAQ started trading the stock. The first BATS trade was at $15.25 a share, but almost immediately market makers on NASDAQ quoted BATS at $10.98 a share, and then at $8.03, and then $4.17, and then ever lower at blazing speed. It took precisely 1.372 seconds for the price to crash all the way from $15.25 to a fraction of a penny a share, a textbook example of a mini flash crash. While BATS was being brutally flayed during its debut, not one of the SEC's reforms instituted since the Flash Crash had any effect at all. Never before had a stock market's own shares flash crashed to oblivion. NASDAQ market makers simply withdrew for "safety," the same reason why Cummings said Tradebot withdrew in the Flash Crash. The episode made headlines around the world and forced BATS to rescind its IPO.

Meaningful stock market reform must reverse at least some of the anarchy of the last 10 years. HFT market maker scalpers should take on material market obligations before they're handed any market privileges. Already the privileges they enjoy have enabled them to insert themselves in up to three-quarters of all stock market trading and to earn more than old-school market makers. Along the way their behavior has destabilized markets.

Regulators must shed light on all these business practices. Regulators should require any firm deploying a market making strategy to register as a market maker, and market makers should post genuinely competitive market quotes at all times. Changes in market maker holdings during the day should be reported to facilitate review by regulators. Most important, market makers must have standards for exactly when and how they can adjust their inventories, and they should be prevented from demanding liquidity if it accelerates price changes. Market makers should also report to regulators when they supplied liquidity and when they demanded it, by security, across all venues, along with their per-trade profits.

Regulators should also carefully evaluate exchange trading rules, particularly the role order time-of-entry plays in trading. Order time priority at a price is behind many of the problems about which critics worry. As a simple reform, giving priority to the public's orders at a price ahead of any professional orders at that price, just as it used to be before deregulation, is better for the market than today's never-ending chase for speed. Bluntly, time priority has lost legitimacy. It lost legitimacy because exchanges learned how to charge for it, so HFT scalpers pay the exchanges for infinitesimal time advantages over other firms and the public and then send and cancel millions of orders a day to game the system.

Over time these firms have expanded their advantages and privileges over other investors, and, as was once true, they should keep those advantages and privileges only if they provide real services to the market in all market conditions. With their many privileges must come responsibilities, something we once understood instinctively. If they can't or won't fulfill those responsibilities, they shouldn't have any of their privileges.

A few hours after the Flash Crash, Senator Kaufman said, "The potential for giant high-speed computers to generate false trades and create market chaos reared its head again today. The battle of the algorithms—not understood by nor even remotely transparent to the Securities and Exchange Commission—simply must be carefully reviewed and placed within a meaningful regulatory framework soon."[18]

Two years later, we're still waiting.

Endnotes

1. CFTC and SEC, "Findings Regarding the Market Events of May 6, 2010."

2. Julie Creswell, "Speedy New Traders Make Waves Far from Wall St.," *The New York Times* (May 16,2010), The New York Times website, http://www.nytimes.com/2010/05/17/business/17trade.html.

3. David Easley, Marcos M. Lopez de Prado, and Maureen O'Hara, "The Microstructure of the 'Flash Crash': Flow Toxicity, Liquidity Crashes and the Probability of Informed Trading," *Journal of Portfolio Management* vol. 37, no. 2, Winter 2011, Social Science Research Network website, http://papers.ssrn.com/sol3/papers.cfm?abstract_id=1695041.

4. Andrei A. Kirilenko et al., "The Flash Crash: The Impact of High Frequency Trading on an Electronic Market" (May 26, 2011), Social Science Research Network website, http://papers.ssrn.com/sol3/papers.cfm?abstract_id=1686004.

5. Nanex, "Flash Equity Failures in 2006, 2007, 2008, 2009, 2010, and 2011" (Nov. 29, 2010, updated Feb. 4, 2011), Nanex website, http://www.nanex.net/FlashCrashEquities/FlashCrashAnalysis_Equities.html.

6. Joint CFTC-SEC Advisory Committee on Emerging Regulatory Issues, "Recommendations Regarding Regulatory Responses to the Market Events of May 6, 2010" (February 18, 2011), Securities and Exchange Commission website, www.sec.gov/spotlight/sec-cftcjointcommittee/021811-report.pdf.

7. Seymour Smidt, "Trading Floor Practices on Futures and Securities Exchanges: Economics, Regulation, and Policy Issues" (1985), American Enterprise Institute for Public Policy Research, Farm Decision Outreach Central-University of Illinois website, http://www.farmdoc.illinois.edu/irwin/archive/books/Futures-Regulatory/Futures-Regulatory_chapter2.pdf.

8. Steven Manaster and Steven C. Mann, "Life in the Pits: Competitive Market Making and Inventory Control" (1996), *Review of Financial Studies* vol. 9, issue 3, 1996: 953-975, EconPapers website, http://econpapers.repec.org/article/ouprfinst/v_3a9_3ay_3a1996_3ai_3a3_3ap_3a953-75.htm.

9. Richard Lyons, "A Simultaneous Trade Model of the Foreign Exchange Hot Potato," *Journal of International Economics* vol. 42, issues 3-4, May 1, 1997: 275–298, Science Direct website, http://www.sciencedirect.com/science/article/pii/S0022199696014717.

10. Joon Chae and Albert Wang, "Who Makes Markets? Do Dealers Provide or Take Liquidity?": 2 (Aug. 24, 2003), Massachusetts Institute of Technology website, http://web.mit.edu/finlunch/Fall03/AlbertWang.pdf.

11. Andrew G. Haldane, "The Race to Zero" (July 8, 2011), Bank of England website, http://www.bankofengland.co.uk/publications/speeches/2011/speech509.pdf.

12. Mary L. Schapiro, "Speech by SEC Chairman: Remarks Before the Investment Company Institute's General Membership Meeting."

13. LaBranche, "Annual Report Pursuant to Section 13 or 159D) of the Securities and Exchange Act of 1934 for the Fiscal Year Ended December 31, 2004," Securities and Exchange Commission file 001-15251 (no date provided), Securities and Exchange Commission website, http://www.sec.gov/Archives/edgar/data/1089044/000110465905016691/a05-6438_110ka.htm.

14. Extrapolated from Jonathan Brogaard, "The Activity of High Frequency Traders" (July 16, 2010), Social Science Research Network website, http://papers.ssrn.com/sol3/papers.cfm?abstract_id=1938769.

15. Tradebot Systems, About Us page, Tradebot Systems website, http://www.tradebot.com.

16. Nanex, "New SEC Limit Up/Down Proposal Would Have Made Flash Crash Worse" (Aug. 2, 2011), Nanex website, http://www.nanex.net/research/LimitUpDown/LUD.Simulated.html.

17. "To Invest or Not To Invest?" video at CNBC website (Dec. 7, 2011), http://video.cnbc.com/gallery/?video=3000061073.

18. Edward E. Kaufman, "Kaufman Statement on European Debt Crisis, Sudden Stock Market Plunge" (May 6, 2010), University of Delaware website, http://green.lib.udel.edu/webarchives/kaufman.senate.gov/press/press_releases/release/-id=3998fbbf-ceb5-4c20-b1d0-11e9c7cbc280.htm.

12

Killing the Stock Market
That Laid the Golden Eggs

Guest Chapter by David Weild and Edward Kim

Introduction by Sal and Joe: *David Weild stepped up to the podium. It was October 2011, and he was about to address a roomful of finance executives in Atlanta at an event called The CFO Roundtable. Behind him, his first slide lit up on the screen: "The Tipping Point: Is Stock Market Structure Causing More Harm Than Good?" Little did they know it, but these CFOs were about to get an eye-opening look at how the stock market has been failing them.*

Weild organized a well-informed panel: Mark Grier, vice chairman of Prudential Financial; Jeff Connaughton, former chief of staff to U.S. Senator Ted Kaufman; and Joseph Saluzzi of Themis Trading. Weild's presentation showed the rapid decline in the number of IPOs and linked that to America's worrisome job loss. The crowd paid close attention when Weild and the panelists described how the stocks of their companies have been tossed around like casino chips by the high frequency trading (HFT) community. Many attendees could not believe how much the market had changed.

One of Weild's goals was to get the corporate investor community to start raising its voice in the market structure debate. By the end of the presentation, he accomplished that as the audience wanted to know more and how they could help. This is just one example of what Weild and his writing partner Edward Kim have been doing for the past three and a half years.

195

Weild and Kim have conducted pioneering research demonstrating that our market structure has harmed the economy, and they have become vocal critics of our one-size-fits-all stock market, calling for a new, parallel market for companies with less than $2 billion in market capitalization. We are honored to include this chapter in our book.

Weild is the founder and chairman of Capital Markets Advisory Partners and heads capital markets at Grant Thornton, a leading audit, tax and advisory firm. He was formerly vice chairman of the NASDAQ Stock Market in charge of the Corporate Client Division where he invented the Market Intelligence Desk that provided real-time insight to listed companies to help them understand why their stocks were trading up or down. Kim is a managing director at Capital Markets Advisory Partners. He was formerly senior vice president at the NASDAQ Stock Market with responsibility for developing new products and services for NASDAQ's Corporate Client Group. He also has worked as a research analyst, equity trader, and investment banker at an array of major Wall Street firms. Their critical and critically acclaimed studies include "A Wake-Up Call For America,"[1] "Why Are IPOs in the ICU?,"[2] and "Market Structure Is Causing The IPO Crisis—And More."[3] The problems documented by these studies led to the JOBS Act (HR 3606), which was approved by Congress with strong bipartisan support. David Weild was invited to the White House when President Obama signed the JOBS Act into law on April 5, 2012.

Stock markets are critical economic infrastructure required to create capital connections and support the acceleration of corporate growth in much the same way that on-ramps, bridges, roads, and tunnels are critical to connecting cities and building commerce. Corporate growth and commerce are the key elements critical for economic growth.

No one would argue that building commerce doesn't require adequate revenue (tolls) to fund the maintenance and development of on-ramps, bridges, roads, and tunnels. Cut too high a percentage of the tolls that fund the "instruments of commerce" and suddenly there is a budget shortfall: The infrastructure goes into disrepair, on-ramps are closed, bridges collapse, and roads and tunnels degrade to the point that traffic and commerce grind to a halt. Companies go out of business. The prices of goods go up. The variety of goods (choice) goes down. Consumers suffer. People lose jobs.

Stock markets exhibit fundamental causal relationships, too. Markets are dying in the United States because of the loss of the necessary tolls (commissions and trading spreads) to maintain proper function. We've stopped investing in the infrastructure required to support the building of corporations. Consumers are suffering. People have lost jobs—millions of jobs. We've killed the stock market that laid the golden eggs of our industrial and technological society for more than four decades.

(U.S. Treasury take note! Changes to stock market structure are exacerbating U.S. budget deficits by undermining tax receipts.)

To understand what makes a stock market vibrant and capable of supporting the financing of corporations and the economy, you must look to the broader ecosystem. This macro system must be constantly funded and grown to create the infrastructure capable of scaling to serve more and more IPOs, more and more publicly listed companies, and more and more investors. Stock market infrastructure doesn't consist simply of trade execution venues such as the NYSE, NASDAQ, BATS, Direct Edge, Liquidnet, ITG, or any of the other more than 50 trade execution venues and dark pools. These are just the "roads." The rest of the infrastructure required—the on-ramps, bridges, and tunnels—consists of investment bankers, equity research analysts, stock brokers, and traders needed to reach investors and support access to equity capital and the growth of corporations.

Just as commerce requires tolls to pay for bridges, roads, and tunnels, the stock market needs adequate tolls to fund investment in the maintenance and development of its on-ramps (investment banks); bridges (market makers committing capital); roads (trade execution venues such as the stock exchanges); and tunnels (analysts giving context for investors and context to brokers to support investors). What happened when the United States stock market cut its "tolls" (commissions and trading spreads) to provide near "free" (no cost) trading? While these changes were implemented with the aim to reduce costs for individual investors, the consequences were disastrous. As shown in Figure 12.1, the IPO market collapsed in 1998 and went into secular decline. Regulation ATS (alternative trading systems) ushered in the age of electronic order books, where customer limit orders could be posted at increasingly narrower increments. Almost immediately, the "tolls" that market makers could charge dropped from $0.25 per share to $0.03125 per share. To stem the subsequent losses, Wall Street cut sales, research, and capital that provided aftermarket support to small capitalization publicly traded companies.

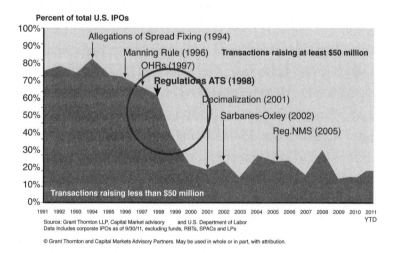

Figure 12.1 The small IPO market collapsed as the order handling rules and Reg ATS (electronic stock markets) cut "tolls" that were required to pay for support

Small investment banks shuttered their doors. Larger investment banks abandoned the once profitable small IPO underwriting business, deciding instead to raise their "minimum deal sizes"[4] to levels that effectively eliminated access to all but the largest private companies (or forced smaller companies to pursue highly dilutive strategies like reverse mergers). Investment banks dramatically cut back capital commitments on their desks, eliminated stock brokers, cut analyst compensation, and cut the depth and breadth of the research coverage offered to investors. Small companies lost support and were delisted. The number of new listings (IPOs) went below the number required to replace what is naturally merged or delisted off the major stock markets. The stock market contracted, and with it, the economy contracted. Companies went out of business.

Sound like a science fiction movie? Hardly. This is exactly what has happened to the U.S. economy: As shown in Figure 12.2, the number of companies leaving the U.S. stock markets has exceeded the number of IPOs every year since 1997, going on nearly 15 years.

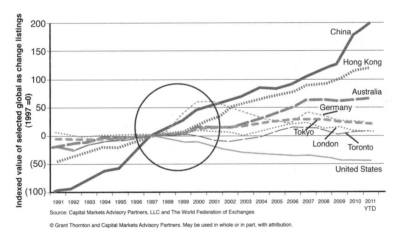

Source: Capital Markets Advisory Partners, LLC and The World Federation of Exchanges

© Grant Thornton and Capital Markets Advisory Partners. May be used in whole or in part, with attribution.

Figure 12.2 The U.S. stock market has shrunk every year since 1997 based on the number of publicly listed companies (down 43% since 1997)

Our low-cost, low "toll taking" stock markets are shrinking the economy, pushing companies out of business. This in turn will cause the price of goods to go up (through lower competition), and the variety of U.S.-derived goods will decline (if it hasn't already). People have lost and will continue to lose jobs. Disposable income has declined and will remain at lower levels than it need be. "Under-employment" is said to be 17%. Many workers have left the work force out of frustration. Consumers have suffered and will continue to suffer. In 1994, the year that professors William Christie and Paul Schultz first challenged why NASDAQ stock spreads all stood still at $0.25 per share,[5] there were 167 different investment banks that acted as a book running manager on at least one IPO that was at or under $50 million in size.[6] By 2004, this number had dropped to only 39 investment banks.[7]

To illustrate how much the IPO "on-ramp" has shriveled, you need to compare only the Microsoft IPO of 1986 to the LinkedIn IPO of 2011. On March 13, 1986, Microsoft went public, raising $58,695,000 through a management and underwriting group led by Goldman Sachs and Alex Brown (no longer in existence) and 114 other underwriters. (Most of these investment banks are also no longer in existence.) On May 18, 2011, 25 years later, LinkedIn went public in an IPO that was six times larger ($352,800,000) and yet was managed by an underwriting group less than one-twentieth of the size. (Only five firms underwrote LinkedIn: Morgan Stanley, Merrill Lynch, JP Morgan, Allen & Company, and UBS.)

Reversal of Fortune

In the 1980s, the annual number of IPOs peaked at 449. By the 1990s, that number had grown to an average of 520 IPOs a year and even exceeded an average of 500 IPOs per year in the five years *preceding* the Dot Com Bubble. Economists will tell you that it is reasonable to assume that the number of IPOs per year should grow in line with the growth of the economy. So, we asked, "How many IPOs should the United States be doing if the economy had grown at 3% per year from the early 1990s to present?" The answer? As shown in Figure 12.3, we would be enjoying 950 IPOs in 2011 growing to 1,000

IPOs in 2013. How many have we averaged since the end of the Dot Com Bubble in 2000? The answer: a paltry 129 IPOs per year.

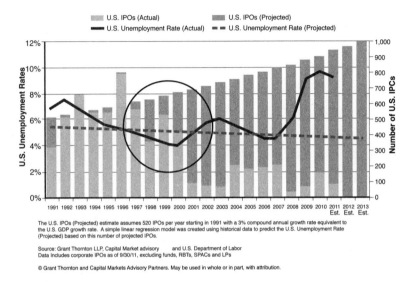

The U.S. IPOs (Projected) estimate assumes 520 IPOs per year starting in 1991 with a 3% compound annual growth rate equivalent to the U.S. GDP growth rate. A simple linear regression model was created using historical data to predict the U.S. Unemployment Rate (Projected) based on this number of projected IPOs.

Source: Grant Thornton LLP, Capital Market advisory   and U.S. Department of Labor
Data Includes corporate IPOs as of 9/30/11, excluding funds, RBTs, SPACs and LPs

© Grant Thornton and Capital Markets Advisory Partners. May be used in whole or in part, with attribution.

Figure 12.3 The IPO deficit: We should be approaching 1000 IPOs/year and <5% unemployment

Today, this IPO deficit has grown to more than 800 per year—that's the difference between the number of IPOs that should have occurred versus the number that actually occurred—and is directly responsible for a major part of the unemployment problem in the United States. Is it any wonder, as seen in the Figure 12.3, that unemployment tends to increase when the number of IPOs declines? We calculate the "loss" or lack of creation of between 10 million and 20 million jobs from the U.S. economy as a result of regulation-mandated changes. The depressive impact has rippled through the equity capital "supply chain," from IPOs to venture capital to start ups, and with it, the economy. Perhaps most notable among these changes was Reg ATS in 1998, which ushered the dawn of electronic trading in pennies (decimalization) and sub-pennies. This pivotal change and its implications were masked in large part by a weakened-credit standards real estate boom. As long as real estate prices were going up and jobs were created, the public and politicians didn't care that we were building our future on economic quicksand.

In each of the decades of the '70s (NASDAQ was started in 1971), '80s, and '90s, the U.S. economy produced in the neighborhood of 20 million net new jobs. It reminds us of that picture book exercise we walk our kids through: Which one of these decades is not like the other decades? Which of these decades had a stock market that was not like the other decades?[8] Today, as a result of unemployment, nearly one in four children in the United States now lives below the poverty line.

The IPO market in the United States was what once made the U.S. stock market the envy of markets and economies across the globe. It was our "Stock market that laid the golden eggs" of American prosperity. It epitomized the American Dream and was a major part of the formula through which we reinvented ourselves when industries matured and the economic baton was passed to lower wage-labor economies.

Today, Wall Street firms, regulators, securities attorneys, the NYSE, and NASDAQ increasingly agree that Reg ATS, which gave birth to electronic markets in 1998, enabled trading interests to proliferate the number of price points at which stock trades could be executed—from four or eight price points per dollar—to thirty-two and then one hundred by 2001 with decimalization. This nearsighted, if well-intended, action destroyed the trading spreads and commission model that paid for the IPO origination network of investment bankers, research analysts, institutional and retail stock brokers, and capital committers (traders) that in turn maintained a large-scale IPO manufacturing capability and aftermarket marketing for these companies' shares after they went public. Reg ATS killed the goose that laid the golden eggs of a U.S. stock market that the rest of the world envied for its capacity to embrace risk and drive entrepreneurship and innovation in ways that gave birth to entire new industries and drove U.S. economic leadership.

The Window Is Open! Oops! The Window Is Shut!

Wall Street likes nothing better than to cheer, "The window is open! The window is open!" They don't make money by telling issuers the truth—that these windows of financing opportunity are getting tougher and tougher to jump through—because their competitors are all too ready to paint a rosy outlook to secure another mandate. After all, mandates are nothing more than options to earn a fee for most investment bankers. The more options (mandates) an investment banker holds, the more fees he is likely to earn. As a general rule, investment bankers inflate valuations, outlooks, and their capabilities as an inducement to create more fee options. They have little incentive to tell issuers the truth: that all investment banks have undermined their equity distribution capabilities by shuttering middle market institutional sales groups and converting retail brokers into asset gatherers. That electronic stock markets and penny pricing, besides degrading their distribution capabilities, have exacerbated volatility (see Figure 12.4) and the incentive to provide aftermarket support. That the days are over when corporate issuers were an investment bank's most valued clients. That the vast majority of issuers today are viewed as product for a bank's most profitable clientele—the hedge funds and other actively trading or large institutions.

Today, IPO "windows" never open quite as wide and they slam shut at ever-increasing speeds. The marketing apparatus of Wall Street has been so degraded that IPOs are most accessible for stocks that have big, visible brand names (for example, LinkedIn, Pandora, Groupon, and Tesla Motors), not the vast majority of companies that need to be fully marketed. Wall Street no longer can afford the investment in aftermarket (post IPO) marketing infrastructure to cater to the thousands of institutional investors and hundreds of thousands of retail investors largely now self-directed due to neglect. It takes more than three times as long to get through the "window" for an IPO as it did 20 years ago (see Figure 12.5).

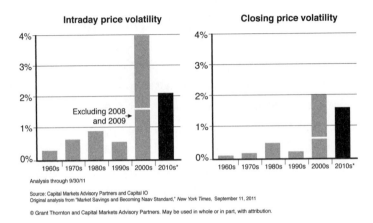

Analysis through 9/30/11

Source: Capital Markets Advisory Partners and Capital IO
Original analysis from "Market Savings and Becoming Naav Standard," *New York Times*, September 11, 2011

© Grant Thornton and Capital Markets Advisory Partners. May be used in whole or in part, with attribution.

Figure 12.4 Unprecedented volatility: Standard & Poor's 500 index moves of 4% or higher

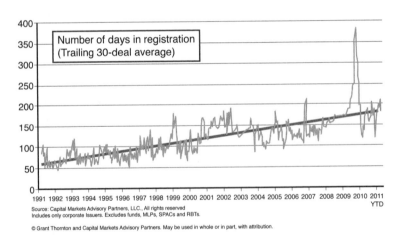

Source: Capital Markets Advisory Partners, LLC., All rights reserved
Includes only corporate Issuers. Excludes funds, MLPs, SPACs and RBTs.

© Grant Thornton and Capital Markets Advisory Partners. May be used in whole or in part, with attribution.

Figure 12.5 IPOs take more than 3x as long to get through the window (filing to pricing) than they did 20 years ago

Winds of Change?

Back in 2008, when we first began writing on this subject, most pundits still attributed the contraction in IPOs to "market cycles" and not "market structure." However, over the past year, our view has been increasingly accepted, and our work has been cited in Congress, the Senate, the SEC, the White House Job Council Report, the IPO Task Force Report to the U.S. Treasury, and an increasing number of academics. A recent Harvard Business School case study on SecondMarket, the secondary market for private stock, featured exhibits from our previous studies. There are now at least five capital formation bills in Congress, three of which may have been directly plucked from our study, *A Wake-Up Call for America*, and all of which were likely inspired by our studies. These capital formation bills were wrapped into the JOBS Act and signed into law by President Obama on April 5, 2012.

Although we are gratified to have ignited forces for constructive change on Capitol Hill, we fear that the bills now considered, although helpful, will miss the mark by treating the *Issuer Cost* problem while largely ignoring the other two problems that are at least as important: *Adequate Tolls* and *Issuer Disclosure*.

The good news is that we are no longer debating *"Did"* we kill the stock market that laid the golden eggs?" but *"How"* did we kill the stock market that laid the golden eggs? And *"What"* can we do to bring the golden egg layer back?

A Blueprint for Effective Stock Markets

All stock markets, private or public, require three legs to their stool:

- **Reasonable issuer costs:** The costs for issuers to raise capital cannot be prohibitive or issuers will stop accessing markets.
- **Adequate tolls:** There must be adequate *tolls* to pay for the investments in infrastructure necessary to sustain large-scale (many deals) capital raising and aftermarket support.

- **Adequate issuer disclosure:** There must be adequate and reliable disclosure (and concomitant enforcement) so that investors and buy- and sell-side analysts can evaluate companies and be kept abreast of their progress.

If our "stool" is lacking any of these legs, our stock market will sputter whether through issuer avoidance (issuer cost), lack of liquidity and a shifting of aftermarket burden onto the backs of issuers (inadequate tolls), or a loss of investor confidence (issuer disclosure and enforcement).

Private markets lack disclosure. Most of the bills in Congress are looking to cut costs for issuers by opening up private markets, whether it is through repeal of the prohibition against general solicitation (making it easier to market offerings) or increasing the number of shareholders before a company must register with the SEC. And although a case can be made that the tolls in the private market are much more adequate than in the public markets (OTC trades in private companies typically command a 2.5% commission on both sides of the trade for 5% of gross proceeds versus 1/10 of 1% for an institutional commission on a publicly traded stock), it is clear that private markets will take a long time to develop:

- Private markets lack *Information Disclosure* standards and apparatus such as the SEC's Edgar filing and dissemination system.
- Many investors are prohibited from participating in private markets.

Public markets lack adequate tolls. The JOBS Act, which passed both the House and Senate in a landslide with bipartisan support, requires the SEC to study the impact of decimalization on capital formation and report back to Congress. We believe this will pave the way for a debate on the much bigger need for adequate tolls to support the requisite infrastructure to build the on-ramps and aftermarket support in our public markets.

How do we know that adequate tolls are the "missing link" to bringing back our IPO markets? Because issuers that have filed to go public have demonstrated that *cost* is not an impediment to them and yet this sample set, which consists of increasingly larger and more mature companies, is failing to achieve a "Successful"[9] IPO at higher and higher rates (see Figure 12.6).

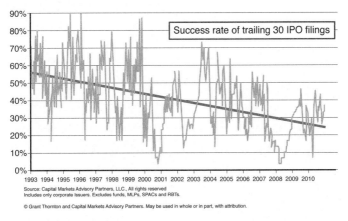

Success rate of trailing 30 IPO filings

Figure 12.6 IPO success rates have been cut in half since the dawn of Reg ATS and electronic markets

Contrary to the advice of many of the large investment banks that argue for larger IPO (fee) sizes, the worst performing (biggest decline) sample set of IPOs has been for the largest sample set of IPOs—deals that are larger than $500 million in size. This group of transactions is now "successful" less than 40% of the time (see Figure 12.7).

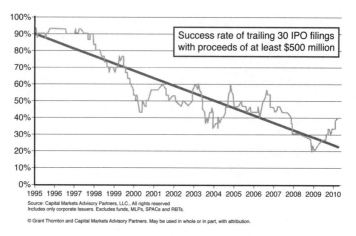

Success rate of trailing 30 IPO filings with proceeds of at least $500 million

Source: Capital Markets Advisory Partners, LLC., All rights reserved
Includes only corporate Issuers. Excludes funds, MLPs, SPACs and RBTs.

© Grant Thornton and Capital Markets Advisory Partners. May be used in whole or in part, with attribution.

Figure 12.7 IPOs > $500 million have demonstrated the steepest decline of all

Alternative Views

There are a number of alternative views of what happened to U.S. stock markets and why. We share them here. Some are quite interesting and may show that the depression in IPOs was an unintended consequence of other actions.

Arthur Levitt

Arthur Levitt was the longest tenured chairman in the history of the SEC. He seized on the study by professors Christie and Schultz in 1994 to attack the NASDAQ quarter point spread model as "price fixing." Levitt's focus, while cloaked in pro-consumer spin, may have been motivated to level the competitive playing field between NASDAQ and the American Stock Exchange; Levitt had previously been chairman and CEO of the American Stock Exchange. The NASDAQ dealer model, which was much more generous to the broker-dealer community than the American Stock Exchange specialist model, effectively destroyed the ability of the American Stock Exchange to win new listings. However, when Reg ATS was implemented in 1998, many new entrants came into the market and began to lobby for access to floor-based markets. An unintended consequence of Levitt's Reg ATS may have been that it backfired on the specialist system, ultimately leaving it vulnerable to Regulation NMS (National Market System), which was finally implemented in 2005.

Professor John Coffee

John Coffee is a professor of law at Columbia Law School. He is a noted expert in securities law and corporate governance. Coffee participated at the SEC Small Business Forum in 2011 and followed our remarks. He took issue with our characterization of Reg ATS (the advent of electronic markets) as being responsible for the loss of the small IPO, countering that, in the year preceding the adoption of Reg ATS, Rule 144 seasoning periods were shortened from two years to one year and that the small IPO market might have shifted over to the private placement market to account for the drop. We researched this and don't find any evidence of a shift into private markets to account for the loss in small IPOs beginning in 1998. Both practitioners and senior regulators that we have spoken to have generally agreed with us that Reg ATS destroyed the economic model that firms depended on to support small IPOs, and as was pointed out to us time and time again, "Private placements have been traditionally priced at significant discounts to public offering prices, so why would rational issuers divert to the private placement market unless the public market was closed?"

Dick Grasso and Richard Bernard

Dick Grasso was chairman and CEO of the New York Stock Exchange for many years. Richard Bernard was general counsel of the NYSE. In separate conversations with us, both shared the view that the NYSE specialist system, before the implementation of Reg NMS in 2005, caused specialists, who were earning excess profits on larger capitalization stocks that were inherently liquid, to reinvest a share of those profits to shore up liquidity in smaller capitalization stocks. This so-called allocation system, as a matter of public policy, recognized that smaller capitalization stocks needed investments made to drive liquidity.

Professor Lawrence Harris

Lawrence Harris is a professor of finance and business economics at USC Marshall School of Business and was formerly the chief economist of the Securities and Exchange Commission. Professor Harris maintained that some regulators sought to cut trading and commissions because it would have two effects:

- Eliminate sales practice abuses. Stock brokers would not earn a living and thus would no longer have an incentive to market stocks.

- Eliminate small IPOs because "Small IPOs fail at higher rates than large IPOs."

Back in 1971, there was a small technology company that was unprofitable on an operating basis. It was only three years old when it went public raising $8 million (about $44 million in today's dollars). It created a revolutionary product: the first commercially available microprocessor chip. After it went public, it actually missed its first delivery date, and investors cut its stock price in half. Talk about risk. That kind of company wouldn't even make it to the IPO stage in today's unforgiving market.

The name of that company? Intel. We sincerely hope that our regulators, in their haste to cut risk and sales practice abuses, didn't also neuter our economy.

The Case for Higher Cost Markets:
The Stock Market Toll Paradox

The Laffer Curve in economics shows that tax revenues drop as the tax rate approaches 100%—people just stop working. A corollary to the Laffer Curve is that tax revenues also decline when tax rates approach 0%. The implication then is that there is an optimum point of taxation.

We argue that like the Laffer Curve in economics, there is an optimum point for spreads and commissions ("tolls") in micro markets. That just like Goldilocks and the Three Bears, one toll rate was too high (pre-Reg ATS), the current toll rate is too low, and there must be toll rates somewhere in between that are "just right" (and will likely vary from stock to stock).

By charging consumers a higher "optimal" toll, we can better support capital formation and dampen volatility and speculation (which improves investor confidence), the combination of which can improve economic growth and investor returns. Thus, paradoxically, higher tolls actually drive higher returns to investors. *There is no free lunch.* If the United States wants to sustain a world-class capital formation infrastructure to fund entrepreneurs, job growth, and the American dream, it must be paid for!

The only question is how we determine what an optimal toll is for any given stock of any given industry. This is not a simple question but the answer is simple: If we create choice in toll rates for issuers and we let issuers decide what sort of toll structure will be applied to their stock, we will usher in a whole series of healthy conversations among issuers, support providers (investment banks, analysts, and brokers), and their investors.

The bet is that *market forces* (the pressure of investors and market makers on issuers) will cause issuers to choose the toll structure that ultimately results in an optimal market and improved cost of capital, and that a lower cost of capital can make American companies more competitive and more likely to access equity capital and to invest.

We have two recommendations that would open up the IPO market again.

Give Issuers Control over Their Tick Sizes

Imagine a department store that carried suits in only size 50 short, in purple tweed. Perfect for a select few—useless for the majority of consumers. Yet this department store is exactly what our stock markets are today. One size fits all. One set of rules for all listed companies, regardless of size, shareholder characteristics, trading volume, or liquidity.

Our markets today are tailor made for a small minority of stocks— those that trade in high volume with high information symmetry. For the vast majority of companies, the rigid regulations not only make little sense, but worse, they also may inhibit access to capital and increase the cost of equity capital, thereby undermining key reasons for listing in the first place.

In 2001, the centuries-old system of fractional price increments began to be phased out in favor of decimal increments, or tick sizes. All stocks, which used to trade in quarters, eighths, and sixteenths, were now living in a penny tick world. Although we do not dispute the move to decimal-based increments, it was senseless to force all companies to endure a minimum tick size of a penny. It's a suit in size 50 short when you're a 44 long.

Worse than senseless, the penny tick size has been destructive for small cap companies and the small IPO markets. It is simply not economically viable for small caps to be publicly traded entities in a penny tick market.

For the most actively traded stocks, yes, we concede a penny tick *may* make sense. But how can the same minimum be applicable to all stocks, regardless of price and trading characteristics? We submit that it would be far more logical to have different tick sizes for different stock prices, and different float values for companies in different industries.

One approach would be a system in which the issuer would determine its own tick size by vote of the board of directors after consultation with their investors, investment banks, research analysts, and stock exchanges. Wear a suit that fits in a color and fabric you like.

Within a decimal framework, issuers could select among several tick sizes, perhaps 1, 2, 3, 5, 10, and 25 cents. Small cap companies in particular may opt for higher tick sizes, recognizing the need to create a toll structure that would support capital commitment in trading, research coverage, and sales. Finally, this would also create a mechanism for issuers to throttle back on domination of their trading volume by high frequency traders.

U.S. Representative Schweikert (R-AZ), vice chairman of the House Subcommittee on Capital Markets, sponsored an amendment incorporated into the JOBS Act that allows the SEC to set higher tick sizes. It gives us great hope that the biggest problem facing capital formation—lack of a viable economic model to support small companies once they are public—will finally get the attention it so rightly deserves.

Call for a New Parallel Stock Market

By creating a new, parallel market for public companies under $2 billion in value and giving a seat at its governance table to institutional investors, member firms, and issuers, we could develop trading rules that allow for optimally higher spreads and commissions, which would balance interests and provide adequate incentives for small investment firms to get back into the business of underwriting and supporting small cap companies. Larger firms that have fled the small cap market might even be incented to return. More firms mean more competitive choice for issuers. Further, issuers would be allowed to choose on which market they list: the traditional penny-spread market or the "New Market." The SEC could use its authority under securities laws to exempt this market from rules standing in the way, or Congress could be proactive and create a legal framework to ease adoption.

This solution adds real substance, process, clarity, and shape to the rebuilding of our IPO market. It would allow issuers to choose the market option that makes the most sense to them while other established markets continue to operate as they do today. Most important, it would reignite the job-creation engine that once made U.S. stock markets the envy of the world.

One-size-fits-all stock trading has become a disaster for all but our nation's largest companies. Our rush to cut trading spreads and commissions has made large caps even more active—but we've abandoned the entrepreneur in the process. These are the people who take on most of the business risk and job creation in this country. With such inhospitable stock markets, mergers and acquisitions have become virtually their only outlet to realize value for their hard work.

And as we've so often seen during this tough economy, M&A generates job cuts, not new jobs.

Issuers need choice in market structure. The American people need issuers to have choice in market structure.

Our futures depend on it.

Endnotes

1. David Weild and Edward Kim, "A Wake-Up Call for America" (Nov. 2009), Grant Thornton International, Grant Thornton International website, http://www.gt.com/staticfiles/GTCom/Public%20companies%20and%20capital%20markets/gt_wakeup_call_.pdf.

2. Weild and Kim, "Why Are IPOs in the ICU?" (December 17, 2008), Grant Thornton International, Grant Thornton International website, http://www.grantthornton.com/staticfiles/GTCom/files/GT%20Thinking/IPO%20 white%20paper/Why%20are%20IPOs%20in%20the%20ICU_11_19.pdf.

3. Weild and Kim, "Market Structure Is Causing the IPO Crisis—and More" (June 2010), Grant Thornton International, Capital Markets Advisory Partners website, http://cmapartners.com/wp-content/uploads/2011/05/Market-structure-is-causing-the-IPO-crisis-June-2010.pdf.

4. Minimum deal sizes of large investment banks in the early 1990s hovered around $10 million. Today, the large investment banks generally cite minimum IPO sizes of $75 million and attribute this increase to institutional investor "liquidity" requirements. However, these minimum deal sizes are more likely reflective of the potential for deal profitability (fee sizes) and the misalignment of investment banks with investors in smaller-sized public companies: In the early 1990s, when NASDAQ traded in quarter point increments, a book running manager could triple its IPO profits during the first year of aftermarket trading, and book running managers typically enjoyed 60% of the IPO economics. Today, most IPOs have joint book runners, and firms may enjoy only 30% of the IPO economics. The combination of loss of aftermarket profitability and multiple managers has the effect of raising the deal size as much as 6x for investment banks to approach comparable aggregate fees in the post RegATS, post-Decimalization environment.

5. William G. Christie and Paul H. Schultz, "Why Do NASDAQ Market Makers Avoid Odd-Eighth Quotes?" 1994.

6. Dealogic, database tool, http://www.dealogic.com.

7. The decline in the number of investment banks acting as book running manager is likely understated since in 1994 it was industry practice to have only one book running manager per IPO while by the early 2000s the practice had changed to include multiple book running managers.

8. Prior to NASDAQ in 1971 (and prior to the deregulation of commission structures commonly known as "May Day" in 1975), growth company IPOs were taken public and traded in the over-the-counter market or on smaller stock exchanges. The NYSE did not generally list IPOs, deeming them as being insufficiently seasoned and too risk for the "Big Board," and broker-dealers enjoyed a regulated commission structure that provided the economic model necessary to support the investment in a standing infrastructure of bankers, analysts, salesmen, and market makers.

9. We define a "Successful IPO" as an IPO priced within one year of filing with the SEC, priced at or above the low end of the original price range filed with the SEC, and trading at or above issuer price 30 days after the IPO. These are minimally acceptable standards for issuers to deem their IPO a success. IPOs that take longer than a year to consummate are priced below the low end of the range or break IPO price generally represent grave disappointment and potential financial disaster for their backers.

13

Call to Action

Get ready, Mark. That incredible company you've been nurturing since Harvard is about to become one of the biggest casino chips on Wall Street.

After trading in "private markets" among only sophisticated investors, Mark Zuckerberg's Facebook plans to go public in one of the largest and highest profile events on Wall Street decades. We recently penned an open letter to the young CEO on our firm's blog about who is likely to dominate the trading of his firm's stock:

> You may be thinking that regardless which exchange you pick, your stock will help investors create wealth by investing in your company for the long term. Ever hear of rebate arbitrage? Latency arbitrage? Colocation? Private data feeds? Actionable IOIs or dark pools? Probably not, but that's what stock trading is all about nowadays.
>
> Your stock will now be traded by high frequency traders who have an average holding period of 22 seconds.[1] The majority of them won't care about your earnings or your new "likey like" button. They won't care about how many gazillion users you signed up or how many eyeballs are on your site. They will care only about flipping your stock for a very small profit—millions of times per day. They will care only about getting paid a rebate of roughly 1/3 penny per share to "add liquidity" in your stock. They are not looking to invest in Facebook; they are looking at

it as a tool to help them make money in their high-speed arbitrage world.

Also keep in mind that one-third of your stock will be traded in dark pools that are off-exchange and away from the public's eye. Know that even though the spread in your stock will be a few pennies (most of the time), your stock will not necessarily be liquid. Sure, your stock will trade a lot of volume, but this is not the same as liquidity. Know that when your stock starts to move around intraday by 3–5%, there will be no one to call to ask what is going on.

In their quest to modernize the stock market, our regulators ended up creating a monster that we doubt they ever could have imagined, although we do think some of the results were intentional. They turned what was once a relatively simple process of matching buyers and sellers into a conflicted, fragmented, algorithmic nightmare where natural supply and demand no longer is responsible for setting prices.

In this book, we have illustrated the damaging effects of the conflicts of interests that are now deeply embedded in the stock market. We have shown how SEC regulations that were implemented over the past 15 years are the origin of many of the current structural deficiencies in the market. We have demonstrated how the role of a stock exchange has changed from an investor protection and capital raising model to a for-profit arms merchant. We have revealed the economic conflicts of interest buried in broker-sponsored algorithms and smart order routers. We have shined a light on the murky practices that exist in dark pools. We have disclosed how internalizing broker/dealers, who supposedly offer price improvement, really harm investors by cherry-picking their orders and financially modeling their behavior. We recapped the events of the May 6, 2010 Flash Crash, chronicling the abusive behavior of these internalizers. And we have shown how the HFT community has been taking advantage of our broken markets with almost no action taken by regulators to protect the investing public.

Get ready, Mark.

We Are Not Alone

Our critics—and we have plenty—say that we are just trying to promote ourselves with this book. They say we are old-fashioned brokers who can't keep up with technology. But pay close attention. Our critics will be the same insiders who wrote comment letters to the SEC exalting our incredibly robust market structure in the weeks preceding the Flash Crash. They were ones "talking their book," and they continue to do so today.

While we are prepared to bear the slings and arrows from this self-interested, short-term profit-oriented community, we are not alone in our opinion. Following is a sample of what other, leading market participants have been saying:

- Mark Cuban, famous entrepreneur, investor, and owner of the Dallas Mavericks basketball team: "The best analogy for (high frequency) traders? They are hackers. Just as hackers search for and exploit operating system and application shortcomings, traders do the same thing. A hacker wants to jump in front of your shopping cart and grab your credit card and then sell it. A high frequency trader wants to jump in front of your trade and then sell that stock to you."[2]

- Michael Price, president of MFP Investors and legendary value investor: "The SEC and the New York Stock Exchange...made a huge mistake allowing these computer-driven, super-high-speed order systems to front-run orders...and then re-offer it up a penny or two, to scarf a penny or two."[3]

- Leon Cooperman, founder of the Omega Advisors hedge fund complex: "The high frequency traders are turning the best capital markets in the world into a casino and scaring the public, and it's not in the public interest."[4]

- Jim McCaughan, chief executive of the asset management arm of Principal Financial Group, the giant insurance company: "High-frequency trading, fundamentally, when you look at what their algorithms are finding, [is] almost a structured way of trying to front-run."[5]

- Roger McNamee, cofounder of Elevation Partners, a private equity firm that owns stakes in *Forbes* and Facebook: "NASDAQ, once it went to flash trading, basically said we're not in capital formation anymore; we're just in the business of letting our market makers front-run their customers."[6]

- Charlie Munger, Vice Chairman of Warren Buffett's Berkshire Hathaway: "I don't think the rest of us have anything to gain in having massive trading between computers which try to outwit one another with their algorithms. To the extent that one succeeds, the rest of us are all paying...."[7]

There Is an Alternative

We realize that we have painted a bleak picture of a system destined to fail again. Poorly designed regulation and embedded industry participant conflicts of interest are going to be difficult to extract from the current equity market. Although we applaud the SEC taking steps to address market deficiencies, we fear that this process will take too much time. No doubt conflicted industry participants, who have been profiting handsomely, will try to slow any corrective reforms. We can no longer wait.

It is time to take our equity market back. We believe an alternative market structure needs to be formed. That is why we support

David Weild and Edward Kim's call in Chapter 12, "Killing the Stock Market That Laid the Golden Eggs," for the creation of a parallel market that offers real choice for the corporate issuer. These corporations have lost their voice in the equity markets. Nowadays, they are merely another observer watching as the high-speed players use their shares like chips at the HFT casino.

Weild and Kim believe the current market structure has eroded the economics of true market makers, resulting in a dearth of initial public offerings. In turn, this has cost the U.S. economy millions of jobs over the past 20 years. Traditional broker/dealers have been squeezed out of the capital formation process, creating a void that has been filled by new high frequency market makers. But unlike broker dealers of the past, these new market makers no longer help companies raise funds for expansion. Nor do they sustain an orderly market by providing research or committing capital to trading. While the ostensible victim has been corporate issuers, the ultimate victim has been you and every other American in the form of lost jobs, lost productivity, lost innovation, and lost wealth creation.

No wonder we are in such a mess.

For an alternative market to succeed, it must offer three incredibly simple features that no longer exist today:

1. Stocks would have to be traded by real market makers with obligations to supply capital at all times. These market makers would have affirmative and negative obligations. They would have to supply real liquidity, not phantom liquidity, and they should not interfere when the market is working without their assistance.

2. There must be minimum quote sizes based on the market cap of the stock and a minimum order life on all orders.

3. To reward market makers for creating a more stable two-sided market, there also needs to be a minimum spread that is wider than a penny.

No doubt, our critics will claim that this alternative is going in the wrong direction. They will say it is a step backward and will bring back all the problems that we had with the old NYSE specialist and NASDAQ market maker systems. They will say that technology has moved us forward and made the markets more efficient. They will tell us that you can't turn back the clock. You can't put the genie back in the bottle. You get the picture.

Getting a new market up and running will probably be extremely difficult. But if there is demand from the true owners of the market (institutional and retail investors) and the true sources of the equity market (publicly traded companies), then this new market has possibility. We have talked to hundreds of CFOs and corporate investor relations departments. They know something is wrong and are yearning for an alternative.

If approved and launched, this new market will have an immediate effect on our capital markets. Trust and confidence will be restored. The many months of domestic equity outflows will start to come to an end. Investors will start to pile back into stocks because they will believe that markets are properly valuing securities and that their orders are not bait for ultra-high-speed traders. Research and stock picking will become relevant again as margin returns to brokers who deploy capital toward the valuation of stocks for the long term. Correlation among assets will fall to more normalized levels as investors focus on individual companies, instead of mindless ETF tracking devices. Ultimately, capital will find its way back to innovative, job-creating companies.

A fantasy?

No.

It's all up to you.

Fight for Your Rights

If you've read this book up to this point, chances are you are as outraged as we are and want to know what you can to do protect yourself. Here is what we recommend.

Retail Investors

Retail order flow is extremely profitable for brokers who internalize it because it is "uninformed" or dumb and easy to trade against or manipulate. When your execution receives a sub-penny price improvement, it is probably because your order was sold by your broker to an internalizer or routed to a dark pool that has intercepted your order before it could go to the displayed market and receive an even better price.

Most online brokers use a smart order router to execute your trades. The router is smart for them because they can maximize their payment for order flow, but it is not necessarily smart for you. Did you ever try posting a buy limit order on the bid and wonder why your order seems to always be last to get executed? Most likely your broker routed the order to an exchange that pays him the largest rebate. This larger rebate means that your order sits on an exchange that is most likely last to interact with cost-minimizing broker smart routers. Your order will probably get filled when the market is about to move against you.

Here's what you can do:

- **Ask your broker whether you can direct your order to a particular exchange:** Most brokers have this ability, but some like to bury the details to try to prevent customers from using it because it is more expensive for the brokers.

- **Never use a market order:** HFT market makers pick off market orders and adjust their quotes to make your order interact with a less advantageous price. The Flash Crash was the ultimate example of why not to use market orders.

- **Find out where your broker plans to execute your order:** Rule 606 reports are where you can find the details of your broker's routing strategy. Rule 606 states: "Every broker or dealer shall make publicly available for each calendar quarter a report on its routing of non-directed orders in NMS securities during that quarter." Be on the lookout for an abnormally high percentage of orders executed on one venue. This may be good for your broker and the payment for order flow that it receives, but it may compromise your order.

- **Ask where your order has been executed:** Rule 606 also states, "Every broker or dealer shall, on request of a customer, disclose to its customer the identity of the venue to which the customer's orders were routed for execution in the six months prior to the request." Here you can see exactly where your orders have been going.

Institutional Investors

Because their order flow is much larger than retail, institutional investors face a different set of issues and need to protect themselves even more. Here's what we recommend to our clients:

- **Know your router:** What is the detailed routing preference of your smart order router (SOR) service? Routers usually preference the cheapest destinations first, but these destinations tend to be filled with high frequency traders trying to sniff out activities through thousands of orders and cancellations every second. In most cases, upon request, your SOR vendor can remove destinations. It might cost a bit more per share in commissions, but your trades will be better executed.

- **Learn whether your router sends actionable indications of interest (IOIs) to dark pools:** Some algorithms claim that these IOIs increase your fill rate, but they also may give a free look on your order flow to other market participants. Demand that your broker does not interact with any dark pool sending or receiving IOIs that may compromise your order.
- **Ask your broker for a daily report where your executions occurred and what type of order was used:** Check whether a majority of your executions are executed in "toxic" pools. Is your broker using a low-cost order that touches multiple venues before executing? Although this may lower your broker's cost, these order types may be "leaking" information on your order.

Publicly Traded Companies (Corporate Issuers)

One of the least talked about participants in the equity market are the publicly traded companies. It is their stock that has been turned into a casino chip over the past decade. The voice of the corporate issuer has been getting louder in this debate, but needs to be heard from more regularly. Here are a few things they should be demanding:

- Accurate, timely, and complete trading data so officials for publicly traded companies can fulfill their fiduciary duty to shareholders to know and understand how the company's currency—its shares—is used. The listing exchange should supply a trade summary that shows where the company's shares were traded, which brokers executed the trades, long versus short volume, and short interest—all in a format that is easy to access and study.
- Direct and advance notification whenever the listing exchange is applying to change the rules governing how stocks are traded.
- Fair access to analytics on the same level as the technological resources that the exchanges provide to parties trading stocks.

Raise Your Voice

You may be thinking that the insiders have the game rigged and your voice will never be heard. Not so. You are reading this book because we started asking questions, finding answers, and talking to people. The lesson we learned is that every voice in the market is important and needs to be heard.

Stay Informed

The market is dynamic. Investors need to keep up to be aware of the trading games that the exchanges and HFTs play. Many trade magazines and blogs offer detailed insight, and they are free. For example:

- **Advanced Trading:** www.advancedtrading.com
- **FT Trading Room:** www.ft.com/intl/trading-room
- **Securities Technology Monitor:** www. securitiestechnologymonitor.com
- **Tabb Forum:** www.tabbforum.com
- **Themis Trading Blog:** blog.themistrading.com
- **Zero Hedge:** www.zerohedge.com
- **Traders Magazine:** www.tradersmagazine.com

Comment

Investors should comment about proposals that they think are unfair. Before new regulations or exchange rules are implemented, there is a public comment period. Look for these proposals on the SEC's website at www.sec.gov and submit an email. Click the Proposed Rules tab and pay particular attention to the "SRO Rulemaking" section.

Demand Change

All investors should demand the following from regulators:

- **Ability to opt-out of private data feeds:** We can understand the exchanges publishing quotes and trades in their direct data feeds because those are visible on most trading systems. But what about all the other information in these feeds, such as data on cancellations and revisions? Why should exchanges be allowed to provide the equivalent of a DVR recording of every movement you make during the trading day? We believe you, the retail and institutional investor, own the data. It is information on your order that is being sold and distributed to high speed traders so they can model your behavior. Exchanges should give investors the ability to opt out of the private data feeds.

- **Eliminate the speed differential between the slower public SIP and faster private data feeds:** Why does the Securities Information Processor (SIP) produce a quote for the general investor that is significantly slower (and thus less accurate) than what HFTs can produce? The answer is that HFTs subscribe to services like colocation and access to private data feeds and can calculate the quote faster than the SIP. This has led to the HFT trading strategy called *latency arbitrage* that has been siphoning profits from investors for years. These two quotes should be synchronized.

- **Eliminate "phantom" indexes:** What you see when viewing an index intraday is different from what most HFTs see, creating additional opportunities for latency arbitrage. Most major indexes contain only trades from the primary listing exchange, which represents only approximately 25% of all trades. In addition, index values are updated only every few seconds, depending on the index. This entire situation raises serious questions

about the reliability and pricing of index-based trading products. Indexes should be calculated dynamically and include all
trades.

- **Real-time identification of which dark pool traded a
  stock:** Only trades that occur on exchanges identify where they
  take place. However, if a trade occurs in a dark pool, it appears
  on the tape only where the trade was printed or reported. For
  example, if a trade occurs in Dark Pool X, which reports the
  trade to the FINRA Alternative Display Facility, market participants will not know which dark pool traded the stock. Knowing which dark pool traded your order can assist investors in
  identifying toxic pools and allow them to get a better execution.
  The SEC raised this issue in 2009 but has yet to take action.[8]
  Considering that more than 35% of all trades now occur off the
  major exchanges, the investing public should demand identification of trade execution venues.

- **Eliminate the maker/taker exchange model:** Many
  exchanges pay brokerage firms to supply bids and offers, and
  thus make liquidity, and charge those who take it. This incen-
  tivizes brokers to send customer orders to venues where the
  broker can collect the best rebate versus best execution for the
  customer. This model should be replaced by a flat fee regardless of whether liquidity is added or removed. This would discourage broker-sponsored smart order routers from sending
  client trades to destinations that benefit the broker's economic
  interests and not their clients.

- **Introduction of an order cancellation fee:** More than 95%
  of orders are canceled primarily because HFTs use the rapid
  fire issuance and revocation of orders to "ping" the market like
  sonar to find real orders and then trade against them. These
  excessive cancellation rates stress the system and could lead

to outages. While some exchanges recently proposed adding a small cancellation fee to a subset of their clients, this does not go far enough. Just like mobile phone carriers that charge for bandwidth, market participants who generate excessive order cancellations should be charged accordingly. That's what the Joint CFTC-SEC Advisory Committee on Emerging Regulatory Issues recommended.[9] Unfortunately, although this was proposed in February 2011, nothing has been done yet.

Repair Our Broken Markets

Our markets will continue to remain vulnerable as long as we as an industry remain in denial that volume does not equal liquidity, and as long as we tolerate the for-profit exchange model, which generates its revenues by encouraging speed above all other concerns and safety.

Many believe that our post-Reg NMS automated market must be more efficient. They believe technology has been good for all investors and all publicly traded companies. We say, think again. Think about the effect this has had on small companies. Think about how many companies have either not grown or have been swallowed up by larger companies because their route to access the capital markets was cut off by the HFT roadblock.

After a decade of misguided regulation, or the unintended consequences thereof, we have been left with a mere shell of an equity market. The slightest hiccup and our new HFT market makers go running for cover. They are not there to profit from the smooth flow of capital. They are there to profit by taking advantage of retail and institutional investors and by scalping wealth from IRAs, 401ks, and government and corporate pension funds.

As this book is about to go to press, we have begun to notice a slight swing in the pendulum. Regulators and legislatures have begun to take some first steps in seriously examining the problem we have articulated in this book. In Europe, the European Securities and Markets Authority has started to analyze the dangerous effects of HFT. In the U.S., the CFTC has set up a Subcommittee on Automated and High Frequency Trading. We were proud to be selected as members and plan to use our voice to represent the retail and institutional trading community. The SEC is also starting to push harder on proposals such as the consolidated audit trail, a critical tool needed to oversee the market properly. These are encouraging signs, but we have seen many initiatives fall by the wayside in the past.

Enough is enough.

Make your voice heard.

It is time to repair our broken markets.

Endnotes

1. Michael Hudson, "History of US Shows Economy Grows When Top Tier Tax Rates and Workers' Wages Are High," Jan. 1, 2011, The Real News Network website, http://therealnews.com/t2/index.php?option=com_content&task=view&id=31&Itemid=74&jumival=6000.

2. Mark Cuban, "What Business Is Wall Street In?" May 9, 2010, Mark Cuban Weblog, Blog Maverick website, http://blogmaverick.com/2010/05/09/what-business-is-wall-street-in/.

3. Frances Denmark, "Five Questions: Michael Price on Problems at the NYSE," Dec. 17, 2011, Institutional Investor website, http://www.institutionalinvestor.com/Article/2950741/Five-Questions-Michael-Price-on-Problems-at-the-NYSE.html?ArticleId=2950741.

4. Lee Brodie, "Billionaire Investor Pens Scathing Letter, Says He's Fed Up," Nov. 30, 2011, Fast Money Halftime Report, CNBC website, http://www.cnbc.com/id/45493113/Billionaire_Investor_Pens_Scathing_Letter_Says_He_s_Fed_Up.

5. Jonathan Spicer and Herbert Lash, "Who's Afraid of High-Frequency Trading?" Dec. 2, 2011, Reuters News, Thomson Reuters website, http://hft.thomsonreuters.com/2009/11/20/quiet-evolution-drawn-into-the-light/.

6. CNBC Video, "Groupon Controversy & Social Media," July 27, 2011, CNBC website, http://video.cnbc.com/gallery/?video=3000034844.

7. CNN Money Video, "Munger: Cut banking sector 80%," May 1, 2011, CNN Money website, http://money.cnn.com/video/news/2011/05/01/n_charlie_munger_banks.cnnmoney/index.html

8. SEC, "Regulation of Non-Public Trading Interest."

9. Joint CFTC-SEC Advisory Committee on Emerging Regulatory Issues, "Recommendations Regarding Regulatory Responses to the Market Events of May 6, 2010."

Appendix

Themis Trading White Papers

This section reproduces some of the key white papers we started publishing in 2008 to explain market structure issues to our institutional trading clients. After posting these papers to the Themis Trading website and blog, many of them caught the interest of the financial media, regulators, and legislators searching for answers to all the volatile market activity we have seen.

—Sal Arnuk and Joseph Saluzzi

Contents

Toxic Equity Trading Order Flow on Wall Street: The Real Force Behind the Explosion in Volume and Volatility

December 17, 2008

Introduction

Retail and institutional investors have been stunned at recent stock market volatility. The general thinking is that everything is related to the global financial crisis, starting, for the most part, in August 2007, when the Volatility Index, or VIX, started to climb. We believe, however, that there are more fundamental reasons behind the explosion in trading volume and the speed at which stock prices and indexes are changing. It has to do with the way electronic trading, the new for-profit exchanges and ECNs, the NYSE Hybrid, and the SEC's Regulation NMS have all come together in unexpected ways, starting, coincidently, in late summer 2007.

This has resulted in the proliferation of a new generation of profitable, high-speed, computerized trading firms and methods that are causing retail and institutional investors to chase artificial prices. These high frequency traders make tiny amounts of money per share, on a huge volume of small trades, taking advantage that all listed stocks are now available for electronic trading, thanks to Reg NMS and the NYSE Hybrid. Now that it has become so profitable, according to *Traders Magazine,*[1] more such firms are starting up, funded by hedge funds and private equity (only $10 million to $100 million is needed), and the exchanges and ECNs are courting their business.

This paper explains how these traders—namely liquidity rebate traders, predatory algorithmic traders, automated market makers, and program traders—are exploiting the new market dynamics and negatively affecting real investors. We conclude with suggestions on what can be done to mitigate or reduce these effects.

To illustrate most situations, we use a hypothetical institutional order to buy 10,000 shares of a stock at $20.00 that has been input into algorithmic trading systems, which most buy-side traders use. Algorithmic or "algo" trading systems chop up big orders into hundreds of smaller ones that are fed into the market as the orders are filled or are in line with the volume of the stock in question. Typically, such orders are easy to spot as they commonly show that the trader has 100 or 500 shares to sell or buy.

Liquidity Rebate Traders

To attract volume, all market centers (the exchanges and the ECNs) now offer rebates of approximately ¼ penny a share to broker dealers who post orders. It can be a buy or sell order, as long as it offers to do something on the exchange or ECN in question. If the order is filled, the market center pays the broker dealer a rebate and charges a larger amount to the broker dealer who took liquidity away from the market. This has led to trading strategies solely designed to obtain the liquidity rebate.

In this case, our institutional investor is willing to buy shares in a price range of $20.00 to $20.05. The algo gets hit and buys 100 shares at $20.00. Next, it shows it wants to buy 500 shares. It gets hit on that and buys 500 more shares. Based on that information, a rebate trading computer program can spot the institution as having an algo order. Then, the rebate trading computer goes ahead of the algo by a penny, placing a bid to buy 100 shares at $20.01. Whoever had been selling to the institutional investor at $20.00 is likely to sell to the rebate trading computer at $20.01. That happens, and the rebate trading computer is now long 100 shares at $20.01 and has collected a rebate of ¼ penny a share. Then, the computer immediately turns around and offers to sell its 100 shares at $20.01. Chances are that the institutional algo will take them.

The rebate trading computer makes no money on the shares but collects another ¼ penny for making the second offer. Net, net, the rebate trading computer makes a ½ penny per share and has caused the institutional investor to pay a penny higher per share.

Predatory Algos

More than half of all institutional algo orders are "pegged" to the National Best Bid and Offer (NBBO). The problem is if one trader jumps ahead of another in price, it can cause a second trader to go along side of the first one. Quickly, every algo trading order in a given stock follows each other up or down (or down and up), creating huge, whip-like price movements on relatively little volume.

This has led to the development of predatory algo trading strategies. These strategies are designed to cause institutional algo orders to buy or sell shares at prices higher or lower than where the stock had been trading, creating a situation in which the predatory algo can lock in a profit from the artificial increase or decrease in the price.

To illustrate, use an institutional algo order pegged to the NBBO with discretion to pay up to $20.10. First, the predatory algo uses methods similar to the liquidity rebate trader to spot this as an institutional algo order. Next, with a bid of $20.01, the predatory algo goes on the attack. The institutional algo immediately goes to $20.01. Then, the predatory algo goes to $20.02, and the institutional algo follows. In similar fashion, the predatory algo runs up the institutional algo to its $20.10 limit. At that point, the predatory algo sells the stock short at $20.10 to the institutional algo, knowing it is highly likely that the price of the stock will fall. When it does, the predatory algo covers.

This is how a stock can move 10 or 15 cents on a handful of 100 or 500 share trades.

Automated Market Makers

Automated market maker (AMM) firms run trading programs that ostensibly provide liquidity to the NYSE, NASDAQ, and ECNs. AMMs are supposed to function like computerized specialists or market makers, stepping in to provide inside buy and sells, to make it easier for retail and institutional investors to trade.

AMMs, however, often work counter to real investors. AMMs have the ability to "ping" stocks to identify reserve book orders. In pinging, an AMM issues an order ultrafast, and if nothing happens, it cancels it. But if it is successful, the AMM learns a tremendous amount of hidden information that it can use to its advantage.

To show how this works, this time our institutional trader has input discretion into the algo to buy shares up to $20.03, but nobody in the outside world knows that. First, the AMM spots the institution as an algo order. Next, the AMM starts to ping the algo. The AMM offers 100 shares at $20.05. Nothing happens, and it immediately cancels. It offers $20.04. Nothing happens, and it immediately cancels.

Then it offers $20.03—and the institutional algo buys. Now, the AMM knows it has found a reserve book buyer willing to pay up to $20.03. The AMM quickly goes back to a penny above the institution's original $20.00 bid, buys more shares at $20.01 before the institutional algo can, and then sells those shares to the institution at $20.03.

Program Traders

Program traders buy or sell small quantities of a large number of stocks at the same time, to trigger NBBO or discretionary algo orders, to quickly juice a market already moving up or down into a major drop or spike up.

Because so many algo orders are pegged and are pushed around by other high frequency traders, program traders are like a fuse. When they light it, that's when things happen. This is especially so in volatile markets when things are shaky and people are nervous like they are now. Many algo orders must achieve a percentage of volume that matches the market in the stock. So if the program traders can increase the volume on an individual stock just enough, they can trigger even more algo buying or selling.

Program traders profit by having an option on the market. Their objective is to push that option into the money by a greater amount than what they used to get the market moving.

Market Center Inducements for High Frequency Traders

Most HFT strategies are effective because they can take advantage of three major inducements offered by the market centers and not typically accessible to retail or institutional investors.

1. Rebate traders trade for free. Because they are considered to be adding liquidity, exchanges and ECNs cover their commission costs and exchange fees. This makes it worthwhile for rebate traders to buy and sell shares at the same price, to generate their ¼ penny per share liquidity rebate on each trade. Exchanges and ECNs view the order maker as a loss leader to attract the order taker. In addition, the more volume at different prices, even if that means moving back and forth a penny, the more money the market center makes from tape revenue. Tape revenue is generated by exchanges and ECNs from the sale of data to third-party vendors, such as Bloomberg for professional investors and Yahoo for retail investors.

2. Automated market makers colocate their servers in the NASDAQ or the NYSE building, next to the exchanges' servers. AMMs already have faster servers than most institutional and retail investors. But because they are colocated, their servers can react even faster. That's how AMMs can issue IOC orders—immediate or cancel—sometimes known as *cancel and replace*. They issue the order immediately, and if nothing is there, it is

canceled. And that's how AMMs get the trades faster than any other investor, even though AMMs are offering the same price. AMMs pay large fees to the exchanges to colocate, but it obviously has a decent return on investment. According to *Traders Magazine*,[2] the number of firms that colocate at NASDAQ has doubled over the past year.

3. People often wonder whether it is fair or legal for program traders to move the market the way they do. Everybody forgets, however, that in October 2007, the NYSE publicly removed curbs that shut down program trading if the market moved more than 2% in any direction. The NYSE said it was making the change because "It does not appear that the approach to market volatility envisioned by the use of these 'collars' is as meaningful today as when the Rule was formalized in the late 1980s." On a more commercial level, the NYSE had been at a competitive disadvantage because other market centers that didn't have curbs were getting the program trading business.

What Is the Effect of All This Toxic Trading?

1. Volume has exploded, particularly in NYSE stocks, but you can't look at NYSE volume on the NYSE. The NYSE executes only 25% of the volume in NYSE stocks. You must look at NYSE listed shares across all market centers, such as ECNs, like the NYSE's own ARCA, or dark pools, like Liquidnet. *Traders Magazine*[3] estimates high frequency traders may account for more than half the volume on all U.S. market centers.

2. The number of quote changes has exploded. The reason is high frequency traders searching for hidden liquidity. Some estimates are that these traders enter anywhere from several hundred to one million orders for every 100 trades they actually execute. This has significantly raised the bar for all firms

on Wall Street to invest in computers, storage, and routing to handle all the message traffic.

3. NYSE specialists no longer provide price stability. With the advent NYSE Hybrid, specialist market share has dropped from 80% to 25%. With specialists out of the way, the flood-gates have been opened to high frequency traders who find it easier to make money with more liquid listed shares.

4. Volatility has skyrocketed. The markets' average daily price swing year to date is approximately 4% versus 1% last year. According to recent findings by Goldman Sachs, spreads on S&P 500 stocks doubled in October 2008 as compared to ear-lier in the year. Spreads in Russell 2000 stocks have tripled and quoted depth has been cut in half.

5. HFT strategies have become a stealth tax on retail and institu-tional investors. Although stock prices will probably go where they would have gone anyway, toxic trading takes money from real investors and gives it to the high frequency trader who has the best computer. The exchanges, ECNs, and high frequency traders are slowly bleeding investors, causing their transaction costs to rise, and the investors don't even know it.

What Can Be Done?

Forget about short sale restrictions. From a regulatory point of view, we believe two simple but powerful rules would help to elimi-nate much of the problem.

1. Make orders valid for at least 1 second. That will eliminate the pinging. High frequency traders will expose themselves. One second would destroy their ability to immediately cancel an order if nothing is there.

2. Reinstate the 2% curb on program trading. When the market is down 3% or 4%, that's when the program traders can juice it. The SEC, however, must institute the curb across the board so that no market center has an advantage over another.

With these two rules, at least half the volume of the exchanges and ECNs might go away. The market centers, however, will surely fight it because they don't want to lose the trading volume and the resultant tape revenue.

Until Then, What Can Investors Do?

Although there's little action that retail investors can take, we urge institutional investors to not "walk away from the machine" after they enter an algo order.

Algo and other electronic trading systems have lulled many institutional traders into a false sense of security. These traders like the electronics because they can enter orders directly and they don't need to bother with sell-side brokers. The trades are cheaper, at 1–2 cents per share versus 4–5 cents. And the performance seems adequate; the trades get done in line with standard metrics, such as the volume weighted average price (VWAP). These traders, however, may not realize that the VWAP might have been 1 to 3 cents per share higher or lower because of toxic order flow. So in the end, institutions might pay 5 cents per share or more for their trades.

We also recommend that institutions use algo systems for only the most liquid of stocks. Anything less must be worked, the same as in the "old days." Institutions need to relearn how to "watch the tape" and take advantage of, or work around, high frequency traders.

Achieving best execution has never been more challenging.

What Ails Us About High Frequency Trading?

October 5, 2009

"What the _____ is going on?" our client asked. "This is screwing our investors!"

It was the mid-1990s, and it was our first experience with High Frequency Trading (HFT), which has since grown to become one of the hottest controversies in securities trading today. Our client was a classic, buy and hold institutional investor, managing money for 401ks and pensions. At the time, we were agency institutional traders working at Instinet.

Our client had begun to notice how the Instinet top-of-book, which was not part of any national quote, was generating automated orders from a handful of firms that shadowed our institutional clients. These automated orders would match or better our clients' orders by an eighth or sixteenth (no decimals back then).

"Why is it that every time I put in an order in ABCD, these guys go behind me, or bid ahead of me, and when I cancel, they do, too?" our client asked. "They are forcing me to pay more to buy or sell for less!" So began our mission to help institutional investors cope with challenges created by HFT. Because HFT represented only approximately 15% of the volume until about the mid-2000s, it was a manageable situation.

Then Something Happened

We began to notice a greater amount of "wiggle" in stock prices when we traded for clients. Our clients would lament to us as well, even as they traded their own orders. Daily we heard how trading had become like a cage match. Daily our clients would detail how they would have to explain to their portfolio managers why they were light on volume—why they got only 2,400 shares bought, with the stock $1.50 higher on only 16,000 shares.

What we learned amazed us. HFT was now accounting for as much as 50–70% of the volume. And under every rock we turned, we found HFT engaged in (1) what clearly looked like a questionable practice that cost institutional investors money or (2) raised questions whether HFT was enjoying an unfair advantage versus classic institutional investors.

In response, we alerted our clients to what we learned. Eventually, others began to raise questions, too, including Senators Kaufman and Schumer. The SEC proposed banning the practice of flash order and has begun to look into other areas, such as dark pools, colocation, and how technology and automated trading have changed the market. HFT is categorized by the rapid trading of thousands of orders systematically and automatically, by computers analyzing instantaneous changes in prices and quotes. We have three issues with HFT.

HFT's Dominance May Be Affecting the Health of the Market

First, at an estimated 50–70% of all equities volume, HFT has gotten too large for the marketplace. HFT volume has exploded because of regulatory rule changes, technological innovations, exchanges going for-profit, and a global stock market sell-off that decimated traditional volume. It is here and now, with HFT so prevalent in this current marketplace, that institutional traders have begun to feel HFT's negative effects in such disproportionate ways.

Although we accept HFT's presence and tolerate it at a "normal" rate and existence in the market, at today's extremely high presence, it deserves a commensurate amount of attention.

We offer this analogy: The market is like an ocean. To the extent that there are many different trading styles and participants trading against and interacting with each other, the market is healthy, like an ocean teeming with many species. But when one participant accounts for so much volume, something is out of balance, the same as an ocean where one of its more predatory species, such as a shark, becomes the dominant inhabitant.

HFT Predatory Trading Taking Advantage of Unfair Practices

The second issue we have with HFT is with the predatory aspects of its practice as opposed to HFT rebate-driven and mean reversion trading. HFT predatory algorithms are proprietary trading engines designed to detect meaningful order flow in the market and trade around it. If all market participants had equal access to all public quotes and trade prints at the same time, you could make the argument that it is just a highly efficient form of day trading. However, if one group of participants had access to order flow before others or makes use of "internalization" dark pools for predatory purposes, those participants, with their low latency, colocated servers, would have an unfair advantage in the marketplace.

Although we believe the NYSE study that demonstrates that the top large cap stocks have benefitted from HFT with increased quote sizes and narrowed spreads, we believe smaller capitalization stocks have suffered with wider spreads, smaller quote sizes, and more volatility.

In the smaller and more difficult trading names of the small and midcap universe, no one extols the virtues of HFT liquidity. Instead, you hear traders cursing as offers get lifted impossibly ahead of them, just as they decide to lift them due to predatory algorithms. The SEC has taken a first major step in controlling predatory trading with its proposed ban of flash order types. Flash orders were a carrot dangled by for-profit market centers in front of high-volume players to entice them to play in one exchange's sandbox over another's. HFT proponents argued flash orders were no different from the old stock exchange floor, where some players got to see or overhear floor brokers before trades hit the tape.

We have a different analogy. Imagine you are at the grocery store. You take your cart to one of five apparently empty checkout lines. Suddenly, nine carts instantaneously appear ahead of you. You scratch your head and move to lane two. The same thing happens. You soon find that whenever you move into a new lane, a multitude of carts appear ahead of you in line.

Why? Because the supermarket has sold the right for those carts to do so. Thus, you can never be at the head of the line, no matter what you do, short of paying the exchanges a large fee to have that same right to cut ahead of someone else. In real life, this enabled HFTs to turn around and buy or sell stock to you for a penny or two more or less than the market was before you submitted your order. Thus, you could never obtain a real NBBO on a reliable basis.

Originally, flashing was defended as offering price improvement to the "flashee" or as being inconsequential. (Only 3–5% of executions are the result of flashing, which takes no account of flashed orders that did not buy or sell at the intended price due to being beat to the quote.) However, as soon as politicians and regulators began to look at it and understand it for what it was, nearly all those defenders have reversed themselves and now say flashing is wrong.

Given that flash was instituted by major exchanges and market centers knowing its unfair nature, what other innovations of recent years are similarly unfair in their nature and contrary to the public's interest? Although many dark pools are valuable to all investors and certainly to large institutions and mutual funds that need to source liquidity in the ever increasingly fragmented marketplace, there is one class of dark pools whose value we question, namely the "internalization" pools.

What toxic and proprietary flow swims in these pools, designed to sniff out intentions of the buy-side? Is this desirable? Is the trade-off (of meaningless 5/1000 of a penny price improvement on 186 shares) worth the opacity we are accepting? Are these pools contrary to Reg ATS and do they offer fair and equal access to prices by all investors (and not just the fastest)? Are these pools fed automatically by your trading system's router? These are valid questions, whose debate we believe would be valuable for the public, similar to the flash debate.

HFT Trading Possibly Affecting Asset Valuations

The third issue we have with HFT is that we are concerned that it causes a disconnect between market prices and real asset values. As everybody knows, the value of security assets is based on the pricing established every day by market trading. But shouldn't we be wary of the pricing of a good if 70% of the transactions taking place are done by a few large players? Would you prefer to buy a diamond in a marketplace controlled by one family or in a marketplace controlled by many players? Given the wild volatility in the oil market in the past few years, and now in currency, commodity, food, and securities, are we avoiding examining another systemic risk?

To conclude, we are not antiprogress or antitechnology. Our entire careers have been spent at firms that have innovated with technology. And we have no issue with any firms that want to spend whatever they choose for better technology. However, we do have an issue if that technology is combined with unfair practices to give an advantage to one group at the expense of the general public.

Finally, we believe in balance. If we were charged with making sure our markets were fair for everyone and a model for the world to emulate, we would examine whether a model and successful marketplace were defined solely by whether it had the speed to execute a million orders per second. Although we believe in free markets, giving up fairness and equal low cost access for all might be a steep price to pay for sub-penny price improvement and increasingly opaque and multitiered markets.

Latency Arbitrage: The Real Power Behind Predatory High Frequency Trading

December 4, 2009

Introduction

In previous white papers, we have discussed several High Frequency Trading (HFT) strategies and tactics, such as Liquidity Rebate Trading, and more predatory styles, such as flash, dark pool pinging, and predatory algorithms (or algos). It is the predatory styles that first alerted us to HFT because of its detrimental impact on traditional institutional and retail investors. In this paper we address the practice of Latency Arbitrage, which is more than a simple case of technological evolution but raises serious questions about the fairness and equal access of U.S. equity markets that have made them the envy of the world.

Most industry professionals have been aware of the term Latency Arbitrage as it applies to HFT. The common assumption is that it refers to the spending or "arms" race in which high frequency traders employ high-speed hardware, software, and bandwidth to execute orders as fast as possible to gain an edge in trading. Because lower latency equals faster speed, Latency Arbitrage was viewed as a natural technological evolution that eventually would translate into more efficiency in the marketplace as the speed cascaded down to all investors. Talk of latency measured in milli-, micro-, and nanoseconds was considered background noise.

At the same time, most industry professionals have been aware of the term colocation as it applies to HFT. This is the practice of market centers, such as the major exchanges, like NYSE Euronext, NASDAQ, BATS, as well as alternative trading systems (ATS), like Direct Edge, to rent out space to HFTs to colocate their servers next to the market center's server, to further reduce latency. Although some industry officials have questioned the fairness of paying for such an advantage, there are no restrictions on which firms can colocate. Theoretically, any institutional or retail brokerage firm could do it to serve clients better.

The Reality of Latency Arbitrage

In practice, however, Latency Arbitrage means something completely different to HFTs.

First, it is about using cutting edge technology and colocated servers at exchanges and ATSs, combined with purchases of raw data feeds from these market centers, to create one's own inside National Best Bid and Offer (NBBO) quote and depth of book substantially earlier than what is publicly available from the Securities Information Processor (SIP) quote. The SIP feeds quotes seen on professional terminals, algo trading systems used by institutions for as much as 50% of their orders, and quotes seen by retail investors on Internet sites.

"It's like you're seeing *The Wall Street Journal* 5 microseconds into the future," said Kevin McPartland, a senior analyst at financial services research firm TABB Group, at a seminar in November sponsored by TABB and Switch and Data, a data center operator.[4]

Second, it is about using HFT techniques, such as Predatory Algos, immediate or cancel (or cancel and replace) orders, and dark pool pinging, to determine what kind of institutional algo orders are in the market, such as those driven by commonly used volume weighted average price (VWAP) formulas, and how those orders will react if the bid or offer of a stock moves up or down. These techniques, all of which also benefit from colocation, were initially outlined in our December 2008 white paper, "Toxic Equity Trading Order Flow on Wall Street."[5]

Armed with all this information, HFTs can achieve "...(almost) risk-free arbitrage opportunities," according to a report by Jefferies &

Company, Inc., an institutional brokerage firm.[6] To put it in layman's terms, "Those are the types of investment strategies that arbitrageurs and hedge-fund managers drool over," Richard Gates, a portfolio manager for TFS Market Neutral fund in West Chester, PA, who has studied latency arbitrage, told a blogger for *The Wall Street Journal*.[7]

Following is an example of how an HFT trading computer takes advantage of a typical institutional algo VWAP order to buy ABC stock:

1. The market for ABC is $25.53 bid/offered at $25.54.

2. Due to Latency Arbitrage, an HFT computer knows that there is an order that in a moment will move the NBBO quote higher, to $25.54 bid/offered at $25.56.

3. The HFT speeds ahead, scraping dark and visible pools, buying all available ABC shares at $25.54 and cheaper.

4. The institutional algo gets nothing done at $25.54 (as there is no stock available at this price), and the market moves up to $25.54 bid/offered at $25.56 (as anticipated by the HFT).

5. The HFT turns around and offers ABC at $25.55 or $25.56.

6. Because it is following a volume-driven formula, the institutional algo is forced to buy available shares from the HFT at $25.55 or $25.56.

7. The HFT makes $0.01–$0.02 per share at the expense of the institution.

It is currently estimated that HFT accounts for 60% of all share volume.[8] Based on our experience trading, we estimate that at least 10 percentage points of that is of a predatory nature. Based on current average daily volume of approximately 10 billion shares, approximately 600 million shares per day are subject to predatory HFT. At $0.01–$0.02 per share, predatory HFT is profiting $6–$12 million a day. At approximately 250 trading days a year, that's $1.5–$3 billion in profit generated from traditional institutional and retail investor assets under management.

The Speed Game

Today, the bulk of trading is not done by professionals analyzing fundamentals, charts, or patterns. It is not done by floor traders, agency traders, sell-side block traders, or institutional buy-side traders. Instead, it is done by proprietary trading firms, where computers analyze quote changes and trade prints. These firms need to receive and analyze an immense amount of data as fast as possible, and they need to generate and deliver orders to market centers equally as fast.

As a result, latency/colocation has become one of the fastest growing mini-industries on Wall Street. Latency has been steadily decreasing as hardware, software, and networking have improved and through the isolation of inefficiencies in circuits and cabling. Now a wide variety of consultants are available to develop ways for corporations and trading firms to reduce latency from endpoint to endpoint. There also is a continuous need to upgrade equipment.

Physical laws apply; reducing this distance can accelerate data input and output. Thus, HFT firms need to be as close as possible to all trading destinations. Jefferies estimates colocation creates a "100–200 millisecond advantage—over a regular vendor-based market data provider."[9] This is why the NYSE is constructing a 400,000 square foot facility in Mahwah, New Jersey and another one outside of London, at a combined cost of $500 million.[10] This is why NASDAQ and Direct Edge have facilities larger than multiple football fields, as well. These facilities all house servers and technology of outside trading firms, as well as the market centers' own data and matching engines.

According to a recent TABB report, "The financial services industry spends $1.8 billion for colocation and private facilities to support fast direct access to market centers. Broker-dealers account for half... exchanges 23%, proprietary trading firms 13%, asset managers 10%, and hedge funds 4%."[11]

Questions

We believe Latency Arbitrage raises three serious questions about market integrity.

1. The primary response from HFTs or market centers is typically "A penny or two should not matter to long-term investors; this is much ado about nothing," to paraphrase the CEO of a major ATS who was addressing a financial industry conference in New York City in early November. We disagree completely. It isn't $0.01–$0.02. It's $1.5–$3 billion. Which leads us to question number one: *Do HFT firms have an unfair advantage?* Most professionals on Wall Street have taken a standard from our past for granted: that everyone sees the same quote and market data at the same time. What if the time differential between what the HFTs see and what everybody else sees were 5 minutes instead of 5 milliseconds? Would that be acceptable? It is not the amount of time that matters. *It's that a differential exists at all.* Who would bet on a horse race if a select group already knew who won?

   Some of the exchanges make sure that each colocated customer receives equal amounts of connecting cable so that a server at the northeast corner of a facility has the same latency as one at the southwest corner. It appears that "fairness" and the equalization of market data speed *among* colocated firms is an important "must" for the exchanges, but not so when it comes to all other institutional and retail investors.

2. Latency Arbitrage has created a two-tiered market of technology-enhanced insiders (composed of a handful of large banks, brokerage firms, and hedge funds) and the rest of us. To be clear, HFTs enjoy this advantage only because market centers are selling them the right to colocate and access raw data feeds. As for-profit organizations, market centers are incentivized to do this. That leads us to question number two: *Is it fair to sell these*

*rights to the highest bidders when market centers are supposed
to be protecting all participants' interests equally?* At the end
of the day, aren't market centers charging HFTs a higher fee in
exchange for giving them an advance look at the NBBO?

3. It is entirely one thing for an HFT firm to use proprietary algorithms to try to predict how an institution's algo will operate so
that the HFT can out-maneuver the institution. And it is the
buy-side trader's fiduciary responsibility to protect his firm's
orders by adjusting execution methods and tactics regularly
to avoid predictability. Jefferies notes in its report that it "has
made a number of adjustments to our algorithms to counter
these issues."[12] That leads us to question number three: *When a
market center provides an HFT with the ability to out-maneuver
institutional orders, is not the exchange putting institutions and
their brokers in breach of their fiduciary responsibilities, especially those institutions managing pension funds governed by
Employee Retirement Income Security Act (ERISA)?*

Growing Institutional Concern

Institutional investors are slowly growing concerned about HFT.

- **Polls:** A recent Greenwich Associates survey found that 45%
of participating institutions believe HFT poses a threat to the
current market structure, whereas 36% believe it benefits the
market and investors by increasing overall liquidity. The balance say they do not know enough to judge.[13]

- **Research:** Quantitative Services Group LLC (QSG), a leading
provider of equity research and trading analytics to institutional
investors, completed a study that found significantly higher
impact costs and trading velocity are incurred for VWAP algorithms when compared to Arrival Price algorithms, especially
when applied to liquid, low-price stocks. "This is contrary to the

popular perception that VWAP strategies reduce trading costs through passive, less detectible, order placement strategies," QSG said. "The results suggest that High Frequency Trading strategies are materially contributing to these increased costs."[14] In addition to Jefferies, BMO Capital Markets has published research exploring the negative aspects of HFT.[15]

• **Media:** Trade media, such as *Securities Industry News*, have published by-lined articles, like "The Un(?)fair Advantage of Latency Arbitrage," by Ralph Frankel, CTO of Solace Systems.[16] As a result, the mainstream media is also becoming more aware of HFT. For example, *The New York Times* published a front-page story on July 24, 2009, titled "Stock Traders Find Speed Pays, in Milliseconds,"[17] and the *Financial Post* in Canada on November 7, 2009, ran a story titled "Traders of the Shadows."[18]

We believe that as more organizations explore HFT and its implications, awareness and concern among institutional investors, especially those responsible for public and private pension funds, will continue to gain traction.

Conclusion

Many professionals believed that Latency Arbitrage referred to the race by HFT firms to be faster than other traders in delivering their orders. We cared little about their technology war, as we thought their game was divorced from executing orders for traditional institutional and retail investors. We always thought HFT advancements in technology would benefit the market in general, as front-end functionality, speed, and efficiency filtered down. We have since found this not to be entirely true.

HFTs use Latency Arbitrage to reengineer the NBBO from end sources directly versus relying on the publically available standard SIP quote. HFTs can do this by paying exchanges and ATSs for the right to locate their servers next to market center data servers and matching engines and the right to access raw data feeds. As a result, HFTs know with near certainty what the market will be milliseconds ahead of everybody else—valuable knowledge that HFTs take advantage of when they trade thousands of stocks, thousands of times, every trading day. For HFTs, it is like shooting ducks in a barrel of honey. For all other institutional and retail investors, it is death by a thousand cuts.

To date, this situation has been tolerated because most investors were unaware that two different quotes existed and could not fathom that those in charge of overseeing the markets would allow this to happen. Why would most investors assume that they looked at different quotes? Why would most investors assume that they weren't watching the same horse race? Now we are at a crucial juncture in terms of our financial market's structure. The time has come for us to ask, "Is short-term fleeting liquidity (in our most liquid names) worth the trade-off to accept a multitiered and unequal market?"

SEC Comment Letter: Regarding File No. S7-02-10, Concept Release on Equity Market Structure

April 21, 2010

Dear Ms. Murphy:

Thank you for the opportunity to comment on the SEC's concept release. Over the past year, we have made it clear what we think about high frequency trading (HFT): that it is rife with problems that negatively affect retail investors and institutional managers of more traditional mutual funds, pension funds and hedge funds.

- We have written several white papers about HFT that can be found on our website at www.ThemisTrading.com.

- We maintain a daily blog (http://blog.themistrading.com) where we confront many issues surrounding HFT, such as whether it truly adds liquidity or shrinks spreads in other than the most active stocks.

- We have authored several articles that have taken on some prominent high frequency proponents and critiqued their defenses of HFT point for point.[19, 20]

We do not want to use our comment letter to review those arguments. Rather, we would like to focus on what we believe is the root of the problem that plagues the U.S. equity market—market structure.

Introduction

Regulations enacted by the Commission over the past decade, particularly Regulation NMS, have led to an enormous amount of unintended consequences, most notably fragmentation and the lack of transparency. The U.S. equity market is now a fragmented web of for-profit exchanges, ECNs, ATSs, and dark pools connected by high-speed, low-latency lines. Visible liquidity in all but the top

volume stocks has essentially disappeared as many market participants elect to hide in dark pools and piece their orders out in small
slices throughout the day. One of the main goals of Reg NMS was to
encourage displayed liquidity. It is now apparent that this goal was not
accomplished.

Traditionally, exchanges have competed for revenues in three
different areas: listings, transaction fees, and market data revenue.
A recent study by Grant Thornton details what the firm refers to as
"The Great Delisting Machine Timeline."[21] It details how a progres-
sion of regulation (including order handling, decimalization, and the
Sarbanes-Oxley Act of 2002) has destroyed the economic incentive
for traditional market making, investment banking, and research.

This lack of economic incentive has caused the removal of support
for capital-raising for small companies—a vital area of our economy.
In turn, this has caused the drying up of the U.S. IPO market and shut
down a major source of revenue for the exchanges. To feed their for-
profit exchange model, the exchanges needed to look elsewhere for
revenue. In the process, we believe the exchanges have sacrificed the
protection of all but a few investors, as follows.

I. For-Profit Exchange Model

The for-profit exchange model is filled with conflicts of interests.

Exchanges were at one time thought to be similar to public
utilities. Their main goal was to attract listings. Becoming a publicly
traded company on a major stock exchange was instrumental for raising capital.

However, with the introduction of Reg NMS, the stock exchange
model changed dramatically. We don't think we need to go through
all the history of what led to this change. (It is well documented elsewhere, and we would like to keep our comments brief.) The main
point is that an exchange model no longer generates most of its revenue from listing fees. Exchanges now receive most of their revenue

from transactions and the sale of market data and related services based on those transactions.

The new exchange model is extremely competitive and filled with new entrants. There are now four major stock exchanges in the United States: NYSE, NASDAQ, BATS, and Direct Edge. Two of these exchanges are publicly traded companies. Based on recent events, it is clear that the primary goal of all these exchanges is to maximize profits. This is normal for a publicly or privately held company, and they have every right to do so. However, when that exchange also has the dual mandate to protect all investors, the evidence shows that these companies have a clear conflict of interest.

Flash Orders

The most obvious example of this conflict occurred last year when flash orders were scrutinized by the public and the media. In June 2009, NASDAQ and BATS began offering their own version of a prerouted order. NASDAQ called its version FLASH, and BATS referred to its version as BOLT.

Both exchanges reacted to a successful program called the Enhanced Liquidity Provider (ELP) launched in 2006 by rival Direct Edge. The ELP program helped Direct Edge grow its market share to 12.9% by August 2009, at the expense of NASDAQ and BATS.

To stop the bleeding, NASDAQ and BATS applied for the ability to preroute orders. Without much discussion, both received SEC approval.

In a comment letter dated June 17, 2009, Morgan Stanley noted that NASDAQ and BATS applied for this new order type under a "noncontroversial" filing:

> NASDAQ and BATS have designated their filings as 'non-controversial' pursuant to Rule 19b 4(f)(6) under the Securities Exchange Act of 1934 (the Exchange Act), which requires that a proposed rule "not significantly affect the protection of

investors or the public interest" and "not impose any significant burden on competition"...Rule 19b-4(f)(6) under the Exchange Act, however, permits filings to become effective immediately without the typical notice, comment, and approval process if the filings are deemed non-controversial.[22]

Were NASDAQ and BATS trying to get a controversial order type approved without the usual comment period? Morgan Stanley seemed to think so:

> The Proposals clearly do not meet the standard of non-controversial in that they have already generated controversy from a diverse group of market participants. Not only have the Proposals generated negative responses from various market participants, but [also] the Commission itself has recently indicated that the appropriateness of the underlying practices permitted by the Proposals is something that the Commission may reconsider in the context of today's electronic market environment.[23]

In early August 2009, the Flash controversy heated up. Senator Charles Schumer sent a letter to Chairman Mary Schapiro urging the SEC to ban flash trading:

> This kind of unfair access seriously compromises the integrity of our markets and creates a two-tiered system where a privileged group of insiders receives preferential treatment, depriving others of a fair price for their transactions."[24]

Unable to withstand the pressure, on August 6, 2009, NASDAQ and BATS voluntarily announced the removal of their preroute order strategy, effective September 1, 2009.

However, this was not the end of prerouted orders. The SEC has proposed banning these order types and issued this proposal for comment, but *prerouted orders are still available on other exchanges* because the SEC has not yet made a decision.

Maker/Taker Model and the Economics of Routing Decisions

"Make-or-take pricing has significantly distorted trading," wrote James Angel of Georgetown University in Washington, Lawrence Harris of the University of Southern California in Los Angeles, and Chester Spatt of Carnegie Mellon University in Pittsburgh in their paper, "Equity Trading in the 21st Century."[25]

Since the early 1990s, when the Island ECN introduced rebate trading, the equity market has used a maker/taker model. Liquidity makers get paid a rebate by the exchange/ECN and liquidity takers pay a fee to the exchange/ECN. Normally, the rebate is less than the take fee. This model has become the standard for all market centers. Almost nobody in the trading community even questions the maker/taker model. It is assumed to be the only way stocks should trade.

Why doesn't anyone question this? The buy-side probably doesn't care much because they pay a flat fee to their broker regardless whether they are making or taking. The brokers who sponsor algorithmic trading systems have figured out a way for this model to be profitable. And the exchanges are content with receiving the spread between the make/take rate.

However, the authors of the "Equity Trading in the 21st Century" believe the maker/taker model has

> ...distorted order routing decisions, aggravated agency problems among brokers and their clients, unleveled the playing field among dealers and exchange trading systems, produced fraudulent trades, and produced quoted spreads that do not represent actual trading costs.[26]

The maker/taker model is at the core of the equity market structure problem. It has influenced how most smart order routers access liquidity. Some orders are not routed to the destination where best execution would dictate but to the cheapest destination first. Most institutional algos use a smart router to route orders in small pieces throughout the day. The pecking order of these routers differs depending on which broker sponsors the algo. But a common goal is to always route to the least expensive destination first. Most of the time this means routing to a dark pool before routing to a displayed liquidity venue. Some of these dark pools are filled with predatory traders "hiding out" electronically, watching for footprints that the algos leave.

We are not the only ones who think that there are conflicts of interest embedded in the maker/taker model. In a comment letter to the SEC on March 4, 2010, Morgan Stanley stated the following:

> The real, underlying problem that needs to be addressed is the conduct of market participants. Diverse market participants are engaging in similar economically driven order handling/routing practices without being subjected to the same regulatory obligations merely by virtue of their respective defined roles in the marketplace.[27]

> We believe that many of these issues, including the Proposal, are symptoms of the larger underlying cause—aggressive order handling/routing practices that have emerged in recent years. These practices, including the aggressive use of actionable Indications of Interest (IOI) and blind pinging, are driven by economic incentives to engage in such practices across many different venues and market participants, not just by dark pools. The economic incentives that exist in the market to reduce execution costs inevitably lead to a race for cheaper execution alternatives.[28]

> The acceptance of the "free look for a free execution" mantra has led to many market participants, including broker-dealers and exchanges, routing their orders to various alternative liquidity providers in lieu of the traditional lit marketplace. Competition and advances in technology have not only permitted, but have also encouraged participants to look for the most

cost-effective execution, many times in conflict with the underlying customer whose order information is 'leaked' to sophisticated market participants and who is not the ultimate recipient
of the resulting economic benefit.[29]

Morgan Stanley is saying that brokers use algorithms that route
to the cheapest venue and not necessarily the venue that provides the
best execution. Brokers are routing to venues where the predators
hide out and take advantage of robotic order flow based on simple
volume weighted average price (VWAP) algos. This has been proven
by recent research from Quantitative Services Group (QSG), a leading provider of equity research and trading analytics to institutional
investors:

> This study reveals that significantly higher impact costs and
> trading velocity are incurred for VWAP algorithms when com-
> pared to Arrival Price algorithms.... The results suggest that
> High Frequency Trading (HFT) strategies are materially con-
> tributing to these increased costs.... The details of the study
> uncover an important artifact from today's trading environ-
> ment: Increased order parceling has three negative ramifica-
> tions. First, more "strikes," or executions per order, increase
> a client's exposure to adverse ticks, and this tick risk translates
> into higher impact costs. Second, more strikes increase the
> chances of leaving a statistical footprint that can be exploited by
> the "tape reading" HFT algorithms. Third, should HFT strate-
> gies identify the order and begin to trade in anticipation of the
> order flow, this will begin a positive feedback loop that can sig-
> nificantly change an algorithm's behavior and invite even more
> predatory order flow.[30]

How much money is made by brokers and exchanges when they
make these routing decisions, which are ultimately hurting their own
clients and helping the HFT predators? Morgan Stanley states the
following:

We estimate that the annual economic benefit for broker dealers aggressively routing in this manner could amount to $63 million (based on a 100 million shares average daily trading volume). Similarly, exchanges that would have otherwise incurred a net loss of approximately $10 million from having to route to other exchanges could turn that loss in an annual economic benefit of approximately $76 million (based on a 100 million shares average daily trading volume) through fiscal routing to alternative liquidity sources. We encourage the Commission to carefully examine the current level of access and market data fees, which we believe are driving the current order handling/routing behavior.[31]

Many institutions use algorithms to receive an average VWAP execution. At the end of the day, they get their VWAP. But what has happened internally? Brokers have profited $63 million and exchanges $86 million due to their poor routing decisions at the expense of the long-term investor. But this is only the tip of the iceberg. The real money is made by HFT firms as they detect the footprints of the algorithm and interposition themselves with the help of their lightning-fast technology and access to direct market feeds from the exchanges. HFT is estimated to be an $8–20-billion-a-year industry. This money comes from somewhere. *We believe that a good part of it is coming from the leakage of institutional algos because brokers and exchanges have an economic incentive to route to the cheapest venue.*

We believe that the maker/taker model needs to be reevaluated. How much liquidity in stocks like Citigroup, which trade close to a billion shares a day, needs to be incented with rebates? With the help of broker-dealer algos and exchanges, the maker/taker model is used to assist high-speed traders in their daily pilfering of millions of dollars from long-term investors. The Commission states clearly in its concept release:

Where the interests of long-term investors and short-term professional traders diverge, the Commission repeatedly has emphasized that its duty is to uphold the interests of long-term investors.[32]

The maker/taker model is a clear example of long-term investors fleeced by short-term traders.

Rebate Arbitrage

NASDAQ, Direct Edge, and NYSE all operate more than one exchange. BATS is currently pending approval from the SEC for a second exchange and NASDAQ for a third one. The U.S. equity market is currently extremely fragmented. Why do our major exchanges want to fragment the market even more? One reason is so that some of their more sophisticated and technologically advanced members can participate in a strategy called Rebate Arbitrage.

For example, NASDAQ OMX operates the NASDAQ system as well as the NASDAQ BX system. Up until April 15, 2010, BX had an aggressive rebate program. This had created a rebate arbitrage incentive in the market. On NASDAQ BX, a rebate of $0.0001/share was given to remove liquidity on shares priced less than $1.00.[33] On NASDAQ, a rebate of 0.20% of the total dollar volume was given to add liquidity on shares priced less than $1.00.[34]

Now look at how this affects the trading of a stock priced under $1.00, such as Sirius XM Radio (SIRI):

- A broker places an order to buy 100k shares of SIRI at $0.8701 on NASDAQ. The order gets hit, and the broker collects a $174 rebate (100k × $0.8701 × 0.002).

- The broker then sells 100k shares at $0.87 on NASDAQ BX and collects a rebate of $10 but incurs a trading loss of $10 (100k ×.0001).

- The broker makes $174 on the transaction but has added no economic value.

It is fair to note that on April 15, 2010, NASDAQ changed its fee schedule to no longer provide rebates for taking liquidity on NAS-DAQ BX. However, a rebate arbitrage still exists because the NAS-DAQ rebate for adding liquidity (20bps) is greater than the NASDAQ BX rate (15bps) for taking liquidity.

II. Latency Arbitrage

Latency Arbitrage has become one of the fastest growing strategies on Wall Street. Latency has been steadily decreasing as hardware, software, and networking have improved and through the isolation of inefficiencies in circuits and cabling. There is now a wide variety of consultants available to develop ways for corporations and trading firms to reduce latency from endpoint to endpoint. There also is a continuous need to upgrade equipment.

HFTs use cutting-edge technology and colocated servers at exchanges and ATSs, combined with purchases of raw data feeds from these market centers, to create their own inside National Best Bid and Offer (NBBO) quote and depth of book substantially earlier than what is publicly available from the Securities Information Processor (SIP) quote. The SIP feeds quotes seen on professional terminals, algorithmic trading systems used by institutions for as much as 50% of their orders, and quotes seen by retail investors on Internet sites.

HFTs can reengineer the quote by paying exchanges and ATSs for the right to locate their servers next to market center data servers and matching engines and by paying for the right to access raw data feeds. They employ technologies such as feed handlers to further speed the receiving of data from the exchanges. Recently, a firm named QuantHouse announced that its feed handler technology, used to standardize exchange raw market data feeds, can decode more than 5.55 million messages per second.[35]

As a result, HFTs know with near certainty what the market will be microseconds ahead of everybody else—valuable knowledge that HFTs take advantage of when they trade thousands of stocks, thousands of times, every trading day. HFTs can then use techniques, such as predatory algos, immediate or cancel (or cancel and replace) orders, and dark pool pinging, to determine what kind of institutional algo orders are in the market, such as those driven by commonly used VWAP formulas, and how those orders will react if the bid/offer of a stock moves up or down.

In its concept release, the SEC asks many questions about market structure. We have a few of our own:

Do HFT firms have an unfair advantage?

Most professionals on Wall Street have taken a standard from our past for granted: that everyone sees the same quote and market data at the same time. What if the time differential between what the HFTs see and what everybody else sees were 5 minutes instead of 5 milliseconds? Would that be acceptable? It is not the amount of time that matters. It's that a differential exists at all.

Some of the exchanges make sure that each colocated customer receives equal amounts of connecting cable so that a server at the northeast corner of a facility has the same latency as one at the southwest corner. It appears that "fairness" and the equalization of market data speed among colocated firms is an important "must" for the exchanges, but not so when it comes to all other institutional and retail investors.

Is it fair to sell these rights to the highest bidders when market centers are supposed to be protecting all participants' interests equally?

Latency Arbitrage has created a two-tiered market of technology-enhanced insiders (composed of a handful of large banks, brokerage firms, and hedge funds) and the rest of us. To be clear, HFTs enjoy this advantage only because market centers are selling them the right to colocate and access raw data feeds. As for-profit organizations' market centers are incentivized to do this.

> *When a market center provides an HFT with the ability to out-maneuver institutional orders, is not the exchange putting institutions and their brokers in breach of their fiduciary responsibilities, especially those institutions managing pension funds governed by the Employee Retirement Income Security Act (ERISA)?*

It is entirely one thing for an HFT firm to use proprietary algorithms to try to predict how an institution's algo will operate so that the HFT can out-maneuver the institution. But it is the buy-side trader's fiduciary responsibility to protect his firm's orders by adjusting execution methods and tactics regularly to avoid predictability. Quantitative Services Group LLC's (QSG) study found significantly higher impact costs and trading velocity are incurred for VWAP algorithms when compared to Arrival Price algorithms, especially when applied to liquid, low price stocks. QSG concluded, "The results suggest that High Frequency Trading strategies are materially contributing to these increased costs."[36]

To further enforce our case that HFTs are paying to see information before the general public, we thought it would be helpful to quote a few paragraphs from the SEC's Concept Release that we are commenting on:

> Exchanges, ATSs, and other broker-dealers are prohibited from providing their data directly to customers any sooner than they provide their data to the plan processors for the Networks. The fact that trading center data feeds do not need to go through the extra step of consolidation at a plan processor, however, means that such data feeds can reach end users faster than the consolidated data feeds. The average latencies of the consolidation function at plan processors (from the time the processor receives information from the SROs to the time it distributes consolidated information to the public) are as follows:

(1) Network A and Network B—less than 5 milliseconds for quotation data and less than 10 milliseconds for trade data and (2) Network C—5.892 milliseconds for quotation data and 6.680 milliseconds for trade data.[37]

The Commission also states

Some proprietary firm strategies may exploit structural vulnerabilities in the market or in certain market participants. For example, by obtaining the fastest delivery of market data through colocation arrangements and individual trading center data feeds, proprietary firms theoretically could profit by identifying market participants who are offering executions at stale prices.[38]

When it adopted Regulation NMS in 2005, the Commission did not require exchanges, ATSs, and other broker dealers to delay their individual data feeds to synchronize with the distribution of consolidated data, but prohibited them from independently transmitting their own data any sooner than they transmitted the data to the plan processors. Given the extra step required for SROs to transmit market data to plan processors, and for plan processors to consolidate the information and distribute it to the public, the information in the individual data feeds of exchanges and ECNs generally reaches market participants faster than the same information in the consolidated data feeds. The extent of the latency depends, among other things, on the speed of the systems used by the plan processors to transmit and process consolidated data and on the distances between the trading centers, the plan processors, and the recipients.[39]

The Commission understands that the average latency of plan processors for the consolidated data feeds generally is less than 10 milliseconds. This latency captures the difference in time between receipt of data by the plan processors from the SROs and distribution of the data by the plan processors to the public.[40]

We could stop our comment letter right here because the Commission has just made our case. They acknowledge that HFTs are seeing information before everybody else because they buy direct data feeds and pay for their servers to be colocated. They acknowledge that HFTs profit at the expense of the average investor. They acknowledge that there are currently two sets of data in the public domain: fast data, which is accessed by privileged firms that can afford all the technology and market data expenses, and slow data, which is what the rest of the investment community receives.

But we also have another topic that needs to be examined.

III. Market Data Revenue

Exchanges generate market data revenue from the sale of quote and trade information to third parties such as Bloomberg and Yahoo Finance. This fee paid by the vendor to the exchange is usually just passed along to all investors. This is a huge revenue-generating business for the major exchanges. Sales of consolidated market data generated approximately $400 million in 2004. This represented about 10–15% of total revenues from the largest exchanges.

In 2006, a debate started by the NetCoalition raged about the amount of fees that the exchanges were charging for their market data. Although most agree that exchanges should be compensated for the service that they provide, the debate centered upon how much was charged. NetCoalition argued that the cost associated with the exchanges obtaining the market data was far lower than the revenue that they were receiving. Exchanges were quick to point out that they were not even required by Reg NMS to supply depth of book information. They argued that it was their proprietary information, and they could sell it if they wanted.

The exchanges won this debate and have been enjoying lucrative market data revenues ever since. The exchanges figured out that to attract more business to their market, they would have to encourage order flow through rebates. We have already detailed the maker/taker model and how it creates incentives for brokers to place orders on the highest rebate system, but not necessarily providing best execution. There is, however, another way that exchanges attract order flow: They rebate back a portion of their tape revenue to the broker who initiated the order flow. This rebate could be up to 100% depending on the level of business that the broker does with the exchange.

In 2007, to further complicate matters as a result of Reg NMS, the SEC changed how market data revenue was calculated. No longer would it be from the volume executed, but now a portion would be credited based on quotes. After the revenue pools are calculated, they are shared with exchanges based on quotes and trades. Quotes at the NBBO and trades are eligible for approximately 50% of revenue. Only exchanges can compete for the quote revenue because trade reporting facilities (TRFs) report only trades and do not quote.

We believe that a good portion of quotes canceled are placed for the sole reason of generating quote revenue. An SRO can generate "quote credits" for each second of time that the SROs quote is at the NBBO. HFT firms have the capability to detect when a stock is moving and cancel their quote before it is executed.

A research paper prepared by the SEC's Office of Economic Analysis concludes

> ...Incentives created by allocation formulas are large enough to have a significant impact on average trade size and revenue-sharing rebate programs are a key mechanism used by exchanges to align the incentives of order-flow providers with the exchange.[41]

> Market data revenue is an impetus contributing to the practices of payment for order flow, internalization, and order preferencing but has largely been ignored in the literature investigating those practices.[42]

Conclusion

Over the past decade, regulatory changes in the U.S. equity market have been dramatic. The market has shifted from a slow-paced auction market with 1/8-point spreads to a high-speed, electronic market where pennywide spreads are common. Consolidated average daily share volume and trades in NYSE-listed stocks increased from just 2.1 billion shares and 2.9 million trades in January 2005, to 5.9 billion shares (an increase of 181%) and 22.1 million trades (an increase of 662%) in September 2009.[43]

On the surface, it appears that these new regulations have been successful and the equity market appears healthy and liquid. But as we have detailed, there are many inequalities now present. Fairness and transparency seem to have lost out to the never-ending quest for profit.

Although we do think that HFT has an unfair advantage in the marketplace, we do not believe that it is the problem. HFT is the symptom of what lies at the heart of the equity market today. In their quest to satisfy the bottom line, the exchanges have sold out the institutional and retail investor. Left unchecked, the exchanges will continue to make choices that cater to a customer base that generates most of their revenue—the HFT community.

HFT is a big bucket that catches many types of trading. For the most part, we don't question HFTs' morality or legality. HFT practitioners, even the predatory ones, are doing what our free market system encourages them to do: make money by all legal and acceptable means—collateral damage be damned. The problem is that our market structure has evolved to cater to them. And to date, our regulatory bodies have rubber-stamped every system and rule change placed in front of them by the exchanges.

We do question a market structure that has allowed predatory HFT to flourish. The predatory trading, which picks off dark pools using a plethora of tools (actionable IOIs, for example) and is amped up with colocated speed, is an issue. But make no mistake: It is a dwarf issue relative to the fact that for-profit exchanges, focused on next quarter's profits, cater to HFT firms at the expense of others.

- Exchanges rolled out flash order types, admitting that they were wrong and unfair.
- Exchanges sell colocation space and data feeds to HFT firms looking for micro- nano- picosecond speed advantages so that they can beat slower orders to the quote.
- Why is the SIP, the public quote that powers the vast majority of institutional buy-side algorithms, operating at a much slower speed than those who pay to colocate?

We believe that our comment letter has clearly illustrated that there are a number of incentives currently in the equity market that are not aligned with the public's interest and the stated goal of the SEC to uphold the interests of long-term investors. We commend the efforts that the Commission has taken thus far in its market structure review and urge the SEC to continue investigating the issues that we have identified in this letter.

Sincerely,

Sal L. Arnuk, cofounder, Themis Trading

Joseph Saluzzi, cofounder, Themis Trading

Exchanges and Data Feeds: Data Theft on Wall Street

May 11, 2010

Introduction

How many average Americans have been victims of identity theft? A Sun Microsystems survey a few years back actually placed that number at 33%. In that same survey a majority of those victims said that "they are likely to stop shopping and banking with institutions that put their personal data at risk."

We can tell you flat out that if an institution played loosey-goosey with our personal data, they would not be earning our business, and we would be lobbying hard to make our outrage known with government regulators and lawmakers so that they could put an end to the malfeasance.

Now, to take this further, what if you found out that an institution, which should be protecting your information and identity, was providing information regarding your transactions in data reports to its other customers as part of their everyday business strategy? Not exactly identity theft, perhaps, but clearly theft of highly proprietary information.

In our previous white paper ("Latency Arbitrage: The Real Power Behind Predatory High Frequency Trading"), we illustrated how the exchanges provide raw data feeds that help high frequency traders figure out market directions. Now, we have discovered that at least two of the exchanges, in addition to providing that information, also provide data that enable high frequency traders to track specific trade orders, putting institutional trading strategies at further risk.

Put simply, every day, certain market centers market and provide data feeds where they reveal more information than just the original order, depth of book, and trade executions. This is done legally as a by-product of a market structure that has gone horribly wrong. However, unlike personal identity theft, where nearly all Americans and stakeholders are aware of the practice, the vast majority of institutional and retail traders are not aware that this is done legally as they enter their order flow.

Thus, instead of traditionally collecting listing and transaction (commission) fees, some market centers are generating revenue by selling colocation and providing low-latency enhanced market data feeds that contain sensitive trader information. Information in these feeds enables high frequency trading (HFT) firms to track when an investor changes price on his order, how much stock the investor buys or sells in accumulation, as well as the ascertaining of hidden order flow. This information assists high frequency traders in predicting short-term price movements with near certainty.

Exchanges argue that this information is public and available to all investors. Technically, this may be true; however, realistically, not many retail or institutional investors have the capital to invest in the type of computer systems needed to access this information, and most are not aware that it exists. They also are not aware that the information provided to high frequency traders reveals critical information about trading intentions. In this report we have identified two situations in which this occurs: the BATS Exchange direct feed known as BATS PITCH and the NASDAQ direct feed known as TotalView-ITCH.

BATS PITCH Feed

BATS supplies an order ID number attached to each order submitted through PITCH. The order ID number is then sent to subscribers of their PITCH feed. From the BATS PITCH specification:

> If an orders Price or Display values change within the BATS matching engine, a Cancel Order Message will be immediately followed by a new Add Order Message with the **same Order ID** as the original order. An order that changes its Display value from "N" to "Y" will not lose its priority.

After a reserve book order (an order that displays only a piece of the entire order) is placed in BATS, the Order ID number tracks cumulative trades over the life of the order. If the quantity or price changes, the order ID number shows that to all PITCH subscribers. Also, any trade execution related to that order has the same order ID number as the original order. High frequency traders who subscribe to the BATS PITCH feed could determine how much an order has traded and if it is changing its price. They can trace the life of an order and decipher valuable information about that order, which helps determine the future price of a stock.

NASDAQ TotalView-ITCH Feed

NASDAQ is supplying information on its TotalView-ITCH product, which reveals information about hidden order flow on its exchange. Every time a nondisplayed (or hidden) order is executed, NASDAQ sends a message that not only identifies that a trade has occurred, but also identifies if the hidden order was a buy or sell. In addition, the trade Order ID associated with that trade is cumulative, which means that every time a trade executes when part of a hidden order, the same ID number is attached to that trade as the original trade, thereby enabling ITCH subscribers to determine how much of the stock in question the hidden buyer or seller has accumulated.

The Trade Message is designed to provide execution details for normal match events involving **nondisplayable** order types.... A Trade Message is transmitted each time a **nondisplayable** order is executed in whole or in part. It is possible to receive multiple Trade Messages for the same order if that order is executed in several parts. Trade Messages for the same order are **cumulative**.

4.6.1 Trade Message (Non-Cross)[44]

TRADE MESSAGE (NON-CROSS)

Name	Offset	Length	Value	Notes
Message Type	0	1	"P"	Trade Message.
Timestamp - Nanoseconds	1	4	Integer	Nanoseconds portion of the timestamp.
Order Reference Number	5	8	Integer	The unique reference number assigned to the order on the book being executed.
Buy/Sell Indicator	13	1	Alpha	The type of nondisplay order on the book being matched. "B" =buy order. "S" =sell order.
Shares	14	4	Integer	The number of shares being matched in this execution.
Stock	18	8	Alpha	The security symbol associated with the match execution.
Price	26	4	Integer	The match price of the order. Refer to Data Types for field processing notes.
Match Number	30	8	Integer	The NASDAQ generated session-unique Match Number for this trade. The Match Number is referenced in the Trade Break Message.

We called NASDAQ and it confirmed that it provides information about hidden order flow. It also confirmed that a buy or sell indicator is attached, and the trade messages are cumulative.

We are not the only market participants who have noticed that the exchanges reveal much more information on their data feeds than most investors realize. In a comment letter to the SEC on its concept release dated April 29, 2010, the Securities Industry and Financial Markets Association (SIFMA) stated

It may, however, be appropriate for the Commission to give greater consideration to the manner in which direct market data feeds may be used by market participants. As noted, direct market data often is faster and more detailed than consolidated data. Also, direct data feed recipients generally are able to more easily trace orders they submit to an exchange or electronic communications network ("ECN") using such feeds—facilitating, for example, their ability to analyze the implications of a particular trading strategy. But some SIFMA members believe that direct market data feeds may be used by third parties to generate more implicit information about the markets. For example, member firms state that direct market transaction information may be linked to particular displayed quotations and, in some instances, direct market data may be used to help discern the presence of reserve orders. As discussed, SIFMA does not believe that the use of trading strategies used to identify potential liquidity in various markets, whether displayed or undisplayed, necessarily requires a regulatory response. However, it might be beneficial for market participants to have a better understanding of the ways in which their market data, if provided to a trading center publishing direct market data, might be used by other market participants.[45]

Conclusion

Most institutional and retail investors have no idea that the private trade information they are entrusting to the market centers is made public by the exchanges. The exchanges are not making this clear to their clients but instead are actively broadcasting the information to the high frequency traders to court their order flow. The exchanges are likely to counter that when a subscriber signs up to their exchange they then allow the exchange to use this data as they see fit. However, how many investors would have signed that agreement knowing that their hidden orders were being exposed? This practice has been going on for years, but not many investors have read the market data specifications. Every day high frequency traders use the information that some exchanges are supplying to disadvantage unsuspecting investors.

Every time a trader places an order in certain market centers, whether at the market centers directly or through a third-party DMA, those market centers collect data regarding the trader's order flow. They supply the information to HFTs that allows them to track when an investor changes price and how much stock has been accumulated. This information helps HFTs predict short-term price movements. Institutional and retail footprints are detected, and "modus operandi" and trading profiles are created. Traders believe that their trading strategies are protected, when actually their strategies (personal data)—including variables such as displayed quantity, timestamp, side, revisions, reserve orders, linked executions, order ID numbers, accumulations, number of shares—are misappropriated by the market centers.

The exchanges believe that they own the data and have the right to distribute it. Why are the exchanges allowed to do this? This is an outrage and demands immediate action by the SEC. How can the public trust the very organizations that are supposed to be protecting them, when these organizations are turning around and providing their personal data? The only difference between personal data theft and the data-feed issue we highlight in this paper is the degree of public awareness.

Phantom Indexes: Major Market Indexes Reflect Only 30% of All Trades Intraday

June 22, 2011

Introduction

The investment world trusts and relies upon indexes such as Dow Jones Industrial Average, S&P 500, NASDAQ 100, and Russell 2000 for gauging market activity. In recent years, this emphasis has become even greater due to the explosion in popularity in tradable index-based products, such as ETFs, futures, and options. In addition, the market has become increasingly dominated by trading volume from arbitraging index, ETFs, and other derivative movements versus the underlying equities.

Surprisingly, we have found that on an intraday basis, these widely watched indexes and possibly others are based on less than 30% of all shares traded, therefore conveying incomplete trading data. We have confirmed in writing with representatives from Dow Jones Indexes, S&P, NASDAQ, and Russell that these indices are calculated using only primary market data. Nowadays, in a world of microsecond trading, these indexes have become phantoms—they reflect some trades involving their components, but not the majority of them.

This situation raises serious questions about the reliability of index-based trading products. The solution? Simple. Indexes should be calculated based on every trade involving a component that crosses the consolidated tape, which includes trades from nonprimary exchanges such as BATS, Direct Edge, and NYSE Arca.

Incomplete Trading Data

U.S. stocks are traded today on more than 50 market centers. According to TABB Group, stock exchanges trade 67% of overall volume. The biggest exchanges are NASDAQ (26% of total U.S. stock exchange share), NYSE (19%), NYSE Arca (19%), Direct Edge (14%), and BATS (12%).[46] The balance of shares traded (approximately 33%) occurs in dark pools, electronic communication networks (ECNs), and broker-internalized alternative trading systems.

As a result, many stocks are traded on exchanges other than where they have their primary listing.[47] NYSE actually trades only 27% of the volume of NYSE-listed stocks[48] and NASDAQ, 29% of the volume of NASDAQ-listed stocks.[49] Most major indexes, however, are calculated intraday using sales from only the primary exchange where the component stock is listed. Thus, they do not incorporate the majority of shares traded. That means that these indexes are based on a little more than one out of every four shares traded.

Dow Jones Industrial Average Components[50]

Ticker	Company	Primary Exchange	% Traded on Primary Exchange
MMM	3M Co.	NYSE	36.87%
AA	AlCoa Inc.	NYSE	15.52%
AXP	American Express Co.	NYSE	26.29%
T	AT&T, Inc.	NYSE	22.02%
BAC	Bank of America Corp	NYSE	15.26%
BA	Boeing Co./The	NYSE	21.69%
CAT	Caterpillar, Inc.	NYSE	19.80%
CVX	Chevron Corp	NYSE	28.75%
CSCO.	CisCo Systems, Inc.	NDAQ	26.52%
KO	Coca-Cola Co./The	NYSE	33.71%
DD	EI du Pont de Nemours & Co.	NYSE	29.01%
XOM	Exxon Mobil Corp	NYSE	34.24%
GE	General Electric Co.	NYSE	20.77%
HPQ	Hewlett-Packard Co.	NYSE	30.14%
HD	Home Depot, Inc.	NYSE	25.05%
INTC	Intel Corp	NDAQ	30.59%
IBM	International Business Machines Corp	NYSE	26.91%
JNJ	Johnson & Johnson	NYSE	28.52%
JPM	JPMorgan Chase & Co.	NYSE	27.30%
KFT	Kraft Foods, Inc.	NYSE	28.07%
MCD	McDonald's Corp	NYSE	29.26%
MRK	Merck & Co. Inc.	NYSE	20.87%
MSFT	Microsoft Corp	NDAQ	30.19%
PFE	Pfizer, Inc.	NYSE	20.50%
PG	Procter & Gamble Co./The	NYSE	30.22%
TRV	Travelers Cos, Inc./The	NYSE	50.29%
UTX	United Technologies Corp	NYSE	28.15%
VZ	Verizon Communications, Inc.	NYSE	20.66%
WMT	Walmart Stores, Inc.	NYSE	27.96%
DIS	Walt Disney Co./The	NYSE	29.83%
	Average		**27.17%**

This index incompleteness is compounded by the number of respective components. There are 30 stocks in the DJIA, 100 in the NASDAQ 100, 500 in the S&P 500, and 2,000 in the Russell 2000. The problem is compounded further by the trading liquidity of each component. In general, the smaller the market cap, the less liquid the trading, and the larger the variances that could occur from one trade on one market center, to the next trade on another market center.

Unintended Consequence of Reg NMS

The Phantom index problem appears to be another unintended consequence of the SEC's Reg NMS. Prior to 2007, approximately 80% of NYSE listed stocks traded on the NYSE, and the majority of stocks in the S&P 500 and the DJIA (the two most watched indexes) were NYSE listed stocks. In 2007, Reg NMS resulted in the equity markets becoming extremely fragmented, spreading trades among a variety of competing market centers.

Almost overnight, NYSE's market share of trading dropped from 80% to less than 30% as faster, cheaper competitors captured share. Indexes, which were calculated intraday based on 80% of all trades, began being calculated based on less than 30% of all trades. Owners of the major indexes, however, have not changed what data they capture to reflect this new paradigm.

NYSE LRPs: Another Source of Index Inaccuracy?

We also believe that during times of market stress, when the whole world is watching, key indexes might reflect an even greater degree of inaccuracy. The conventional belief is that on May 6, 2010, the DJIA, under selling pressure due to a plethora of reasons, plunged nearly 1,000 points and then recovered much of that loss within 20 or so minutes. Some speculate, however, that the DJIA actually fell 25% lower.[51]

One reason could be NYSE's Liquidity Replenishment Points (LRPs). According to the NYSE, an LRP is "A volatility control built into the Display Book to curb wide price movements resulting from automatic executions and sweeps over a short period of time. When triggered, LRPs automatically convert the market temporarily to slow or Auction Market only mode, allowing specialists, floor brokers, and customers to supplement liquidity and respond to the stock's volatility."[52]

During the May 6 Flash Crash, many LRPs were activated. Most trades that were executed at extreme prices, such as $0.01 per share, did not occur on the NYSE. For example, NYSE-listed Proctor & Gamble (PG)—a DJIA component—traded as low as $39.37 on nonprimary exchanges.[53] However, because LRPs were activated, the low of the day on the NYSE was only $56, or 42% higher. Any trades below $56 were not included in index calculations because they were traded off the primary exchange.

In times of extreme volatility, NYSE LRPs will likely be activated, but nonprimary exchanges may continue trading NYSE stocks. However, intraday trades from these nonprimary exchanges will not be reflected in the indexes. Thus, investors who rely on index values in times of market stress could be relying on data that varies widely from reality.

Conclusion

Would you bet on the Kentucky Derby (legally, of course) if the results reflected only some of the horses in the race? Would you have confidence in a publicly traded company that reported results from only some of its subsidiaries? This is currently the case with the major stock indexes in the United States. The indexes that everyday retail and institutional investors rely upon are calculated on an intraday basis without a full deck, so to speak.

In a post Reg NMS world, fragmentation among market centers has reduced the amount of trades that occur on the primary exchanges. The primary market is no longer a complete enough source of data when calculating an index value because it represents only about one in four trades. Index suppliers must adjust their methodology to accurately reflect all trades intraday in a timely manner. If they don't, they risk regulators or Congress doing it for them.

Endnotes

1. Michael Scotti, "At the Speed of Light," Traders Magazine.com (October 2008), Traders Magazine website, http://www.tradersmagazine.com/issues/20_287/102252-1.html.

2. Ibid.

3. Ibid.

4. Nina Mehta, "High Frequency Trading Is a Tough Game," Traders Magazine.com (November 24, 2009), Traders Magazine website, http://www.tradersmagazine.com/news/high-frequency-trading-tough-game-104672-1.html.

5. Arnuk and Saluzzi, "Toxic Equity Trading Order Flow on Wall Street."

6. Electronic Trading Desk, "A Report on Information Arbitrage (IA) & Its Impact on Execution Quality: 2" (Jefferies & Company, November 3, 2009).

7. David Gaffen and Rob Curran, "Measuring Arbitrage in Milliseconds," Wall Street Journal (March 9, 2009), Wall Street Journal website, http://blogs.wsj.com/marketbeat/2009/03/09/measuring-arbitrage-in-milliseconds.

8. Ivy Schmerkin, "High-Frequency Trading Controversy Continues to Swirl," Wall Street & Technology (November 23, 2009), Wall Street and Technology website, http://www.wallstreetandtech.com/electronic-trading/showArticle.jhtml?articleID=221600663.

9. "Electronic Trading Desk, "A Report on Information Arbitrage: 2."

10. Scott Patterson and Serena Ng, "NYSE's Fast-Trade Hub Rises Up in New Jersey," The Wall Street Journal C1 (July 30, 2009), The Wall Street Journal website, http://online.wsj.com/article/SB124890969888291807.html.

11. Mehta, "High Frequency Trading Is a Tough Game."

12. Electronic Trading Desk, "A Report on Information Arbitrage: 7."

13. Greenwich Associates, "High-Frequency Trading: Lack of Data Means Regulators Should Move Slowly" (October 21, 2009), Greenwich website, http://www.greenwich.com/WMA/in_the_news/news_details/1,1637,1851,00.html?

14. Quantitative Services Group, "QSG® Study Proves Higher Trading Costs Incurred for VWAP Algorithms vs. Arrival Price Algorithms, High Frequency Trading Contributing Factor" (Nov. 24, 2009), Quantitative Services Group website, http://www.qsg.com/PDFReader.aspx?PUBID=722.

15. Quantitative Execution Services, "The Impact of High Frequency Trading on the Canadian Market," (BMO Capital Markets, July 22, 2009).

16. Ralph Frankel, "The Un(?)fair Advantage of Latency Arbitrage" (July 24, 2009), Traders Magazine.com, http://www.securitiesindustry.com/issues/19_100/-23732-1.html.

17. Charles Duhigg, "Stock Traders Find Speed Pays, in Milliseconds," *The New York Times* A1 (July 23, 2009), *New York Times* website, http://www.nytimes.com/2009/07/24/business/24trading.html?_r=1&scp=1&sq=%22Stock%20Traders%20Find%20Speed%20Pays,%20in%20Milliseconds%22&st=cse.

18. Karen Mazurkewich, "Traders of the Shadows," *Financial Post* (November 6, 2009), Stockhouse website, http://www.stockhouse.com/Bullboards/MessageDetailThread.aspx?p=0&m=27615398&r=0&s=APG&t=LIST.

19. Sal Arnuk, "Rebuttal: Some High Frequency Trading Is Good, Some Is Bad" (Mar. 18, 2010), Traders Magazine.com, http://www.tradersmagazine.com/news/agency-brokerage-high-frequency-trading-105382-1.html.

20. Sal Arnuk and Joseph Saluzzi, "What Ails Us about High Frequency Trading?" (Sept. 30, 2009), Advanced Trading website, http://www.advancedtrading.com/algorithms/showArticle.jhtml?articleID=220300593.

21. Weild and Kim, "A Wake-Up Call for America," p. 21.

22. William P. Neuberger and Andrew F. Silverman (Managing Directors, Morgan Stanley Electronic Trading), letter dated June 17, 2009 to Elizabeth M. Murphy (Secretary, Securities and Exchange Commission), Securities and Exchange Commission website, http://www.sec.gov/comments/sr-nasdaq-2009-043/nasdaq2009043-5.pdf.

23. Ibid.

24. Schumer, "Schumer Urges Ban on So-called 'Flash Orders.'"

25. Angel, Harris, and Spatt, "Equity Trading in the 21st Century," p. 42.

26. Ibid.

27. William P. Neuberger and Andrew F. Silverman (Managing Directors, Morgan Stanley Electronic Trading), letter dated Mar. 4, 2010 to Elizabeth M. Murphy (Secretary, Securities and Exchange Commission), Securities and Exchange Commission website, http://sec.gov/comments/s7-27-09/s72709-74.pdf.

28. Ibid.

29. Ibid.

30. Quantitative Research Group, "Beware of the VWAP Trap" (November 2009), Zero Hedge website, http://www.zerohedge.com/sites/default/files/RN%20Nov%2009%20-%20beware%20the%20VWAP%20trap.pdf.

31. Neuberger and Silverman, letter dated Mar. 4, 2010 to Elizabeth M. Murphy.

32. SEC, "Concept Release on Equity Market Structure," p. 34.

33. NASDAQ OMX Trader, "NASDAQ OMX BX Price List – Trading & Connectivity," NASDAQ OMX Trader website, http://www.nasdaqomxtrader.com/Trader.aspx?id=bx_pricing.

34. NASDAQ OMX Trader, "Price List—Trading & Connectivity," NASDAQ OMX Trader website, http://www.nasdaqomxtrader.com/Trader.aspx?id=PriceListTrading2.

35. Automated Trader, "QuantHouse Breaks the 5.55 Million Market Data Messages Decoded per Second" (April 19, 2010), Automated Trader.com, http://www.automatedtrader.net/news/quant-news/37724/quanthouse-breaks-the-555-million-market-data-messages-decoded-per-second.

36. Quantitative Research Group, "Beware of the VWAP Trap."

37. SEC, "Concept Release on Equity Market Structure," p. 24.

38. Ibid., 52.

39. Ibid., 62.

40. Ibid.

41. Cecilia Caglio, "Equity Trading and the Allocation of Market Data Revenue: 6" (Mar. 4, 2008), University of Mississippi website, http://faculty.bus.olemiss.edu/rvanness/Speakers/2008-2009/MayhewCaglio-tape_shredding.pdf.

42. Ibid., 7.

43. Securities and Exchange Commission, "Large Trader Reporting System" 17 CFR, parts 240, 249, rel. 34-61908, file S7-10-10, RIN 3235-AK55 (April 14, 2010), Securities and Exchange Commission website, http://sec.gov/rules/proposed/2010/34-61908.pdf.

44. NASDAQ Trader, "NASDAQ TotalView-ITCH 4.1.: 10."

45. Ann Vlcek (Managing Director and Associate General Counsel, Securities Industry and Financial Markets Association), letter dated April 29, 2010 to Elizabeth Murphy (Secretary, Securities and Exchange Commission), Securities and Exchange Commission website, http://sec.gov/comments/s7-02-10/s70210-167.pdf.

46. TABB Group, "Liquidity Matrix: Volume Summary April 2011," TabbFORUM website, http://mm.tabbforum.com/liquidity_matrices/66/documents/original_TABB_Group_LiquidityMatrix_April_2011.pdf?1305559304

47. Larry Harris, "The Exchange Where a Corporate Stock Issue Is Primarily Listed Is the Primary Listing Market," *Trading and Exchanges* (New York: Oxford University Press, 2003).

48. BATS Trading, "Market Volume Summary: 5 Day Avg.," BATS Trading website, https://batstrading.com/market_summary/.

49. NASDAQ OMX Trader, "Market Share Statistics – May 2011," NAS-DAQ OMX Trader website, http://www.nasdaqomxtrader.com/Trader.aspx?id=MarketShare.

50. Fidessa, "Dow Jones Industrial Average Components" (% Traded on Primary Exchange from May 01-May 31, 2011), Fidessa Fragmentation Index, Fidessa website, http://fragmentation.fidessa.com/fragulator/.

51. John Melloy, "Did Dow Actually Drop 1250 in 'Flash Crash'?" (May 12, 2010), CNBC, FAST Money, Behind the Money, CNBC.com, http://www.cnbc.com/id/37109515/Did_Dow_Actually_Drop_1250_in_Flash_Crash.

52. Dino Sola, "When Liquidity Evaporates" (May 7, 2010), Market Melange website, http://www.market-melange.com/2010/05/07/when-liquidity-evaporates.

53. David Goldman, "P&G Stock Drops 37% – Not Really" (May 6, 2010), CNNMoney,CNNwebsite,http://money.cnn.com/2010/05/06/markets/procter_and_gamble_stock/index.htm?postversion=2010050619.

INDEX

FINANCIAL TIMES

In an increasingly competitive world, it is quality
of thinking that gives an edge—an idea that opens new
doors, a technique that solves a problem, or an insight
that simply helps make sense of it all.

We work with leading authors in the various arenas
of business and finance to bring cutting-edge thinking
and best-learning practices to a global market.

It is our goal to create world-class print publications
and electronic products that give readers
knowledge and understanding that can then be
applied, whether studying or at work.

To find out more about our business
products, you can visit us at www.ftpress.com.